T0388339

City, Environment, and Transnationalism in the Philippines

Seki presents an ethnography of uncertainty and precarity experienced by people in urban, rural, and transnational, communities in the Philippines as a case study of social protection without the possibility of a robust welfare state.

He deals with topics including urban poverty, natural resource management, and transnational migration. Throughout these chapters, Seki elaborates on the modes of security and protection that people living at the margins of global capitalism create through mobilizing their sociality and networks. He traces the emerging configuration of "the social", a collectivity and connectedness that ensures a sense of security in life among people. The social can be defined as an idea or institution, which had enabled formal and impersonal solidarity such as that which provided the underpinnings of the modern welfare states of the West during the mid-20th century. In the 21st century, however, the social in this context is experiencing a fundamental reconfiguration as it faces deepening insecurity, risk, and the precariousness under the neoliberal governmentality. What are the contours of the social emerging in an "unlikely place" of the Philippines amid contemporary insecurity and precariousness? The book tackles this question squarely through the analytical concept of the "vernacular public sphere".

A vital resource for scholars of the Philippines, and of anthropology of development, social policy, and civil society in the Global South more widely.

Koki Seki is Professor of cultural anthropology and Southeast Asian studies at the Graduate School of Humanities and Sciences, Hiroshima University, Japan.

Routledge Studies on Asia in the World

Routledge Studies on Asia in the World will be an authoritative source of knowledge on Asia studying a variety of cultural, economic, environmental, legal, political, religious, security and social questions, addressed from an Asian perspective. We aim to foster a deeper understanding of the domestic and regional complexities which accompany the dynamic shifts in the global economic, political and security landscape towards Asia and their repercussions for the world at large. We're looking for scholars and practitioners – Asian and Western alike – from various social science disciplines and fields to engage in testing existing models which explain such dramatic transformation and to formulate new theories that can accommodate the specific political, cultural and developmental context of Asia's diverse societies. We welcome both monographs and collective volumes which explore the new roles, rights and responsibilities of Asian nations in shaping today's interconnected and globalized world in their own right.

The Series is advised and edited by Matthias Vanhullebusch and Ji Weidong of Shanghai Jiao Tong University.

Eldercare Issues in China and India
Edited by Longtao He and Jagriti Gangopadhyay

The Shanghai Cooperation Organization
Exploring New Horizons
Edited by Sergey Marochkin and Yury Bezborodov

Humour in Asian Cultures
Tradition and Context
Edited by Jessica Milner Davis

City, Environment, and Transnationalism in the Philippines
Reconceptualizing "the Social" from the Global South
Koki Seki

Find the full list of books in the series here: https://www.routledge.com/Routledge-Studies-on-Asia-in-the-World/book-series/RSOAW

City, Environment, and Transnationalism in the Philippines

Reconceptualizing "the Social" from the Global South

Koki Seki

Routledge
Taylor & Francis Group

LONDON AND NEW YORK

First published 2022
by Routledge
4 Park Square, Milton Park, Abingdon, Oxon OX14 4RN

and by Routledge
605 Third Avenue, New York, NY 10158

Routledge is an imprint of the Taylor & Francis Group, an Informa business

British Library Cataloguing-in-Publication Data
A catalogue record for this book is available from the British Library

Library of Congress Cataloguing-in-Publication Data
A catalog record has been requested for this book

ISBN: 978-1-032-12382-0 (hbk)
ISBN: 978-1-032-12383-7 (pbk)
ISBN: 978-1-003-22427-3 (ebk)

DOI: 10.4324/9781003224273

Typeset in Galliard
by KnowledgeWorks Global Ltd.

For Keiji, Ryoji, and Chat

Contents

Figures

Pictures

Maps

Tables

Preface

This book is mostly based on the papers published in the past ten years of my research, now rewritten in a new context. They focus on governmentality in specific settings of urban poverty, resource management, and transnational migration in the Philippines. While some data collected within this decade need to be updated, I believe the included ethnographies still reflect the fundamental aspects which define the contemporary Philippines. Having been put in a new theoretical context in this book, these ethnographies will be reintroduced and interpreted in a new light. Here, the theoretical discussion brings into sharp relief the process of neoliberal restructuring of social policies and development, in various settings of the Philippines, and subsequent emergence of alternative public sphere, which I refer to as the "vernacular public sphere". Thus, the book seeks to utilise the past ethnographies in order to reconceptualise "the social"; that is, the possibility of broader mutuality in the Global South.

I will also argue the contemporary configuration of precarity and uncertainty emerging in such process of neoliberal restructuring of "the social". Considering the fundamental paradigm shift of contemporary anthropology since the "ontological turn", inquiries into precarity, uncertainty, and reconceptualizing "the social" should be pursued by focusing more on the deep entanglement between humans and non-humans. While the book tries to avoid grasping "the social" as a given entity, *a priori*, and rather focuses on its emergence in interactions with specific institutions, a further discussion on "the social", and sociality, emerging in interaction, and entanglement, between humans and non-humans will remain a future task.

This is mainly an English version of my book published in the Japanese language in 2017. While most of the data and ethnographies are based on this Japanese publication, the theoretical discussions have become clearer and sharper after incorporating critiques and my own reflections on the former Japanese version.

Various people in the Philippines helped me to make the fieldwork for this study possible. Quite regrettably, some of those people have already been passed away. I would like to mention only a few among them, who offered indispensable help to me. Mr. Anastacio Fajardo of Puerto Princesa City, Palawan, who had been passed away in 2019, and his wife Mrs. Columba Fajardo, and their family in Palawan. Mr. Serafine "Nonong" Esperancilla, a former Barangay captain of Barangay Panacan, Municipality of Narra, Palawan. Mr. Joseph Buriones, who was a former barangay captain of Baranay Malanday, Marikina City, and passed away in 2019. Mrs. Juliet Reyes and her family of Barangay Malanday, Marikina City. My heartfelt gratitude is for those who accepted me into their communities. Finally, part of the research in this publication project is supported by JSPS KAKENHI Grant Number 19K01226.

January 2022
Saijo, Hiroshima
Koki Seki

1 Introduction

Towards the "Vernacular Public Sphere" in the Global South

This book has a two-pronged task: to identify the process of neoliberal restructuring of "the social" observed in the social policies and development in the Global South, and to discuss what kind of alternative public sphere, which will be conceptualised as a "vernacular public sphere" later in this introduction, is emerging in such restructuring. In this study, "the social" is considered as an assemblage of ideas and institutions to nurture mutuality and solidarity for the security of people's lives. It is based on the formal and impersonal mutuality that lies at the basis of redistribution, under which, people accept that the money they earn will be paid for services to someone they have never known or met. Originally, in the history of the West, "the social" was "invented" to deal with various risks found in the process of industrialization during the 19th century in Western Europe (Donzelot 1984).[1] Accordingly, mutual associations, insurance, and social welfare were institutionalised to mitigate the risks of industrialised society, which could no longer be tackled by mutuality based on primordial attachments, such as those among kinsmen and neighbours, or based on charity from the wealthy or the Church. Under contemporary globalization, however, and particularly with the progress of the neoliberal restructuring of "the social", widespread arguments have emerged on the "withdrawal", "shrinking", "loss", and "collapse" of "the social". Although the potential contours of alternative institutions and ideas after such restructuring remain unclear, we are increasingly reminded that our existence faces precarity and uncertainty, particularly by unpredictable incidents, such as the COVID-19 pandemic. It is hence an urgent task to reimagine and reconceptualise "the social" in times of precarity and uncertainty. The present work deals squarely with this task by shedding light on the emergence of the alternative public sphere in the Global South.

The different historical paths and discrepant experiences of modernity between the West and Global South do not necessarily indicate that "the social" is absent in the latter. Even without the welfare state established in modern Western countries, various social policies and development projects, accompanied by nation-state building, indicate attempts to expand and strengthen "the social". This work maintains that the reconceptualization of "the social" from an unexpected place of the Global South sheds new light on the issues of mutuality, solidarity, and security for not only the Global South, but also the Global North.

DOI: 10.4324/9781003224273-1

As such an "unexpected place", this book focuses on the Philippines as an ethnographic field. In particular, it presents an ethnography of the communities, both local and transnational, and the connectedness of the people, which interact with various social policies and development projects. While the question of how a welfare state can be built as an embodiment of "the social" in the Philippines and other parts of the Global South is quite intriguing and significant to ask, it is beyond the purpose of this book, and beyond my ability as well, to make practical policy recommendations regarding the institutional aspects of the welfare of the people. Rather, this book attempts to decentralise the model of "the social", which has been based on the experience of the modern West, by examining the concrete ethnographies of development and globalization in the Philippines. In other words, I attempt to "provincialize" (Chakrabarty 2000) the seemingly universal concept of "the social" by showing that it is always bound by local specificity and emerges as situated knowledge. Through this, while avoiding privileging the concept rooted in the specific history and space of the modern West, this book sheds light on the plurality and multivocal character of this concept, as well as the rich possibilities inherent in it.

Invention of "the Social"

As has been convincingly discussed by those scholars as Donzelot and Castel, "the social" as an assemblage of ideas and institutions had been "invented" in the specific historical experience of Western Europe since the mid-19th century and developed and established by the mid-20th century. Historically, it was an ideology that called for solidarity to deal collectively with risks that had been newly found in the process of rapid industrialization in Western Europe during this period. Castel (2003), for example, argued that the place of "the social" had been clearly noticed for the first time in the 1830s, particularly in France, when pauperism became prevalent as a "social question". Donzelot, on the other hand, emphasises the importance of the February Revolution of 1848 in France in terms of the invention of "the social" (Donzelot 1988). According to him, the cause of the Revolution was the widely shared recognition among the people regarding the contradiction between the formal equality of the citizens promised by the French Revolution on one hand, and the actual mass poverty seen among the labourers on the other. Thus, "the social" was invented as a solution to this contradiction between the promise of the republic and the misery of the people.

This "social question" was closely connected to "an awareness of the living conditions of populations who were both the agents and the victims of the industrial revolution", and was "the question of the place to be occupied by the most desocialized fringes of workers in an industrial society" (Castel 2003: xx).

The discovery of "social questions" was at the same time the discovery of new risks arising from the environment of factory work and urban life in particular, such as accidents, injuries, diseases, mass poverty, and unemployment. These risks are no longer covered by the "primary sociability" argued by Castel (2003: 10) such as family, the community, or religious and charitable organizations, which provided the "protection of proximity", meaning a "system of rules linking directly the members of a group on the basis of their familial belonging, locality, work, and by weaving networks of interdependence without the mediation of particular institutions" (Castel 2003: 10). Compared with this "protection of proximity" based on "primary sociability", or informal and personal mutuality, protection by "the social" enabled the formal and impersonal mutuality that was institutionalised in the social state or welfare state in the early part of the 20th century in the West, which matured into a stable regime by the 1970s.[2] Through this process, "the social" was embodied into a system that enabled risks to be insured and managed collectively by people who shared national solidarity and identity.

"The Social" as Governmentality

As another important aspect of "the social", it should be mentioned that it represents not only ideas and institutions to protect life and security, but also an aspect of power to govern people. In this sense, "the social" contains ambivalent power relations. On the one hand, it is the workings of power that protect our lives and enable us to be freed from various constraints. On the other hand, it makes us governable subjects by disciplining, normalising, and controlling our lives. As pointed out by Tanaka, a political scientist, the expansion of "the social" liberates the individual from dependence on, and bondage to, various traditional groups, such as the community and family, yet, it also re-embeds them in new social relations, under which they are disciplined to become conducive to the maintenance of social order (Tanaka 2006: 256). In other words, the individual is guaranteed the right to survive by being conducive to such social order, while at the same time, their everyday lives, including education, hygiene, food and nutrients, and relationships among families and friends, are meticulously monitored and collectively controlled so that they become responsible for minimizing various risks that would be a threat to the social order (Tanaka 2006: 180). Simply put, "the social" is an assemblage of the ambivalent powers of "liberation" and "disciplining" (Tanaka 2006). In a similar vein, anthropologist Majima argues that inherent in "the social" is the ambivalence of "oppressive disciplining" and "emancipating freedom", "subjection" and "subjectification", and "bureaucratization" and "solidarity" (Majima 2006). What is needed is a framework for deciphering the complicated entanglement of disciplining and freedom and subjection and subjectification as a duality inherent in "the social".

Such aspect of ambivalent power of "the social" is also discussed by Dean (2010), who states that the reconfiguration of "the social" today is accompanied by the emergence of a new disposition of power and subjects. Under this disposition, the subject is "a free subject of need, desire, rights, interests and choice" (Dean 2010: 193). Such freedom, however, has subjection as a condition. Dean argues that "in order to act freely, the subject must first be shaped, guided and moulded into one capable of responsibility exercising that freedom through systems of domination" (Dean 2010: 193). In other words, a free subject becomes possible only when it is steered, taught, and forged to bear the responsibility for exercising freedom. As free subjects, non-state actors such as individuals, families, neighbourhood associations, and communities are empowered, activated, and motivated on one hand. On the other hand, the performance of these actors is monitored, measured, and rendered calculable by various "norms, standards, benchmarks, performance indicators, quality controls and best practice standards" under this new disposition of power and subjects (Dean 2010: 193).

In considering "the social" as an assemblage to govern people, the concept of governmentality coined by Foucault provides compelling analytical importance for this work. According to Foucault, governmentality is a form of power that originated in the political economy of liberalism emerging in Western Europe in the late eighteenth and nineteenth centuries. To govern the population, it does not take the form of a "regulatory system of injunction, imperatives, and interdictions" (Foucault 2009: 352), but rather it aims to "arouse, to facilitate, and to laisser faire, in other words to manage and no longer to control through rules and regulations" (Foucault 2009: 353). For Foucault, the aim of governmentality is not to disturb the natural processes of the population, economy, and society by "clumsy, arbitrary and blind intervention", but rather to ensure natural regulation to work in such a way that those natural phenomena "do not veer off course" (Foucault 2009: 353). As such, governmentality is a mode of power that utilises and mobilises the natural processes inherent in the population, economy, and society that were found to have their own autonomous functions and mechanisms, particularly in the historical processes of urbanization and industrialization in Western Europe since the end of the 18th century.

As already made clear, governmentality differs from the government by empirical institutions such as law, administration, or the state; it is "a way of framing human actions to be guided in a certain direction" (Yoneya 1996: 81), especially through "educating desires and configuring habits, aspirations and beliefs" (Li 2007a: 5). Thus, governmentality can be understood broadly as "a form of activity aiming to shape, guide or affect the conduct of some person or persons" (Gordon 1991: 2). Foucault himself states that governmentality does not "refer only to political structures or to the management of states; rather, it designated the way in which the conduct of individuals or of groups might be directed" (Dreyfus & Rabinow 1983: 221). It is directed towards various populations, as in "the government of children, of souls, of communities, and of families, of the sick" (Dreyfus & Rabinow 1983: 221). Government in this sense does not "only cover the legitimately constituted forms of political or economic subjection, but also modes of action, more or less considered and calculated, which were destined to act upon the possibilities of action of other people. To govern, in this sense, is to structure the possible field of action of others" (Dreyfus & Rabinow 1983: 221).

The concept of governmentality urges us to reconsider fundamentally the conventional view of power. Governmentality is not power emanating from the "centre" or the "above", but rather "a form of power that regulates social life from its interior" (Hardt & Negri 2000: 23). It works not through a unidirectional vector of domination and subordination, but as a sort of magnetic field that entangles all actors alike and makes their lives possible. In other words, governmentality is not a power that oppresses, exploits, or constrains, but rather a power that produces and reproduces life itself, through which society, the economy, and the population as a whole are animated. To put it differently, the paradigm of power inherent in governmentality is biopower, described by Foucault as something qualitatively different from conventional sovereign-juridical power, which is "exercised mainly as a means of deduction, a subtraction mechanism, a right to appropriate a portion of the wealth, a tax of products, goods and services, labor and blood, levied on the subjects" (Foucault 1990: 136). In contrast to sovereign-juridical power, biopower is "a power that exerts a positive influence on life, that endeavors to administer, optimize, and multiply it, subjecting it to precise controls and comprehensive regulations" (Foucault 1990: 137). As Negri and Hart state, "the highest function of this power is to invest life through and through, and its primary task is to administer life" (Hardt & Negri 2000: 24). It is a power that aims to make people live rather than threaten them with death, and it demonstrates its effectivity by guiding them towards how to live a "better life" through a mixture of discipline, surveillance, and control.

What is significant to note here is that on the one hand, a regime of biopower works to "make people live", while on the other hand, those who do not follow, or are perceived as "unfit" to the regime, are "let die" (Li 2009). Whether such power is "good" or "bad" is not actually relevant to ask in the context of the present argument (Higaki 2011: 11–12). Whether it is good or bad, we have already and always lived in, and been entangled with, such a field of power. Rather, the questions to ask are as follows. What is produced and reproduced by such power? What is failed to be produced? And what, as well as who, is marginalised or even left to die under such a regime of power? Similarly, the question of "who" holds power does not make sense here. Rather, the questions are "how", and "in what way", does power flow and operate?

"The social" as argued in this book is considered to be a realm permeated by the power of governmentality delineated above. The actions and behaviours of each one of us entangled in this realm are framed and guided by the subtle workings of power that infiltrate all corners of everyday life in order for us to be moulded into governable, or self-governing, subjects. As such, "the social" is a regime of governmentality as a power that works to produce subjects capable of dealing with contemporary precarity and uncertainty, not through command and regulation, but through structuring the environment in which we, as free actors, navigate to act.

Neoliberal Restructuring of "the Social"

The rise of neoliberalism in the contemporary world resulted in the fundamental restructuring of "the social" as governmentality and biopower discussed so far. Here, I delineate first how neoliberalism and governmentality penetrate each other to constitute the contemporary regime of power. I then argue how "the social" as a mode of intervention by the government was restructured with the progress of neoliberalism.

Neoliberalism, according to Harvey, is "a theory of political and economic practices that propose that human well-being can best be advanced by liberating individual entrepreneurial freedoms and skills within an institutional framework characterized by strong private property rights, free markets, and free trade" (Harvey 2005: 2). However, neoliberalism is not only a theory of political economy, but also a power that penetrates into the most internal and intimate spheres of our being, such as relationships with others, identity, and personality. It is a power that shapes the self and being according to a certain logic of political economy. Foucault describes the implication of neoliberalism on our being as a "generalization of the 'enterprise' form" that "involves extending the economic model of supply and demand and of investment-costs-profit so as to make it a model of social relations and of existence itself, a form of relationship of the individuals to himself, time, those around him, the group, and the family" (Foucault 2008: 242). As the thing that is brought out by this power of neoliberalism penetrating into our most personal relationships, life itself becomes a "permanent enterprise" and society is given a new form based on the model of enterprise "down to the fine grain of its texture" (Foucault 2008: 241). Hence, neoliberalism precisely becomes an object of anthropological inquiry as a cultural device to shape individuals and society according to the norms and values optimal for the self-regulating market, such as self-help, self-reliance, resilience, self-responsibility, self-activation, self-monitoring, entrepreneurship, audit, evaluation, and accountability.

Now, it is widely recognised that the rapid and widespread penetration of neoliberalism in Europe and the US since the late 1970s has led to the withdrawal of the welfare state and the decline of "the social". What occurred there, however, was not simply the irreversible decline and hollowing out of the welfare state, but rather a restructuring of the modes of intervention by the state in response to new risks. Simply put, it was a realignment from direct state intervention to intervention through the activation and mobilization of various non-state actors, such as citizens, neighbourhood associations, communities, civil society organizations, and so on.

Such restructuring has proceeded concomitantly with the entrenching impact of "risk society" discussed by sociologists such as Beck and Giddens. As discussed by Beck (1992), ironically, these new risks are created by modernity itself, under which, advanced technologies and institutions were thought to reduce the risks inherent in modern society, such as mass poverty. Such modern institutions include the nation-state, full employment, the nuclear family (made up of a male breadwinner and female homemaker), class (and class identity), and science and technology. It is widely felt and recognised, particularly among people in the West, that those institutions are now gradually collapsing and ironically creating new risks, a typical case being a nuclear power plant failure. The new risks are no longer specific to a certain collectivity, such as a nation or social class, as they once were, but are now fragmented according to individualised lifestyles, life courses, identities, and preferences. In the face of the prevalence of such fragmented and individualised risks, the protection of people's lives and survival is no longer effectively secured by a universal safety net and national insurance by the state, but rather by the creation and mobilization of various non-state actors such as active citizens and productive communities. The state no longer governs by directly intervening through sanctions and regulations, but rather by creating subjects who are capable of governing themselves.

Relatedly, it is discussed that the contemporary risk society attempts to govern by creating "risk-conscious subjects" who problematise daily life as consisting of risks and act to avoid or reduce them (Azuma, Ichinosawa, Kimura, & Iida 2014). Thus, neoliberal governmentality, as a cultural device, shapes the individual into not only an "enterprise" as discussed above, but also a "risk-conscious subject" who does not allow vague fears about future dangers to be left untouched yet tries to calculate, quantify, and visualise risks in order to control, manage, and tame them (Hacking 1990). The predominance of a "risk-conscious subject" brings into sharper relief the ambivalent nature of the subject, which is shaped by both freedom and constraint, subjectification and subjection, under the neoliberal governmentality of contemporary times.

As discussed so far, the neoliberal restructuring of "the social" resulted in a mode of intervention through activating and mobilizing non-state actors. Such intervention has been described as "government at a distance" (Miller & Rose 2008: 34) or "governing through free subjects" (Rose, O'Malley, & Valverde 2006: 90–91). This can be realised through "autonomizing" (Burchell 1996: 27) and "mobilizing" (Donzelot 1991) society. Under a new mode of intervention, the state becomes "*l'Etat animateur,* or animator state" (Donzelot & Estebe 1994)[3], which puts greater emphasis on encouraging and incentivizing people and other non-state actors than on providing broader protection. This is a shift from a "passive" to an "active" welfare state. This reconfiguration of the welfare state necessitates new citizenry subjects. As argued by Muehlbach for the case of contemporary Italy, "the state shifts the burden of the reproduction of solidarity onto a citizenry conceptualized as active and dutiful, solidarity is outsourced [...] onto citizens, every one of which is now coresponsible for the public goods" (Muehlebach 2012: 11–12).

I have delineated thus far the "inventions of 'the social'" which contains the ambivalent power of governmentality, and how it has been restructured with the progress of neoliberalism. As is clear from the discussion above, however, the concept of "the social" and theory of neoliberal governmentality have been heavily based on the experience of the modern West. Rose, one of the main discussants of neoliberal governmentality, admits that the study of governmentality does not deal with empirical diversity and specificity at the local level of various organizations and their operations; instead, it is the study of a particular way of knowing and acting, or a particular regime of truth based on the historical experience of the West (Rose 1999: 19). This view has a risk of reducing, and simplifying, variegated forms of power under the monolithic category of "the neoliberal governmentality". Instead, this book, which considers "the social" as being situated in a concrete ethnographic setting, attempts to relativise and decentralise the concept of governmentality by contextualizing it in the specific practices and narratives of people in the Philippines.

Anthropologies of "the Social"

This section reviews major studies of cultural anthropology dealing with the aspects and consequences of the neoliberal restructuring of "the social", whereby I set a broader context in which the ethnographies of the Philippines in the following chapters can be properly situated. It is only in the 2000s, especially in the political-economic context since the September 11 attacks in the US, that "neoliberalism" has emerged as a key concept in anthropological research that seeks to understand the dynamism of post-Cold War global transformations, replacing such concepts as "globalization" and "transnationalism" (Ganti 2014). It was a response from cultural anthropology to the new uncertainties and insecurity created in the situation of various parts of the world involved in the drastic marketization of everyday life, financial crises, the fight against terrorism, and so on. While it is true that the tendency to group variegated phenomena under the umbrella category of "market fundamentalism" is often criticised, neoliberalism has indeed become a key word that any anthropological studies seriously tackling the contemporary world cannot avoid mentioning (Allison & Piot 2011: 5).

Among the diverse and cumulative studies on the cultural anthropology of neoliberalism and its influence on the restructuring "the social", a series called the "anthropology of policy" is highly relevant to the discussion in this book (Shore & Wright 1997; Russel & Edgar 1998; Shore, Wright & Però 2011; Clarke, Bainton, Lendvai & Stubbs 2015; cf. Okongwu & Mencher 2000). The pioneering work in these studies was a volume edited by Shore and Wright in 1997 titled *Anthropology of Policy: Critical Perspectives on Governance and Power* (Shore & Wright 1997). They argue that policies, like "family" and "society", are "inherently and unequivocally *anthropological* phenomena" (Shore & Wright 1997: 7, italic in original). Policies, they continue, can be read "as cultural text, as classificatory devices with various meanings, as narratives that serve to justify or condemn the present, or as rhetorical devices and discursive formations that function to empower some people and silence others" (Shore & Wright 1997: 7). The process of governance focused by the anthropology of policy is not something imposed on the people from "outside" or "above" through benefits and sanctions, but rather the complex processes that "influence people's indigenous norms of conduct so that they themselves contribute, not necessarily consciously, to a government's model of order" (Shore & Wright 1997: 6). It is "a type of power which both acts on and through the agency and subjectivity of individuals as ethically free and rational subjects" (Shore & Wright 1997: 6). As can be clearly seen, the discussion of the anthropology of policy, while being heavily influenced by the Foucauldian notions of governmentality and biopower, considers policies as powerful discourses that shape subjectivity and identity and as a cultural device that privileges certain normative claims to frame problems and their solutions while marginalizing or silencing other claims.

A follow-up to the above volume, titled *Policy Worlds: Anthropology and the Analysis of Contemporary Power*, was published in 2011 (Shore, Wright & Pero 2011). The relationship between the governmentality inherent in social policies and neoliberalism, which was not thoroughly dealt with in the previous work, is discussed in more detail. In particular, the paradoxical situation, under the heightened surveillance and obsessive security and risk management in Western societies after the September 11 attacks, in which the effects of state disciplining and control are strengthened while the state's functions are outsourced to the private sector, sets the backdrop for the volume. In this context, it argues that policy is an "art of politics" that consists of today's biopower working as a new way of managing populations, achieving its aim under the guise of scientific objectivity and neutrality while hiding a specific political agenda behind it.

Sharing basic concerns with the anthropology of policy is a series of studies on "audit culture" (Strathern 2000) as a defining feature of governance that has permeated various public institutions in the West, such as health care, the judicial system, and higher education, since the 1990s. These studies argued the new character of governmentality, focusing on how people are constructed as subjects who monitor, audit, and evaluate their own performance in terms of economic efficiency. The state no longer intervenes through guidance and regulation, but rather governs through creating new kinds of subjectivity that involve "self-managing individuals who render themselves auditable" (Shore & Wright 2000: 57).

Relatedly, there is a substantial accumulation of anthropological research on the "new poverty" that has emerged accompanied by the new risks created under the post-welfare state in Europe and the US since the 1990s (Good & Maskovsky 2001; Kingfisher 2002, 2013; Morgan & Maskovsky 2003; Muehlebach 2012; Mori 2014). In particular, research on Anglo-Saxon countries, including the US, Canada, and the UK, argues that the consequence of neoliberalism is never homogenous in various societies and has variegated effects specific to race, ethnicity, class, and gender (Good & Maskovsky 2001). It is argued that neoliberalism as a cultural classificatory system results in a "feminization of poverty" through extolling identities as healthy workers and flexible entrepreneurs, on the one hand, and marginalizing identities as mothers and housewives on the other. Such a system creates a binary representation between the "deserving poor", who are willing to work and pay taxes, and the "undeserving poor", who are dependent on welfare, and further links the latter with images of blacks (especially women), single mothers, and urban ghetto dwellers. It also creates discourses that naturalise poverty (particularly women's poverty) as a matter of personal pathology rather than as structurally produced and reproduced (Kingfisher 2002, 2013). Relatedly, Muehlebach argues that, with the background of Italy, where the state social services have recently been in decline, an emotional commitment to "service", "sacrifice", and "volunteering" has been exalted and internalised by the people, creating a subject called "ethical citizenship", in which citizens are mobilised as pro bono providers of welfare. Paradoxically, in this situation, neoliberalism mobilises people as bearers of the post-welfare state through activating a particular ethic and morality, as well as the emotions that support them (Muehlebach 2012). Finally, the volume edited by Mori asks how "the social" is constituted as a connection between people in today's European regional contexts (Mori 2014). The idea of solidarity and insurance systems to deal with "traditional risks" or "industrial-welfare state risks" in Europe up to the first half of the 20th century failed to deal with today's "new risks" characterised by "unpredictability, unanticipated scale, and complicated causal relationships", and new forms of security and solidarity to deal effectively with these new precarities have yet to emerge. Recognizing this situation, Mori and others examine the emergence of a new mode of "the social" as a fluid, situated, and diverse connection between people, which is in contrast to the conventional concepts of "welfare" or "society" as an objective entity, based on ethnographic details across Europe. It is argued that what is occurring in Europe, which is experiencing a crisis of the welfare state, is a shift in the arrangement of respective actors such as the state, market, and community, as well as a blurring of the boundary between the public and private, or intimate, spheres (Mori 2014).

The literature reviewed so far shares a basic concern with this book in that it traces various consequences of the neoliberal restructuring of "the social". However, it cannot be denied that these studies lean heavily towards the Eurocentric view. In this regard, Kipnis, a cultural anthropologist who focuses on contemporary China, has criticised the so-called "governmentality school", which includes Rose, Dean, and others mentioned above, for a critical lack of a "comparative perspective" (Kipnis 2008, 2011). According to Kipnis, the elements of neoliberal governance, such as "government at a distance", privileging the practices of "self-cultivation", "self-discipline", and emphasis on "calculability", must have existed in a wide range of places and times, with a variety of meanings and interpretations, outside the modern and contemporary West. It is thus futile, Kipnis argues, to frame supposedly diverse techniques and practices of government under the monolithic category of "neoliberal governmentality" without appropriate perspective for and interest in comparison (Kipnis 2008: 284, 2011: 5–8). For example, Kipnis continues, in contemporary China, the so-called audit culture, in which each person's performance is quantified and subject to audit, has permeated every nook and cranny of education and local administration by Communist Party officials. However, people do not speak of this tendency as neoliberal governmentality, but rather interpret it as stemming from a socialist collectivist system of production. This book, while sharing the critique by Kipnis, adopts a comparative view, which can decentralise the Western experience of "the social", and focuses on its plurality.

It is clear from the review above that we need a perspective on the neoliberal restructuring of "the social" that does not privilege the modern and contemporary West. In the following, I would like to touch on four studies based on such a perspective. The first is Ong's study of the neoliberal situations emerging from the specific context of the Asia–Pacific Rim made up by the various transmi-grants, which include temporary migrant workers, highly skilled professionals, and international students, among others (Ong 2006). Ong argues that neolib-eralism always entails "multiple, often contradictory strategies that encounter diverse claims and contestations, and produce diverse and contingent outcomes" (Ong 2006: 7) according to the unique ethnographic settings in which it operates. Focusing on various concrete ethnographic contexts reveals that the encroachment of neoliberalism always proceeds in a haphazard manner that cre-ates various enclaves and zones, that is, "exceptions". In these exceptions, the everyday lives of people are not governed solely by neoliberal calculations and choices, but rather are untamed by market-driven logic and rationality while rely-ing more on intimate, and primordial, attachment based on religion (particularly Islam), ethnicity, and informal connectedness such as *guanxi* among Chinese migrants. Thus, neoliberalism as an anthropological object always emerges as "exceptions" since the effect of neoliberal governmentality on subjects is not at all uniform, but rather "graduated" (Ong 2006: 78–79). As a result, such "neoliberalism as exception" produces at one end of the scale excludable subjects who, as "exceptions to neoliberalism", are denied protection and security, but works at the other end to promote selected populations who act according to neoliberal rationality. Ong thus argues that the possible contribution of anthro-pology lies in the exploration of "the dynamic tension between neoliberalism as exception and exceptions to neoliberalism" (Ong 2006: 25).

Next, I examine Ferguson's exploration of the burgeoning, and alternative, welfare states in the Global South, focusing on various cash transfer programme for poverty reduction that have recently been introduced in southern African countries (Ferguson 2015). The crux of Ferguson's argument is that the prem-ise of the social development of the poor countries should shift its focus from "production" to "distribution". According to his discussion, the welfare state and "the social" originating in Western modernity presuppose a nation-state in which men engaging in wage labour under formal employment support the nuclear family. This model, however, is not valid in southern African countries, where unemployment, underemployment, and employment in the informal sec-tor are common phenomena. The predominant labour under such a situation is "distributive labour" as a practice of distributing goods and services produced in other places by others, rather than "productive labor" in which workers produce some goods and services by themselves. In this sense, street vendors, beggars, hawkers, prostitutes, and others engaging in various informal sector jobs are all distributive labourers. Generally, distributive labour has been negatively valued compared with productive labour, but its aspect as labour should be reevalu-ated as it provides significant survival security made possible by the active and careful maintenance of social relations by the poor. Relatedly, the cliché of the development industry, "give a man a fish and you feed him for a day. Teach him how to fish and you feed him for his lifetime", emphasises production, and skills training for that purpose, rather than the distribution of goods. But such an approach is not always effective in today's world, where the production of wealth, and the employment opportunities for it, are very unevenly distributed. Rather, in the context of southern African countries, where formal employment opportunities for productive labour are limited, how to distribute fairly goods that are unevenly distributed (i.e., how to give a fish fairly) becomes the target of social policy. The introduction of various noncontributory and unconditional cash transfer policies (specifically, old-age pensions, maternal and child benefits, and basic income benefits) in southern African countries today is an example of how social policies in these places suggest that the primary focus of social policy is shifting from developing human resources suitable for productive labour (i.e., "teach a man to fish") to secure the right to the distribution of wealth that is unevenly distributed across the globe (i.e., "give a man a fish"). Furthermore, according to Ferguson, this situation is anthropologically interesting because it suggests, for both people and the state, a new way of conceptualizing "(re)distribution" and "recognition", and a new "distributive politics" based on these concepts. Under such new "politics of distribution", recipients of cash benefits (or those who further depend on these beneficiaries) can claim a "rightful share" based on the mere fact of "being present" in a certain community, even without engaging in any kind of productive labour or feeling indebted or stigmatised as a recipient of doles or the benevolence of welfare. An important point made by Ferguson is that the resources mobilised by people in such "distributive politics" are not abstract ideas of the modern West, such as "human rights", "citizenship", and "freedom", but rather tangible and personal interdependence with others, particularly with superordinates, where people try to engage in distributive labour and gain their "rightful share" for survival by actively inserting themselves into subordinate positions in the hierarchical social order.

The next two studies are the cases from South America. Both are concerned with the possible mode of the welfare state in South America and the concept of "the social", based on a reexamination of the norms of clientelism among the poor, in the regional context of neoliberal social policies during the 1990s and their criticisms in the 2000s. Clientelism is an individualised and personal exchange of votes and goods, as well as favours, based on loyalty and patronage between the poor (clients) and political elites or political brokers (patrons) who bridge the two. The research discussed here is a rethinking or reappraisal of the patron–client relationship, which has traditionally been viewed negatively as a private diversion of public resources. First, the study of Auyero, an ethnography of the slums of Buenos Aires, the capital of Argentina, criticises the understanding of the patron–client relationship in terms of mere privatization of public resources and, instead, focuses on why this type of relationship persists (Auyero 2001). According to Auyero, clientelism is a personal network that provides for the survival needs of the poor and solves their daily problems. Furthermore, it is not only a distribution network of goods and services, but also a symbolic system through which people order their reality, whereby the poor understand the meanings of their own experience of poverty, and even construct their identity. This patron–client relationship as a "problem-solving network" of the poor is not peripheralised or eradicated with the modernization of politics or the growth of the economy, but rather is a sustainable and pervasive institution that lies at the basis of "the social" among the poor in Argentina (Auyero 2001).

Second, Ansell's study examines a social policy package centred on conditional cash transfers (CCTs) in northeast Brazil, the area with the highest poverty rates in the country (Ansell 2014). In the implementation of the policy package, called "Zero Hunger", the importance of "efficiency", "transparency", and "accountability" is espoused by government staff to achieve policy objectives. At the same time, the patron–client relationship between beneficiaries and political brokers is denounced with the aim of eliminating it as much as possible. However, according to Ansell, with social policy packages based on normative democracy offering no real solutions for the suffering of the poor, patronage and clientelism are not eradicated; instead, such a personalised relationship reaffirms the moral value of "intersubjective compassion" based on an "intimate hierarchy" between the powerful and the weak. As such, clientelism, far from being the vestige of feudal time, is deeply ingrained in the everyday psyche of the people.

The common argument in the four studies reviewed so far is the limitation of the concept of "the social" based on a privileged model of the modern West that presupposes a nation-state consisting of citizens employed in formal, permanent, wage labour. In societies where formal institutions, such as permanent employment, transparent markets, and liberal democracy, have difficulty functioning, more effective and pervasive institutions for the sustenance of the people are instead constructed through various informal ties. These studies, while focusing on the resilience of such ties, can be seen as attempts to explore the process of the neoliberal restructuring of "the social" and the burgeoning mode of a public sphere in the Global South made possible by such a process. While this book shares the arguments made by these studies, it would not be sufficient, or unique, to point out simply that the alternative mode of the public sphere is realised by informal and personal ties in countries where formal and impersonal institutions are weak. It is surely too naïve, and even too retrogressive, to evaluate the resilience of intimate dyadic relationships in the local community, such as patron–client ties, as a solution to people's survival. In other words, aside from merely discussing the "persistence", "endurance", or "resilience" of informal networks, what should be discussed are the dynamics of interactions between, and entanglement of, the informal and the formal, in which the informal networks articulate with the formal ones such that they emerge as an alternative mode of the public sphere that is more effective and inclusive. To put it differently, the focus should be on the alternative public sphere that emerges at the interface where informal/personal mutuality articulates with formal/impersonal mutuality in the concrete interactions of the people entangled with the encroaching influence of globalization and neoliberalism in the Global South. At the same time, we need to elaborate on the ways in which informal ties, such as the patron–client relationship, are reinterpreted and given new meanings, alternative values, and norms by people faced with various types of precarity (see Chapter 3), and the process through which these informal networks are activated as a resource to support the emerging mode of the alternative public sphere. This book attempts to tackle this aspect squarely as it has not been adequately addressed in previous studies.

Towards the "Vernacular Public Sphere" in the Philippines and Global South

The discussion so far has clarified the focus of this study—the interface between the formal/impersonal mutuality called "the social" and informal/personal mutuality. It has further delineated that "the social" is deeply penetrated and restructured by neoliberal governmentality in contemporary times. However, regarding the restructuring of "the social" and the consequent emergence of the alternative public sphere, the Philippines might be an unlikely place, or "strange vista" (Claudio 2017: 2).[4] This is because the country is often spoken of in terms of a "weak state" and "underdeveloped public sphere". In the following, I attempt to answer why, then, I considered the Philippines a case study for the theme of this book.

For this purpose, I deal first with the country's modern and contemporary history to elaborate further on the significance of the Philippines as a case. According to Abinales and Amoroso, throughout its modern and contemporary history, the Philippines has never formed a public sphere based on the nation-state; instead, personalised exchange relationships of goods and services have prevailed, particularly private networks of resource distribution through patronage and clientelism (Abinales & Amoroso 2005). As a backdrop, Abinales and Amoroso also point out that throughout its modern and contemporary history, there has been a "dilemma of state-society relations", or a tug-of-war for predominance between the state and society, in the Philippines. It is important to note here that the term "society" in studies of the Philippines generally refers to the opposite of what is referred to as "the social" in this book. It is typically used in the same sense as "social forces", meaning forces that are constituted by a bundle of rather informal, personal, and individualised relationships, such as the family, relatives, and patron–client relationships with influential politicians, that are opposed to the public sphere, particularly the state. What, then, does the "dilemma", or tug-of-war, between society and the state mean in this sense?

To begin with, it should be pointed out that there has been a persistent criticism, mainly from the middle class, of the prominence of "social forces", the primary concern of which has been the pursuit of personalised interests that can impede the state's pursuit of public interests. At the same time, people have had a strong aversion to the tendency for the state to become strong enough to counter such "social forces" and thus, it should be similarly avoided. To understand this aversion to the "strong state", we need to look back to the administration of President Ferdinand Marcos (1965–1986) because it created a collective memory of dictatorship that remains ingrained into the Filipino people up to the present day. In the 1970s and 1980s, when many Asian countries adopted the so-called developmental dictatorship, a similar political system was inaugurated in the Philippines under President Marcos. In fact, it can be argued that this developmental dictatorship was the most comprehensive and visible realization, or a trial at least, of the idea and institutions based on "the social" in the contemporary history of the Philippines. For example, during this period, advocating the *"Bagong Lupunan"* (New Society), the Marcos administration promoted urban planning, social housing, infrastructure, and social services, as well as the disciplining of the people to maintain social order through strong state intervention. However, this iron-fisted development of "the social" traumatised, rather than benefited, the people through brutal human rights violations and the suppression of democracy. In the subsequent political regimes, this trauma, created by the experiences of the dictatorship, led the people to hold strong fears, suspicions, and criticisms against the state as soon as it became so powerful that it could contend with, or oppress, the interests of "social forces", and often resulted in widespread movements to demand the resignation of the incumbent president (Abinales & Amoroso 2005: 9).

In other words, throughout the contemporary political history of the Philippines, this "dilemma", or tug-of-war, between the state and "social forces" has prevented the formation of a robust idea of "the social", which could have been realised in the concrete public policies of social welfare and development. In fact, various studies have defined Philippine society by the lack or absence of "the social". For example, McCoy and others argued that politics in the Philippines is characterised by powerful local political families that have survived for several generations, and their rent-seeking activities, which is the pursuit of particular interests that certain groups can enjoy exclusively through the state's restriction and regulation of competition in a free and fair market (McCoy 1994a). According to McCoy, what is created by the competition of these families is an "anarchy of families", which has consequently eroded and appropriated the public sphere of the Philippine nation-state (McCoy 1994b). The Philippines can be characterised by a weak state and bureaucracy on the one hand, and by strong families and local bosses on the other, where the "privatization of public resources strengthens a few fortunate families while weakening the state's resources and its bureaucratic apparatus" (McCoy 1994b: 10).

In a similar vein, Hutchcroft (1998) argued that Philippine society, and especially its government-business relations, reflected "booty capitalism" that shared common characteristics with the Weberian patrimonial state. Under this regime, "the state apparatus has repeatedly been choked by an anarchy of particularistic demands from, and particularistic actions on behalf of, those oligarchs and cronies who are currently most favored by its top officials" (Hutchcroft 1998: 13–14). The state displays a "weak degree of autonomy" and a "high degree of favoritism", wherein "oligarchs and cronies plunder the state apparatus for [their] particularistic advantage[s]" (Hutchcroft 1998: 15). These discussions have provided a powerful paradigm for interpreting Philippine society, with "the social", deemed a formal and impersonal mutuality and solidarity, being fragile and "hard to imagine" at best (Anderson 1998: 235), or simply nonexistent.

However, a scathing criticism of this paradigm has been levelled by the Filipino historian Reynaldo Ileto, who argued that a paradigm in which Filipino society is conceived of as "an anarchy of families" signals the "reproduction of colonial images and discourses" (Ileto 1999: 46) by Americans in relation to cultural "others" whose "true" and "essential" behaviour is "codified in ways that reflect the desires and fears" inherent in the postcolonial gaze (Ileto 1999: 41). Ileto further argued that this paradigm works through essentialist binaries of family versus state, particularist versus nationalist, violence versus law, and clientelism versus genuine democracy, wherein the former within each binary is always ascribed with a negative value of feudalistic backwardness (Ileto 1999: 61). Countering the "anarchy of families" paradigm, Ileto insists that political behaviour within Philippine society seeks to "simultaneously occupy, or oscillate between the public (i.e., nationalist) and private (local and familial) spheres" (Ileto 1999: 61). The perspective posed by Ileto allows us to avoid a simplistic view of Philippine society based on the dichotomy of the "weak state/strong society" and enables a more nuanced understanding of "the social" created through the articulation, or entanglement, of the public and private spheres.

Ileto's critical argument offers valuable suggestions for the discussion of this book. Features such as the fragile state and public sphere, the severe disparities and fragmentation between social classes, the politics of clientelism, and the prominence of the informal sector have led to the facile conclusion of the lack or absence of "the social" modelled on the welfare state that typically appears in the modern West. Often, such features of Philippine society have even been pathologised as "aberrance" or "damaged culture" (Fallow 1987). As mentioned earlier, however, this book maintains that "the social" is constituted not only by the formal state institutions of universal welfare and social security, but also by various attempts for inclusion of marginalised people through social development projects by the state, private business sector, nongovernmental organisation (NGOs), and civil society, which are also considered an assemblage called "the social". When such assemblage is considered, the Philippines not only provides long and variegated experiences of the attempts to construct and expand "the social", but also indicates how "the social" is fundamentally penetrated and restructured by neoliberal governmentality. Thus, the Philippines offers a valuable case for studying the process of the neoliberal restructuring of "the social" and the emergence of an alternative public sphere.

Figure 1.1 shows the framework of this study, which can be induced from the discussion so far. It shows, firstly, that the focus of the following chapters is the interface between "the social" and localized mutuality. In this schema, "the social" is an assemblage of ideas and institutions embodied in the various social policies and development projects. On the other hand, localised mutuality consists of informal/personal ties such as families, kinship, neighbourhoods, communities, and patron-client relationships. In the neoliberal restructuring of "the social", social policies and development projects mobilise those informal and personal ties to achieve their purposes. Such articulation between and entanglement of "the social" and localised mutuality induces re-interpretation,

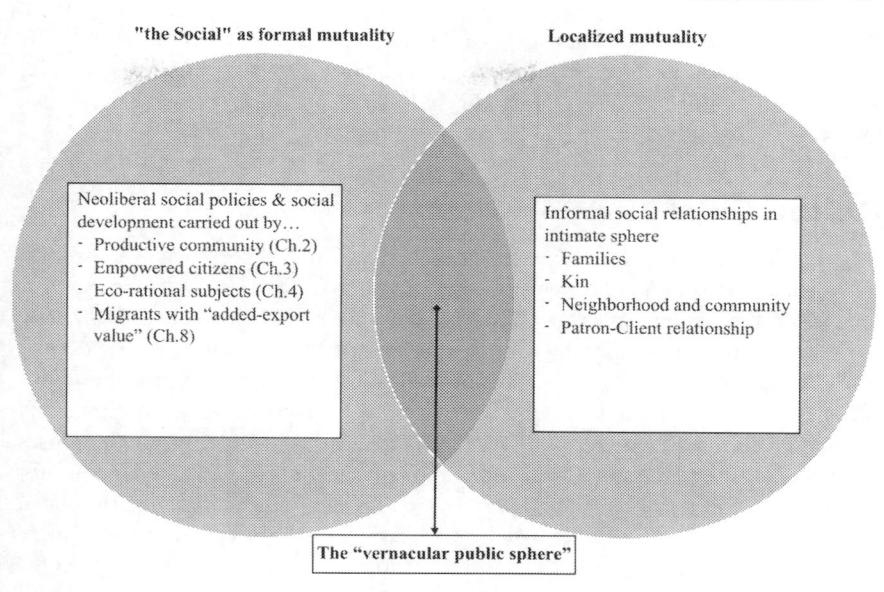

"the Social" as formal mutuality   Localized mutuality

Neoliberal social policies & social
development carried out by...
- Productive community (Ch.2)
- Empowered citizens (Ch.3)
- Eco-rational subjects (Ch.4)
- Migrants with "added-export
  value" (Ch.8)

Informal social relationships in
intimate sphere
- Families
- Kin
- Neighborhood and community
- Patron-Client relationship

The "vernacular public sphere"

Figure 1.1 The "vernacular public sphere" as the focus of this study

re-activation, or even reinvention, of those localised social relationships. The book seeks to identify the contour of the alternative public sphere emerging in this process of reconfiguration of localised mutuality.

As the cases of social policies and development projects, the chapters of the book will deal with poverty alleviation and security (Chapters 2 and 3), natural resource conservation (Chapters 4–6), and overseas employment and transnational emigration (Chapters 7–10). These social development policies are motivated and mobilised by such neoliberal rationales as "productive community" (Chapter 2), "empowered and active citizens" (Chapter 2 and 3), "manager of nature" (Chapter 4), and "migrants with 'added-export value'"(Chapter 8). The chapters will argue; firstly, how, and in what way, the social relationships of localised mutuality are re-interpreted, re-activated, and re-invented through the interaction, and negotiation, with the neoliberal social policies and development; and secondly, what is the emerging contour of alternative public sphere at the interface between the "social" and localised mutuality. In this study, the alternative public sphere is conceptualised as, and used interchangeably with, the "vernacular public sphere" to emphasise that the focus of this study is neither on the formal civil society nor the informal social relationships, but rather, as discussed by Ileto, on the public sphere which "simultaneously occupy, or oscillate between the public (i.e., nationalist) and private (local and familial) spheres" (Ileto 1999:61). The author believes that the elaboration of the vernacular public sphere entails broader implications which go beyond the context of the Philippines. It has been quite some time since serious doubts were raised, not only in the Global North but Global South as well, about the sustainability of the welfare system based solely on "the social" as formal/institutional mutuality. This study wishes to contribute to conceptualise a more robust, sustainable, and inclusive public sphere amidst the precarity and uncertainty that current human society faces.[5]

Organization of the Book

This book is composed of nine chapters, divided into three parts, in addition to an introduction and a conclusion. Part I, "Urban Poverty and Clientelism", focuses on the uncertainties faced by the urban poor living in slums, particularly those arising from their extremely limited access to basic life resources and opportunities, such as land, employment, and education. It then examines the implications of clientelistic networks between people and those with resources, such as local politicians. Part II, "Conservation and Emergent Community", focuses on the small-scale fishermen who experience uncertainty due to the depletion of marine resources in rural fishing communities. It examines the role of networks in addressing such uncertainties, which, while being rooted in the intimate sphere of the community, is articulated with the various actors beyond the closed community. Finally, Part III, "Mobility and Connectedness in Transnational Social Fields", focuses on the uncertainties inherent in the expanding transnational social field as people migrate from the Philippines to other countries as workers and immigrants. It examines the mutuality that emerges from the intimate ties of community, family, and fellow compatriots. The final chapter, as a conclusion, considers the implications of the ethnographic cases of these chapters for the concept of the "vernacular public sphere".

Chapters 2 and 3 focus on the government's social policies that target residents of poor neighbourhoods of Marikina City in Metro Manila. Chapter 2 examines the Community Mortgage Programme (CMP), which aims to create legitimate landownership among slum dwellers, often derogatorily referred to as "squatters", indicating their illegal occupancy of the land. While the details of the programme are described in the main text, this chapter views the CMP not simply as a social policy to provide land, but also as a citizenship project to foster the ethics, morals, values, and lifestyles deemed appropriate for land-owning citizens among the residents. The homeowners associations organised by the beneficiary residents themselves are considered a principal actor in terms of its implementation. In the process of land acquisition, these organizations foster values such as hard work, thrift, and responsibility among their members (especially for repaying the loans). In other words, the CMP relies on the activation and empowerment of residents through the formation of their own organizations. However, the material in this chapter suggests that while the CMP creates a certain number of legitimate landowners, it also creates new conflicts, divisions, and peripheralization among residents, as some are personally linked, or suspected of being linked, with local politicians through patron–client relationships. In other words, it becomes clear that social development programmes, which are intended to be self-activating and empowering in their institutional design, coexist with, and are being penetrated by, a vastly different logic of clientelistic ties based on private and individual exchanges in the process of implementation. However, this chapter does not conclude with only one aspect of the erosion of public policy by such clientelism, but rather argues that it is precisely these informal ties that enable the urban poor to access external resources.

Chapter 3 deals with the case of a Conditional Cash Transfer Programme (CCT), which is a policy for alleviating poverty among slum dwellers by supplementing their meagre incomes. Through this case, it is argued that clientelistic linkages, and the direct provision of particular goods and services mediated by them, are actually requested and desired by the population, even in the face of criticism against such personalised exchange by the government and middle-class people of the country. The crux of CCT policies is that cash is provided by the government on the condition that the residents themselves maintain and promote their children's education and their family's health and hygiene, and actively "invest in human capital". In the process of implementing these policies, people are urged to become active citizens who internalise appropriate values and morals and voluntarily seek and practice "investment in human capital" rather than simply being dependent on government dole-outs and charity. However, such policies are limited in their ability to ensure people's survival against the risks inherent in the everyday realities of the slums, such as natural disasters, precarious informal sector work, and family breakdowns owing to poverty. In the face of these realities, critical voices from beneficiaries are calling for more direct and generous benefits to the poor, rather than for imposing stricter conditions. These voices, while being critical against government programmes that rely on self-activation and self-help, call for alternative logic and ethics in terms of redistribution between the haves and have-nots, which is akin to patronage based on more intimate and personal ties.

The chapters in Part II present cases mainly from a coastal fishing village in the Province of Palawan in the western part of the Philippines. Since the enactment of the "Philippine Fisheries Code of 1998", various resource management practices have undergone the institutionalisation process. The resource management regime institutionalised by the Code is characterised by the devolution of state authority over resource management to local governments and the mobilization of resource user communities. Under this regime, waters that used to be open access are bounded and enclosed as a space for exclusive use by a limited number of resource users, and are further divided and classified according to the market value of the resources. Such a resource management regime involves the management of the natural environment, and at the same time, or even more than that, encourages the self-management of resource users themselves through internalizing a particular rationality for conservation. Such a regime, to put it differently, constitutes a device for moulding the coastal residents into the subject as a "manager of nature". In Chapter 4, the process of institutionalization of marine resource management is delineated in detail, followed by an argument for how such institutionalization often conflicts with traditional resource use patterns in villages, constrains fishermen's livelihoods, and creates new divisions and marginalization among fishermen.

Chapter 5 presents the case of the reorganization of resource use patterns observed in the process of institutionalization explained in the previous chapter. Through this case, this chapter deals with how the institution of resource management is "contextualized" in the sense that fishermen interpret and appropriate the formal resource management regime in a way that becomes more compatible with the specific resource uses of their own communities. Such a contextualization process can be seen as a response by communities to the new risks posed by the resource management regime. Community, in this case, is not a self-contained community marked by boundedness and homogeneity, but rather a community that is open to a variety of actors, such as local governments and NGOs. This chapter thus avoids a dichotomy of community versus civil society and instead examines the "vernacular public sphere" that emerges at the interface between localised mutuality in communities and policies and the institution of coastal resource management.

In Chapter 6, the focus shifts from the community to the individual level and presents the life history of a fisherman. The transition of livelihood activities as seen in his life history shows that the resource management regime discussed in Chapters 4 and 5 largely constrains and restricts his fishing activities, while at the same time, he makes use of the new livelihood opportunities created by the regime. What can be understood from his life history is that the fishermen in the field site are not subjects who thoroughly internalise the norms and discipline demanded by the resource management regime or, conversely, actors who squarely resist such a regime. Rather, what is emerging is an agency that tides over in everyday life while making do with the various livelihood opportunities available at hand. The various connections and networks that this fisherman maintains with fishing communities are what makes such a flexible livelihood strategy possible. In this way, the chapter addresses again, with a microscopic lens focused on a certain individual, the question asked in Chapter 5 of what kind of mutuality, or "vernacular public sphere", is emerging among the people for coping with the uncertainties posed by contemporary resource management regimes in the rural Philippines.

Part III deals with the transnational social field, which has expanded as a result of continuous overseas migration from the Philippines. In the Philippines, the state, particularly the Philippine Overseas Employment Administration, actively encourages its own people to work abroad. However, this does not necessarily mean that the state prepares robust welfare and security for such overseas migrant workers. Rather, the government, through providing various opportunities for skills seminars and qualifications for migrants, encourages them to become risk-conscious and preventive subjects who can adapt to volatile migrant labour markets and survive abroad by their own responsibility. The uncertainties inherent in the transnational social field are exacerbated by the retreat of the state in providing a safety net for overseas migrants. Such uncertainties include, for example, civil wars and conflicts in host countries, abuse by employers, and a breakdown of the family due to long-term separation. With the inability of the state to provide adequate security against these uncertainties, a kind of mutuality and form of "the social" emerge to enable survival in the precarity of the expanding, and deepening, transnational social field of the Filipino people. With this as a basic line of inquiry in Part III, Chapter 7 examines the life history of a woman, the wife of an overseas migrant worker, living in an urban poor neighbourhood. Based on her life history, the chapter depicts how individuals access necessary goods and resources by activating and utilizing networks "from below" (e.g., neighbourhoods, grassroots community organizations, NGOs, and the media).

In contrast to the relatively lower-class labour migration discussed in Chapter 7, Chapter 8 deals with the migration of the middle class. What is the motivation behind the desire of those in the middle class, many of whom have formal professional jobs in the Philippines, to migrate to Western countries? Interviews reveal that their migration is not necessarily motivated by economic necessity, but rather by a distrust of the state and its constituent classes, both upper and lower, and by family strategies to provide a better future for their children, who are still of school age. The uncertainties posed by a fragile state are experienced by middle-class people with a sense of insecurity and hopelessness due to an uncertain future. For them, migration abroad can be understood as an act of risk-avoidance through securing a more desirable education and living environment for their children.

Chapter 9 focuses on children who have been brought to the US by such middle-class parents and examines the difficulties they experience in this host country. While these children experience conflicts with other ethnic groups and marginalization in the mainstream White society of the US, they also face various difficulties within their own ethnic group, the Filipino immigrant population. This chapter argues that the identities of so-called "1.5 generation" children, who left the Philippines at school age and immigrated to the US with their parents, are constructed in contrast to the second generation, who are the same age as the 1.5 generation but were born in the US. In relation to the Filipino second generation, who have internalised the values and behaviours of mainstream American society, 1.5 generation children, who are forced to experience a double-identification process between the Philippines and the US, often have feelings of inferiority, insecurity, and marginalization. Yet, it is remarkable that they speak of "family", emphasised as a core value of "We, the Filipino", as a symbol to differentiate themselves most sharply from the second generation. It is argued that the "family" in this context is a representation of their identity constructed in opposition to the second generation, which works as a symbolic resource to secure their position in the immigrant society of the US. The cases of Chapters 8 and 9 reveal that, in response to the risks and uncertainties posed by globalization and a weak state, people are choosing to migrate abroad as a family life strategy and attempting to adapt to a transnational social field by utilizing family and kinship networks. Thus, intimate ties with family have become a resource for constructing identities amid the conflicts and marginalization they experience in the transnational social field.

Chapter 10 examines the emergent form of the "vernacular public sphere" which, while based on family and kinship ties, goes beyond the personal sphere of intimacy and is linked with a broader mutuality of various actors in the transnational social field. Specifically, I present some cases of middle-class people who have the same class background as those covered in Chapters 7 and 8, who plan to migrate abroad as a family strategy, but stay in the country while engaging in NGO activities for the welfare of overseas Filipino migrants. Overseas migration, as an act of differentiation and distinction by the middle class, does indeed produce disparities and division between the middle and other classes in the Philippines. However, middle-class people, precisely because of their position as "middle", cannot help but entertain the "fear of falling", and overseas migration, rather than being an act of guaranteed success and upward mobility, has a risky aspect for them in that they may experience downward class mobility or lose the status and property they accumulated before their departure from the country. The chapter argues that such uncertainty inherent in the migration of the middle class prevents them from completely severing their ties with others in the Philippines, including those in other classes, and further urges them to seek connection and solidarity with the people remaining in the country. However, in a contemporary transnational social field, where the state is withdrawing from its role of providing the people with social protection and uncertainty is accordingly increasing, strong and lasting solidarity based on class identity is no longer possible. What can be found from these cases is a mutuality of loosely connected networks, or transient solidarity, that contains aspects of both articulation and disarticulation with others. Such articulation and disarticulation appear alternately according to specific circumstances. We can find in such loose networks and transient solidarity not only the selfish interests of the middle class, but also their genuine desire for connection with their compatriots (*kapwa*).

The concluding chapter discusses the implications of the cases presented in each chapter with regard to the theme of the emergence of the "vernacular public sphere". What emerges from the ethnographies of the preceding chapters is that, in today's Philippines, the state has increasingly withdrawn from being the core actor that provides "the social", and has instead sought to achieve its purpose of dealing with various precarities and uncertainties of the people through activating and mobilizing various non-state actors such as individuals, families, neighbourhood associations, communities, and NGOs. In this sense, the argument in these chapters can be seen as just another example of neoliberal governmentality made possible through "government at a distance" and "governing through free subjects" adopted as an analytical lens in this book. What previous studies of governmentality have not discussed, however, is how localised mutuality that is reactivated through interactions with the neoliberalised ideas and institutions of "the social" could actually create broader associations and solidarity, that can be called the "vernacular public sphere".

Among the urban poor, for example, patronage and clientelism based on informal and private ties were being reinterpreted as a desirable network to tide them over in their predicament. In the fishing village under the resource management regime, mutuality rooted in community ties is articulated with the neoliberal social policy of resource management and mobilised to create the vernacular public sphere. Furthermore, the migrants living in transnational social fields created new meanings of "family" and "compatriot (*kapwa*)" that were mobilised as symbolic resources to deal with the precarity and uncertainties inherent in overseas migration. Thus, the final chapter elaborates, as a conclusion, the way in which these informal ties and mutualities negotiate with, and even appropriate, the penetrating power of neoliberal governmentality so that it creates the "vernacular public sphere" for the people living in the Philippines and other parts of the Global South to tame contemporary precarity and uncertainties.

Notes

1. The discussion of "the invention of the social" is based on works by Jacques Donzelot (1984, 1979). His major work in French (*L'invention du Social: Essai sur le déclin des passions politiques*) is partially translated in English (Donzelot 1988, 1991). Since I am not able to read French, I owe much to the recent Japanese translation of the whole text by anthropologist Ichiro Majima (published in 2020).
2. Thus, while "the social" was invented during the 1830s and 1840s in Western Europe, as discussed by Donzelot and Castel, its development and establishment as a concrete institution was a long and gradual process. There were some epoch-making thinkers and thoughts during this long history of the deployment of "the social", which spans more than 100 years. Some of those thinkers and thoughts include Léon Bourgeois' "solidarism" at the end of the nineteenth century (Omoda 2010), some thinkers during the Third Republic in France (1870–1940), such as Émile Durkheim's discovery of the society as "organic solidarity", Marcel Mauss' discussion of the gift as "total social fact" and his advocacy for cooperatives based on it, and William Henry Beveridge's "Beveridge Report" in 1942; these thoughts converged into the concrete institution of the welfare states in Western Europe that had blossomed during the 1950s, 1960s, and 1970s. In a similar vein, according to Esping-Andersen (1999: 33), "what we call the welfare state may have its roots in, but certainly does not begin with, late nineteenth-century social reformism. The welfare state is a peculiar historical construction that began to unfold between the 1930s and 1960s".
3. My quote of the work by Donzelot and Estebe (1994) is based on Castel (2009). Since I am not able to read French, I relied on its Japanese translation by Toru Kitagaki, which was published in 2015.
4. Claudio attempts to update the discussion of liberalism based on the postwar political history of the Philippines. Although the Philippines is an "unlikely place" and "strange vista" for a discussion of liberalism, Claudio argues that "narrating a history of liberalism outside the so-called 'liberal-democratic West' will allow us to view it askance" (Claudio 2017: 2). The justification of the case study of this book overlaps with his standpoint.
5. The concept of the "vernacular public sphere" owes match to the existing anthropological discussions such as the "indigenous public sphere" by Comaroff and Comaroff (1999), the "alternative mode of civil society" by Hann (1996), the "political society" by Chaterjee (2004), and "vernacular democracy" by Tanabe (2007). I noticed the discussion by Tanabe and others on "vernacular public arena" in India (Neyazi and Tanabe 2014) only after completion of the draft of this book. The concept is a further development from the notion of "emergent sociality" that I discussed in Seki (2020).

Prologue to Part I

Urban Poverty and Clientelism

The two chapters that make up Part I argue for the neoliberal restructuring of "the social" in the setting of the urban poor community of Metro Manila. The chapters present concrete cases of social policies that aim to alleviate the plight of the urban poor and discuss how these policies are permeated by the logic of neoliberal governmentality, under which, residents restructure their mentality and practices in their everyday lives. In particular, I examine how formal institutions to promote the project and informal institution of clientelism are mutually inseparable. Clientelism is defined as an interdependent relationship between the poor and the political elite which consists of a personal exchange of loyalty and votes from the poor on the one hand, and protection and benefits from the political elite on the other. It is true that such personal relationships have always been subjected to harsh criticism, especially from the country's middle class, for being a breeding ground for graft and corruption, an obstacle to the development of civil society, and the root cause of the "weak state". Here, however, I would like to consider the implications of the intimate interdependence and reciprocity between the weak and powerful that is suggested in the narratives and practices of the poor.

As an introduction to Chapters 2 and 3, this prologue provides some basic perspectives on the neoliberal urban governance that has a significant impact on the urban space and lives of the poor in the Philippines today. I then review some of the major literature on urban communities in the Philippines.

In general, neoliberal urban governance can be summarised as a shift from "urban managerialism" to "urban entrepreneurism" (Harvey 1989)—a shift from centralised and highly subsidised urban planning based on state regulation to a more diffuse, fragmented, and flexible governance utilising non-state entities such as voluntary associations, private firms, communities, and individuals. To put it differently, urban entrepreneurism is about the "public sector running cities in a more businesslike manner, in which institutions of local governance operate like the private sector or are replaced by private sector-based system" (Swyngedouw, Moulaert & Rodriguez 2002: 573). However, this process does not simply mean the "political withdrawal" or "abstentionism" of the state (Osborne & Rose 1999: 751); rather, the state actively seeks new partnerships with the above-mentioned non-state entities through "facilitating, enabling,

DOI: 10.4324/9781003224273-2

stimulating, shaping, and inciting their self-governing activities" (Osborne & Rose 1999: 751). As such, neoliberal states do not abandon "the will to govern" (Rose 1996b: 53); rather, "they seek techniques of government that create a distance between the decisions of formal political institutions and other social actors, conceive of these actors in new ways as subjects of responsibility, autonomy and choice, and seek to act upon them through shaping and utilising their freedom" (Rose 1996b: 53–54). In a word, it is a "government at a distance" (Rose 1999).

Particularly, in the urban poor slum communities such as those dealt with in this study, the poor residents are mobilised as effective and productive labour power. This promotes a shift from subjectivities dependent on social welfare into those more suited to "workfare" (Peck 2001). Such workfare policies denounce welfare dependency while trying to deter welfare claims, and encourage people to accept even low-paying and unstable jobs. In truth, it should be noted that "workfare is not about creating jobs for people that don't have them; it is about creating workers for jobs that nobody wants. In a Foucauldian sense, it is seeking to make 'docile bodies' for the new economy: flexible, self-reliant, and self-disciplining" (Peck 2001: 6).

Entangled with such a workfare regime, the residents of urban poor neighbourhoods are encouraged not only to maximise their marketability and employability, but also to manage risks in their community. A community of so-called "productive citizens" can be maintained through continuous monitoring and risk assessment in the neighbourhood and an active adoption of risk reduction strategies. Hence, the residents are urged to not only enhance the well-being of the communities, but also police them. Such policing considers certain groups of residents, such as the unemployed, vagrants, or potential criminals, to be a risky category, eventually stigmatising and consequently excluding them. This governing through exclusion not only polices the risk in the community, but also, by means of setting specific standards, models, and norms, ultimately creates a category of "undeserving" or "uncivil" residents who fail to live up to these set standards, models, and norms.

The urban governance that has emerged in the Philippines since the 1990s, which shares the neoliberal logic summarised above, can be framed as an "enablement model" realised within a context of political decentralisation, democratisation, and economic liberalisation (Shatkin 2000, 2004).[1] Under this model, the national government avoids intervening too much in urban governance, limiting its role to enabling local government, markets, the private sector, NGOs, neighbourhoods, and community-based organisations to distribute social welfare provisions, development services, and resources such as housing and land. With this mode of urban planning, the major cities of the Philippines, particularly Metro Manila, have experienced a huge influx of investments in infrastructure by mainly the private sector, notably Light Rail Transit, over/underpasses at major thoroughfares, and shopping malls and high-rise condominiums catering mainly to the emerging middle class, sometimes called the "new rich" (Pinches 1999). A potentially unintended effect of this urban development, identified by

Shatkin (2007, 2008) as "bypass-implant urbanism", is that it almost exclusively benefits the urban middle and upper classes while "bypassing" the well-being and interests of the poor and lower labour class.

In the two chapters of Part I, we examine specifically the social policies developed against the backdrop of such neoliberal urban governance based on fieldwork carried out in a poor neighbourhood in Marikina City, Metro Manila. Though studies on slum and urban poor communities in the Philippines include the now-classic anthropological ethnography by Jocano (1975), a majority are policy-oriented surveys based on the evaluation of government programs on urban land reform and social housing.[2] As an exception to those policy oriented studies, the anthropological study by Pinches is a valuable contribution to the understanding of complex interactions between the lower working and middle classes, as well as the resultant identity of the lower class urban poor observed in one of Metro Manila's slum areas (Pinches 1992a, 1992b). Some sociological studies deal with the activities of the local people's organisations demanding residential rights and entitlements, particularly in regard to the agency of local residents (Berner 1997, 2000, 2001; Parnell 2002). Studies carried out by political scientists have produced remarkable insights into the political participation of the urban poor and their views on democratic politics. Schaffer's study, for example, which was based on the voters' education campaign in urban poor areas in Metro Manila, describes how the view of the current state of Philippine democracy and characteristics of individual politicians is significantly different between the poor and the upper and middle class, and that such differences have resulted in a severe and deep class divide and conflict among different classes in the contemporary Philippines (Schaffer 2005). In a similar vein, Garrido's study deals with symbolic boundary-making between the poor and upper/ middle classes, which is often expressed explicitly and, at the same time, contested during major political rallies and street demonstrations (Garrido 2008, 2019). Further, Hutchison focuses on the limitations of the societal incorporation of the urban poor, even under the democratisation process, since the late 1980s, and on the "disallowed" political participation of the NGOs working for the rights of those urban poor (Hutchison 2007). Finally, Kusaka, based on fieldwork involving street vendors in Metro Manila, discusses the deep divides among the urban social classes, particularly between the "masses" (the poor labour class) and the "citizens" (the middle class) (Kusaka 2017). He points out the predominance of a "dual public sphere" emerging from the moral conflict between the "masses" and "citizens".

While owing much to the existing literature, the following two chapters try to bring sharper relief to an aspect of urban governance, described by Cruikshank as "technologies of citizenship", that governs and shapes people to become autonomous, self-sufficient, politically engaged, and participatory, while, at the same time, making visible the segment of the population who failed to be such citizens (Cruikshank 1999). The following chapters particularly elaborate the emerging form of the vernacular public sphere observed in the process of the making and unmaking of citizens and their communities, which is realised through the dual processes of inclusion and exclusion of the urban residents in Metro Manila.

Notes

1. See Bird and Rodriguez (1999) and Eaton (2001) for a more general discussion of decentralisation in the Philippines and its institutional limitations in terms of poverty reduction.
2. As examples of urban studies on policies and their evaluations, see Lee (1995), Rebullia et al. (1999), Casino (2001), Llanto and Orbeta (2001), Manasan (2002), Antolihao (2004), Porio (2004), Veneracion (2004), Ballesteros (2005), Murphy (2008).

2 Association Eroded?
Land Tenure Programme for Slum Residents and the Clientelistic Connection

This chapter focuses on a government project aimed at providing land for slum dwellers.[1] Particularly, it examines the situation where a resident association organised as a formal institution to implement the project actually coexists, and interpenetrates, with the informal institutions of clientelistic connections. In the beginning, it delineates the characteristics of local governance of Marikina City, Metro Manila, in the context of the neoliberal urban governance elaborated in the prologue, particularly since the 1990s. Additionally, an overview is provided of Barangay Malanday in Marikina City, where I conducted intensive fieldwork. The subsequent section provides an overview of the Community Mortgage Programme (CMP), a social policy that this chapter deals with as the main case. Particular focus is placed on the role of the homeowners association, which is the driving force behind the CMP, and traces how such associations have been incorporated into, and mobilised by, government policy in the process of the state's decentralisation since the 1990s. The next section, the central part of this chapter, consists of data obtained during fieldwork in Barangay Malanday. It first examines the progress of the CMP in the study area. Particularly, it identifies the factors that determine the success or failure of the CMP based on the cases of several associations. This is followed by the specific ethnographic case of an association of street vendors who have not fully benefited from the CMP, but rather have become further marginalised within their communities in the process of the programme's implementation. In particular, we examine how these street vendors attempt to improve their peripheral position by organising an alternative association among their peers. Furthermore, as the main argument of the chapter, the urban governance of the slums, which attempts to achieve land tenure security for slum dwellers, is, on the one hand, enabled by the mobilisation of the associations among the residents who are nurtured to become citizenry subjects and have internalised a spirit of self-help and self-reliance, and on the other hand, intermingles with the clientelistic connection between local politicians and residents, which is somehow considered to be an erosion of formal institutions by informal ones. As a conclusion, while avoiding the conventional interpretation of such erosion as a negative aspect that brings only the failure to the programme, I propose a more complicated, and nuanced, view regarding the implications of coexistence of the seemingly conflicting logics of the association

DOI: 10.4324/9781003224273-3

of active citizens on the one hand and clientelism on the other in the progression of the CMP.

Urban Governance in Marikina City in Barangay Malanday

Here, I would like to examine the characteristics of urban governance in Marikina City in Metro Manila. Since the enactment of Republic Act No. 7160 in 1991, commonly known as the Local Government Code of the Philippines (hereinafter, the "Local Government Code"), many of the functions and powers previously carried out by the central government in the Philippines have been delegated to the local governments, and the discretion of the heads of the local governments have been expanded. With this institutional transition as a background, Bayani Fernando came into power in the city government of Marikina. He was in power from 1992 to 2001, and his wife, Marides Fernando, was the mayor from 2001 to 2010. In the May 2010 election, an anti-Fernando candidate was elected to the post, defeating a candidate from the Fernando camp. The style of governance initiated by Bayani and Marides Fernando, however, was influential and has shaped the mode of local governance of Marikina City to this day. Hence, the characteristics of the "conjugal leadership" by Bayani and Marides carried out during the two decades since the beginning of the decentralisation is quite significant in discussing today's local governance in Marikina City, which is delineated in detail below.

Marikina City, located on the eastern edge of Metro Manila, had a population of 496,206 and 105,351 households as of 2009, when the fieldwork for this study was most intensively conducted.[2] When Bayani Fernando started his career as a mayor in 1992, a conspicuous feature of Marikina was the huge slum areas spread along the Marikina River running through the centre of the city that absorbed a huge number of internal migrants from rural areas (Picture 2.1). According to the residents, at that time, Marikina was known to be a "*talahiban*" (a vacant field where only coarse grass can be found) and "*tambakan ng bangkay*" (an illicit dumping site for corpses involved in crimes). Being such, Marikina was perceived by its own people as rather disorderly and dangerous. Bayani, who ran for his mayorship with such slogans as "Squatter-free community" and "Let us set our community right" (*Ayusin natin ang ating komunidad*), was elected to the city administration in 1992. "Community", and particularly an "orderly community (*maayos na komunidad*)", was a motto in his local governance. What, then, was the "orderly community" sought after by Bayani's administration? In order to understand this point, various city ordinances issued during the terms of office of Bayani and Marides are examined here. As Table 2.1 indicates, ordinances that were intended to regulate various aspects of community life in Marikina were frequently issued during the Fernando administration.

What is noteworthy in the table is that in these ordinances, "community" is used interchangeably with "public space". The ordinances issued under Bayani

Picture 2.1 Settlement along the river in Marikina City (Barangay Tumana)

and Marides tried to regulate, sometimes meticulously, the people's behaviour in the community as a public space.

Interestingly, the prefaces to these ordinances reiterate and emphasise certain terms. Some of the "keywords" are, for example, "health", "safety", "security", "order", and "sanitation". These aspects should be realized and maintained through the "discipline", "propriety", and "higher morals" of the residents. The ordinances continue to underscore that the "proper conduct of its citizenry" should be achieved for this purpose. The ordinances also delineate, sometimes even meticulously, what kind of acts are deemed to be a "public disturbance", "public nuisance", and "violence". Finally, they advocate that an "orderly community" can be realized only through the exclusion of these acts from "public places". Thus, the "orderly community", which was sought after by the Fernandos, was no longer a community bound by the primordial attachment of slum dwellers who shared homogeneous demographic backgrounds, but rather expected to be a civil space connected through the public interests of urban society transcending personal and parochial concerns; this was the "orderly community" envisioned by the Fernandos, often dreamed to be a "sanitary" and "peaceful" so-called "Little Singapore" and founded under a spirit of "discipline" and "self-help" of "healthy citizens".

Further, the style of administration by Marides Fernando is often called the "corporate approach" (Gonzalez 2009: 68). In this approach, the citizens' lives

Table 2.1 Major City Ordinances of Marikina Regulating the Activities in "Public Spaces" Issued Under the Administration of Bayani and Marides Fernando

Ordinance number (year of issuance)	Title of the ordinance	Objectives and major stipulations of the ordinance
#59 (1993)	ORDINACE REGULATING THE USE OF STREETS AND SIDEWALKS IN THE MUNICIPALITY OF MARIKINA	• "It shall be unlawful for any person to occupy any portion of the streets and/or sidewalks within the Municipality of Marikina for purposes other than for purely pedestrian walk" (sec. 2). • The following acts are prohibited: "vending or selling of foods, magazines, newspapers etc.; conduct of shoe-shine occupation; conduct of religious activities such as preaching and seeking alms; doing house chores such as washing clothes, hanging clothes, and bathing" (sec. 2).
#86 (1994)	ORDINACE PROHIBITING THE REMOVAL, DEFACEMENT, AND OTHER FORMS OF VANDALISM ON ALL MUNICIPAL SIGNBOARDS, STREAMERS, TRAFFIC SIGNS, STREETNAMES, AND PUBLIC OR NATIONAL MARKERS POSTED ON STREETS AND OTHER OFFICIALLY DESIGNATED PLACES IN THE MUNICIPALITY	• To preserve all government-funded properties which includes signboards, streamers, traffic signs, street names, markers. • "It shall be unlawful for any person to remove, deface, or commit other forms of vandalism on public or national markers posted on streets or other officially designed places" (sec. 1).
#74 (1996)	ORDINANCE PROHIBITING THE DRINKING OF INTOXICATING LIQUOR ON SIDEWALKS, STREETS, ALLEYS, PARKS, AND OTHER PUBLIC PLACES WITHIN THE MUNICIPALITY OF MARIKINA AND PRESCRIBING PENALTY FOR THE PURPOSE	• To penalise the drinking of alcohol in the public places. • "it has been of common knowledge that many unnecessary noise, community disturbance and violence in public places are committed by intoxicated people who hold drinking sessions in sidewalks, streets, alleys, parks and other public places".

(Continued)

Table 2.1 Major City Ordinances of Marikina Regulating the Activities in "Public Spaces" Issued Under the Administration of Bayani and Marides Fernando *(Continued)*

Ordinance number (year of issuance)	Title of the ordinance	Objectives and major stipulations of the ordinance
#57 (1999)	ORDINANCE PROHIBITING THE BURNING OF GARBAGE, TRASH OR ANY OTHER REFUSE MATERIALS IN STREETS, SIDEWALKS AND OTHER PUBLIC PLACES	• 2,000 pesos for the first offense. 5,000 pesos for the subsequent offenses.
#116 (2001)	MARIKINA SETTLEMENT CODE OF 2001	• Provision of land reform and social housing programmes, including the CMP, for the urban poor communities. • Establishing the Marikina Settlement Office (MSO) for the task of these programmes. • Comprehensive stipulation of the prohibited acts in community such as drinking alcohol, gamble, illegal parking, and so on. • Injunction to install the toilet for each household. Penalty for the offender.
#163 (2001)	ORDINACE IMPLEMENTING A CITYWIDE CURFEW, BANNING MINORS FROM LOITERING FROM 11 P.M. TO 4 A.M.	• "In a serious effort to promote discipline and proper conduct to its citizenry, most specially to its juvenile sector, the city government deems it necessary to implement a citywide curfew, imposed on minors who place themselves within the territorial jurisdiction of Marikina, as maybe further classified in public places".
#73 (2002)	ORDINANCE ADOPTING THE ANTI-LITTERING CODE OF MARIKINA 2002	• To prohibit the littering, particularly the cigarette, in the public space.

(Continued)

Table 2.1 Major City Ordinances of Marikina Regulating the Activities in "Public Spaces" Issued Under the Administration of Bayani and Marides Fernando *(Continued)*

Ordinance number (year of issuance)	Title of the ordinance	Objectives and major stipulations of the ordinance
#108 (2002)	ORDINACE ADOPTING THE MARIKINA CITY DRESS CODE IN PUBLIC PLACES 2002	• "To strengthen the city's drive towards orderliness, propriety and discipline to bring about an atmosphere of decency and to uphold higher morals among Marikeños". • "No person shall move about (i.e. walk, jog, run, or the like) in public places and outside his private residence topless" (sec. 3). • "Market vendors must be attired as follows: a.) T-Shirt, Blouse or any top apparel with sleeves, b.) Pants or Skirt, c.) Shoes, sandals or step-in, d.) Apron, for vendors in the wet section" (sec. 4).
#67 (2003)	ORDINACE ADOPTING THE NEW MARIKINA ANIMAL CODE OF 2003	• Stipulation on animal care and protection, responsible pet ownership, as well as sanitation and cleanliness. • "Dog owners taking their pets out for a walk or on strolls shall ensure that their dogs are properly restrained with a leash of two (2) meters long and properly muzzled" (sec. 18). • "Straying or roaming of animals in public spaces, streets or plaza is prohibited" (sec. 19). • "The dumping of carcass of dead animals such as dogs, pigs, cats, rats, among others in drainage, canals, rivers, and other waterways is strictly prohibited including all public places such as roadways, sidewalks, publicly owned vacant lots, etc." (sec. 20). • "All dog owners are required to submit their dogs for anti-rabies vaccination every six (6) months" (sec. 24).
#145 (2006)	MARIKINA PEACE, ORDER, PUBLIC SAFETY AND SECURITY CODE OF 2006	• "To promote health and safety, maintain peace and order, and preserve the comfort and conveniences of their inhabitants" (sec. 2). • Comprehensive provision and penalties regarding the peace, order, public safety, and security in Marikina.

in Marikina are managed as if they were a corporation, and what is given the most priority is the enhancement of the market value of the whole city and its residents in order to entice investments (Gonzalez 2009: 68). Visitors to Marikina City Hall will invariably notice the motto of Marides inscribed on the inner wall of the reception hall, which reads, "We manage our city like a private corporation. One where there are stakeholders, workers, and customers. We treat them as our clients whom we want not only to satisfy but also to delight". Thus, the residents of Marikina are expected to be "entrepreneurs", "customers", and "consumers", and the purpose of city governance is to "satisfy" and "delight" these customers and consumers.

In sum, the conjugal governance by the Fernandos pursued the creation of "citizens" who, as members of a private corporation, have high productivity and market value in order to "satisfy" consumers and, similarly, investors. Only such citizens may be deemed entitled to an "orderly community" as a civil public sphere transcending the parochialism of a community of primordial attachment. As such, since the 1990s, Marikina typically embodied the neoliberal urban governmentality discussed in the prologue. The following part examines the flagship programme of Bayani and Marides' government for realizing such an "orderly community" and "citizens".

Two chapters in Part 1 present the case of Barangay Malanday, one of the 16 barangays that make up Marikina City.[3] As of 2009, Barangay Malanday had a population of 53,907 and 11,452 households. Its distinguishing feature is that about half of the inhabitants, or 6,000 households, are squatters or informal settlers who do not have legal land ownership rights (Pictures 2.2 and 2.3). Until

Picture 2.2 Informal settlement in Barangay Malanday

Picture 2.3 A family in informal settlement (Barangay Malanday)

the early 1990s, many of them made their living by subcontracting or sub-subcontracting shoemaking, a local industry in Marikina.[4] Today, however, due to the importation of cheap shoes from China, the shoe industry in Marikina has become a completely shunned industry. As a result, many residents who have lost their jobs are employed in the urban informal sector, with jobs such as street vendors or jeepney and tricycle (a small motorcycle with a sidecar) drivers (Pictures 2.4), and most of them earn less than the legal minimum wage of about 430 pesos per day (1 peso was about 0.02 USD in 2011).

The CMP and Homeowners Associations

The CMP is a nationwide programme initiated under the presidency of Corazon Aquino in the late 1980s that is intended to provide legally secured land titles for slum residents who have informally settled on either public or private land.[5] Specifically, the CMP capitalises on "self-help", "competition", and "peer-pressure" among residents in order to transform squatters into legal landholders (Lee 1995). In a broader context, the programme was based on the "enabling approach" recommended by the United Nations, under which the emphasis is to "coordinate community mobilization and organization, and to make the argument for state withdrawal from the delivery of housing goods and services in favor of providing support for local determination and action. Enabling

Picture 2.4 Tricycle drivers waiting for the passengers (Barangay Malanday)

policies ... recognize that, to be efficient, decisions concerning the investment of resources in domestic economic, social and physical development have to be taken at the lowest effective level" (United Nations Human Settlements Program 2003, quote from Hutchison 2007: 862; cf. Shatkin 2000; Reid 2005).

Figure 2.1 outlines the basic process of the CMP. The actors, or stakeholders, of the programme include the residents, the landowner, and the mediator between the two, who is referred to as the "originator". To be a beneficiary of the programme, the residents are required to organise community associations called homeowners associations. The number of members of one community association is limited to a maximum of 200 households, with each association having 15 core members, called "officers", including a president, secretary, treasurer, and board of directors.[6] The reason for this limitation is, according to the explanation of some officers of the associations, to allow an easier way to control and monitor the proper observance by every member of the procedures of the programme, particularly the requirement for monthly amortisation payments.

The originator, another stakeholder of the programme, is basically tasked with mediating between the landowners and residents. In the other cases where the CMP was adopted in the Philippines, the originators were mostly NGOs, whereas in the case of Marikina, the local government organised an agency called the Marikina Settlement Office that was exclusively tasked with carrying out the functions of the originator. Taking on the important role of the originator, this office explains

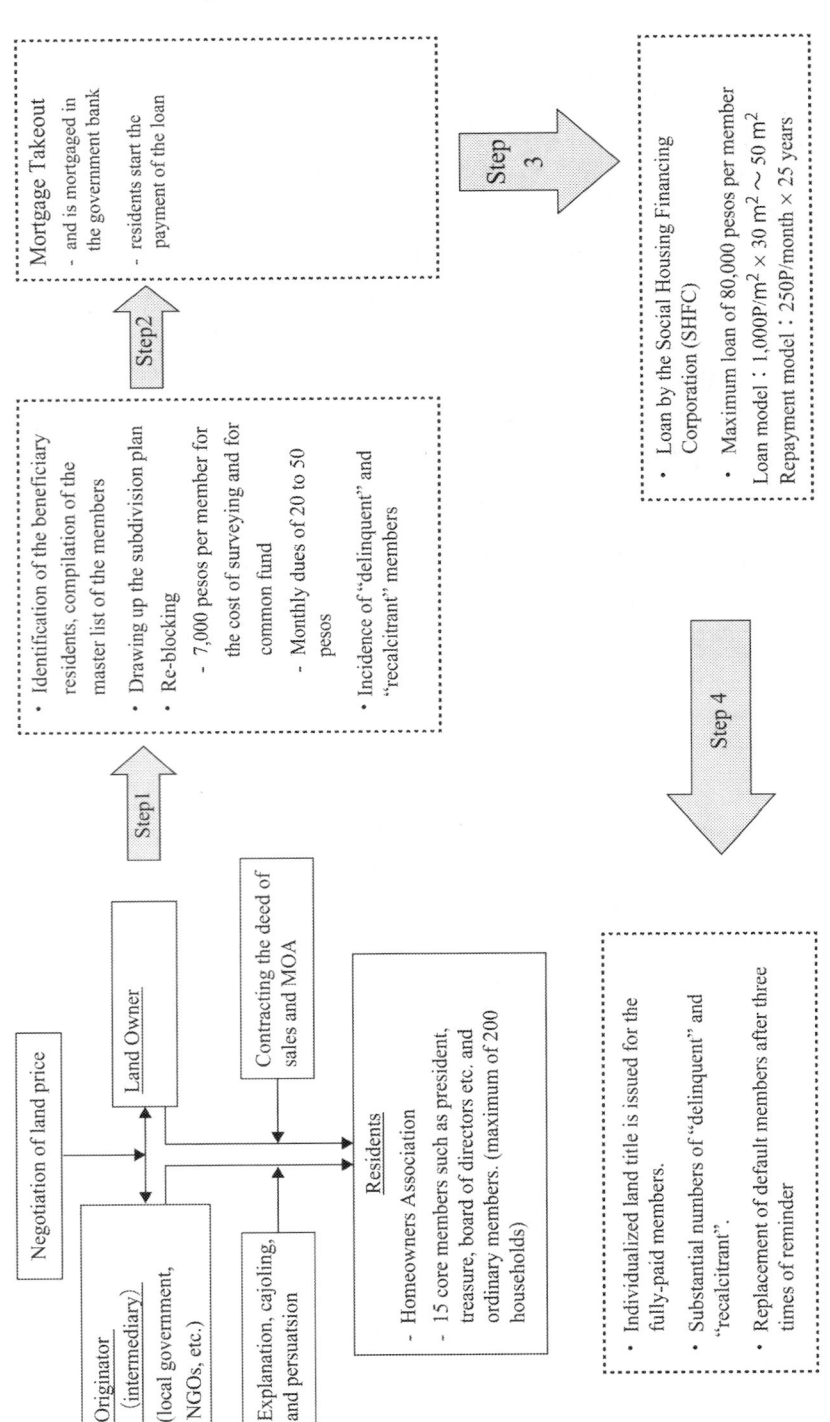

Figure 2.1 Actors and flow of the CMP as of 2009

the principles, significance, and mechanics of the CMP to the residents, as well as the benefits and rights that the residents are entitled to under the programme. It also negotiates an acceptable price with the landowners for them to sell their property. Once a landowner agrees on the price, a Deed of Sale and Memorandum of Agreement (MOA) are executed between the landowner and residents.

Here, it is interesting to note a certain stipulation in the MOA between the residents and landowner, which is provided as follows: "Should a close/distant relatives of the beneficiary intend to stay with him/her, the CA (Community Association, that is, Homeowners Association) should notify the mobilizer (i.e., Marikina Settlement Office [MSO]) in writing of the intended arrival date of the relative. The relative can only stay with the beneficiary within a maximum period of one (1) month from the date of arrival". Further, "In case of the need to temporarily leave the allocated lot due to work in far areas, the awardee through the CA shall notify the Mobilizer in writing within five (5) days prior to the intended departure date. The Mobilizer will conduct a regular occupancy check of the assigned lots. Occupant of the subject property should be the immediate family members of the beneficiary only". What can be read into these provisions is that the project tries to encourage the beneficiaries on the master list and their immediate family members to settle permanently in the designated plots, and conversely, to constrain the flexible, and uncontrollable, mobility of the people moving into and out of the community, which is actually the norm in slum communities. Specifically, the CMP suggests an aspect of the state's technology of development argued by Scott, which is enabled through transforming the complex and "messy" reality of the community into "legible" orderliness (Scott 1998).

Nurturing trust and building cooperative relationships among the residents are strongly required in every step of the programme. Throughout the procedure, the homeowners associations are charged with ongoing responsibilities to encourage, monitor, and discipline the residents for the accomplishment of the programme. First of all, a master list of the household heads who would be the beneficiaries of the programme is drawn up. It is stipulated that to be a beneficiary, one has to be an owner of a house, thus inevitably ruling out non-owners, such as tenants, as possible beneficiaries. In this regard, some critics argue that the CMP excludes tenants and renters who are among the poorest of the slum dwellers (Berner 1997). It is a difficult task to accomplish even this first step of compiling a master list and identifying the rightful beneficiaries in the milieu of informally settled areas, where urban–rural mobility is high and where ordinary households include not only a nuclear family, but also various relatives and friends who have in-migrated from the same provinces.

The next step involves the engagement of an engineer for the purpose of making a subdivision plan, based on which, a "re-blocking" of the settlement is carried out. The purpose of re-blocking is to secure access roads with sufficient width and some space for public purposes such as evacuation centres, day-care, and multi-purpose halls. In this process of re-blocking, the space characteristic of a slum, consisting of a maze of narrow, winding streets, and crowded houses, is transformed into an orderly space divided by a grid of roads with good visibility (Pictures 2.5(a, b, and c)). Every member of the Homeowners

Picture 2.5 (a) Congested community before the re-blocking, (b) A house being demolished because of the re-blocking, (c) A neighbourhood which completed the re-blocking *(Continued)*

Picture 2.5 (Continued)

Associations is required to pay more or less 7,000 pesos, which would cover the survey fee for the engineer, including an allotment for a common fund for use by the association. Additionally, a monthly payment of 20–50 pesos is required from each member to cover the various expenses entailed in the negotiations and procedures between the officers of the association and the local government or landowners. It is not easy for the residents, many of whom are underemployed in the informal sector, to make regular payments religiously, and consequently, many residents who are not able to pay regularly fall into the "delinquent" category, and many who refuse to pay these monthly dues, insisting that "We have been living here free for so many years; why should we pay now?" (Lee 1995: 536), fall into the "recalcitrant" category.[7] Lee, who also conducted research on communities covered by the CMP in Metro Manila, pointed out that the "treasurers (of community associations) need a fair amount of skill to explain, cajole and work with defaulters to persuade and help them to pay or reschedule their repayments" (Lee 1995: 536). As shown in the cases of Marikina presented later, such schemes definitely require social norms such as discipline and responsibility to be nurtured among the residents.

The following step is the stage of taking out a mortgage, the most difficult to fully execute, in which the Social Housing Financing Corporation (SHFC), a government-owned financial institution, purchases the land from the landowner and mortgages it to the homeowners associations of the communities, which in turn start collecting monthly repayments, on heavily subsidised terms, from the association members. In this study, the associations which reached the stage of mortgage takeout are considered as successful cases. As of 2010, however, very few homeowners associations in Malanday have succeeded in taking out mortgages. The loan from the SHFC is equivalent to 80,000 pesos maximum per household, which should be repaid over a period of 25 years. The price of lots covered by the CMP in Marikina, for example, is set at 1,000 pesos per square meter, and each household is allowed to secure a land area of 30–50 m². On average, a member pays 250 pesos as monthly amortisation under this scheme. While most of the members avail themselves of this highly subsidised long-term 25-year loan, some residents who are relatively financially well off are able to pay the loans off quickly so as to acquire titles to their own plot of land more quickly.

The homeowners associations impose sanctions against those who default on their monthly amortisations, either as "delinquent" or "recalcitrant", in the form of community pressure. The officers of the association periodically visit those in default and give them "friendly reminders", "offers of assistance", and finally "threatening letters" (Lee 1995: 536). Should this series of demands fail, the unresponsive defaulters are to be evicted from their homes by their homeowners association and replaced by a substitute household that is considered to be financially fit under the programme.

The CMP in Barangay Malanday, Marikina City

This section presents the case of Barangay Malanday, which is one of the 16 barangays—the smallest administrative unit of the Philippines—comprising Marikina City. Barangay Malanday had a population of 53,907 and 11,452 households as of 2009, including 27 Homeowners Associations. I interviewed some of the officials and members of all 27 associations. Some remarkable features can be pointed out with regard to those associations involved in CMP. Firstly, there is a substantial number of "delinquent" households in every association. Among 27 associations, five even became unable to continue the programme further owing to the substantial population of members who could not pay, or who refused to pay, the common funds or monthly dues. On the contrary, there are four associations that succeeded up to the stage of taking out mortgages and started to receive loans from the SHFC. Even among these apparently successful associations, however, there are not a small number of defaulters. This fact shows that it is not easy for the members to comply with the terms of payment, which requires financial ability as well as diligence and responsibility to pay religiously for a long period of time. One association, which took out a mortgage in 2002, thus considered as relatively successful one, for example, has more than 300 "delinquent" households. Further, another association, which took out a mortgage in 2004, has 40 "delinquent" and 13 "recalcitrant" households. On the other hand, the other two associations, which just took out their own mortgages in 2009, only a few delinquent and recalcitrant households remain. Nonetheless, it cannot be denied that, for any of these associations, the number of members in default can further increase in the coming years. A rather contrastive feature to this is that there are some members in associations that have been taking out mortgages who have completed their loan repayment and already succeeded in securing their individual land titles.

It can also be understood based on the interviews that the core members of most of the associations express political support for Mayor Marides Fernando and the city councillors who are allies of the mayor.[8] It is suggested in the following cases that the homeowners associations, in a certain context, function as a strong political machine for garnering the residents' votes in favour of specific local politicians. In this sense, the CMP, rather than being a nonpartisan and impartial urban land reform project, has become seemingly coloured with personal favour by the mayor and her allied city councillors, and the success of the programme would thus hinge on the constituent's political support for the city administration. Before we proceed to examine the cases of some associations, let us take a look at a case (Case 2.1) that shows how the associations work as a lubricant to articulate people (voters) and local politicians in a clientelistic network.

Case 2.1: Feast with local politicians (March 2016)

In the Philippines, national elections for the Presidency, Senate, and House of Representatives, as well as local elections for city and town mayors and councillors, were scheduled for May 2016. On the morning of March 3, 2016, the presidents and officers of the three neighbouring associations in Barangay Malanday were summoned to a public meeting place by officials of the Marikina Settlement Office. The officers had been instructed to call a minimum of 20 members from each association to welcome the candidates for city councillors and congressmen who were planning to run for the coming election. However, when the expected number of association members could not be assembled as noon approached, an MSO official started to express his frustration and rushed the chairman to call the members quickly. Near noon, the members finally gathered. Then came the current mayor and vice-mayor of Marikina, as well as the city council and congressional candidates running under their camps. When these local politicians came to the meeting place, they greeted the association members by walking among them with a smile and shook hands with each of them. Then, one by one, the candidates spoke, emphasising how the current mayor was good, compassionate, and tolerant, and how voting for a candidate from the opposing camp was the wrong choice. Afterwards, food prepared by the candidates was laid out on banana leaves on a long table, and the candidates and residents enjoyed eating together with their hands.[9]

As indicated by the case above, associations are often mobilised as a tool of governance, with a vote collection function at its core, which is particularly evident during election seasons. The three cases of associations examined below show that, contrary to the official rationale of the CMP as an impersonal and equitable social policy, the actual process of programme implementation indicates the production and reproduction of the networks involving the private exchange of goods and services and political support between certain local politicians and the core members of the association. The following cases of three associations call for particular attention to the social hierarchy in terms of the members' occupations and economic status, as well as the social relationships and networks among the members, especially those maintained between the president and the other board members. In addition, whether they have worked abroad or have relatives who have migrated abroad, from whom they can expect help, is a significant factor impacting the dynamism of economic status and social stratification in the Philippines today, and is therefore given a substantial focus in the cases below.

Case 2.2: "Industriousness", "discipline", and "publicness" as admirable values: Santa Maria Homeowners Association[10]

The Santa Maria Homeowners Association comprises 269 household members and took out a mortgage in May 2009. For the past 11 years, the position of president of this association has been occupied by Victor Punzalan, a former scout ranger of the Philippine Army who was in his mid-40s at the time of the interview. Since he left the military, he has been engaged in various occupations, such as a security guard and driver. He currently works as a school bus driver for a local elementary school, where he also sometimes sells food and snacks. His social network extends overseas because his sister, who is married to an American, a member of the US Navy stationed in the Philippines, and his parents currently live in New Jersey and hold US citizenship. In addition, his daughter is currently studying at a school of nursing and planning to migrate abroad as a nurse to Australia, Dubai, or Canada, where her cousins reside.[11]

For Victor, the association is an "ally" of the city administration, and he expresses his full support for the city mayor, particularly for ex-mayor Bayani Fernando. According to him, "Without BF (the nickname of Bayani Fernando, as endearingly known to his constituents), there would be no CMP". Victor continues, "BF taught us how to be sensible and responsible citizens", and "(because of Bayani Fernando) we learned how to become something from nothing". He criticises members in default, saying, "The CMP will not work for you, you should work for the CMP" because the "government will not give you property for free. If you want your own land, you have to learn how to be responsible". Referring to Aesop's classic fable "The Ant and the Grasshopper", Victor emphasises the ethics of diligence and hard work required from residents to enable the association to enter into a mortgage takeout. In fact, if the negotiations with the landowner take longer owing to a lack of unity and hard work among the community members, it will become more difficult to proceed because the land price will have appreciated.

Further, what Victor emphasises is a space of "community" that is clearly differentiated from the private space, and this sense of community leads to an idea of "publicness" that should be shared by the neighbourhood as a whole. He stated, in English with local accents, "You are king of your own domain. But once you step outside, that's our association's property. Community's property. So, you have to behave properly", or "This road is 'our' property. Not the government property. It's our road. That's why you shouldn't litter. Be a good neighbor, be a good co-owner".

The narratives of the other core members of the Santa Maria Homeowners Association are examined here. The core members of the association, 15 in all, are engaged in various occupations such as a manager of a *sari-sari* store (a small-scale neighbourhood grocery shop), a craftsman and mechanic, employees of private companies, and clerks in retail shops. Characteristically, half of the core members have either worked abroad as contract workers, or otherwise, their spouse or children are currently working abroad. As in Victor's case, most of them maintain transnational networks with families and close relatives who work and live abroad. As such, the core members of the association in this case can be considered as coming from the middle class and having access to a steady cash inflow from not only their employment in the formal sector, but also overseas remittances.[12]

According to one of the officers of the association, "To be a beneficiary of the CMP, the requirement is for you to have a job, regardless of the kind of employment. If you don't have a job, you have to think of what you can do. *Basurero* (garbage collector), *labandera* (laundry woman), *botero* (recyclable bottle collector), any kind of job: what is important is to work, even in a low-level kind of job (*kahit mababang antas na trabaho*). It is unacceptable for you to say you are not capable (*hindi pwedeng hindi mo kaya*)".[13] Another officer says, "What is needed for the association to successfully take out a mortgage is a concern for your own community (*malasakit sa komunidad*)". He further explains that if he sees a suspicious person in his community, he will contact Victor, the president of the association, and ask him to investigate. In this way, he continues, "the residents learn how to be disciplined in the process of the CMP".

Case 2.3: Emphasis on "transparency" and "accountability": San Pedro Homeowners Association

The San Pedro Homeowners Association, which is composed of 381 households, successfully took out a mortgage in May 2009. According to the president of the association, Anita Cruz, most of the members pay their monthly amortisation on time, and 19 members have already paid off their loan and secured their individual land title. However, she admits that there are about ten delinquent and five recalcitrant members in this association.

Anita, who has been the president since 1999, is an employee of the Marikina City government. Similar to the president of the Santa Maria Homeowners Association presented above, Anita is also a close "ally" of Mayor Fernando. According to Anita, every time there are meetings of various kinds, such as a political rally, election campaign, or food provision organised by Mayor Marides Fernando, she is approached by the mayor for help, particularly for facilitating the mayor's access to the people and community, and she is always present in these meetings in order to coordinate with the mayor's camp.

According to Anita, what is required most by the association members is "transparency" and "accountability". She emphasises that she makes sure to hold general assembly meetings regularly and, on these occasions, makes the treasurer clearly explain the monthly financial report of the association in front of the members. In addition, in these meetings, she tries to make the residents understand how monthly dues and other payments, such as the cost for the engineer, are necessary expenses and how collecting these from the residents is legally permitted under the CMP scheme. In this way, the residents are made to understand the importance of the programme and the need for cooperation among themselves. With regard to the unsuccessful associations, Anita suggests that these have failed so far to take out a mortgage because of a lack of "transparency" and "accountability" and the fact that their treasurers are often accused of misuse and unexplained spending by the members.

The above two cases dealt with associations that have already completed taking out a loan and are making good progress in their programmes. The chairman and other executives are considered to be full-time workers in middle-class jobs with stable incomes. They also maintain a network of relatives living abroad who can be expected to remit money on a regular basis. In contrast to these associations, many of the members of the next case, the San Jose Homeowners Association, including the board members, still maintain strong ties to their home rural villages, and are connected to each other through hometown and kinship ties in the community. The San Jose Homeowners Association has yet to take out loans and, furthermore, has been at a standstill, unable to proceed with its programmes because of a failure to collect monthly dues and utility fees from its members. Therein we can see distrust among the members brought about by a lack of "transparency" and "accountability", as pointed out by Anita above.

Case 2.4: Prevailing distrust and conflict: San Jose Homeowners Association

In sharp contrast to the two cases presented above, the San Jose Homeowners Association is unable to collect monthly dues and common funds effectively, a necessary preliminary stage for taking out a mortgage. Thus, the association currently cannot advance the programme any further. The president of the San Jose Homeowners Association, Cardo Reyes, was born in 1955 in the province of Western Samar, an island province of the central Philippines. The association is composed of 152 households, and, characteristically, most of them are im-migrants from two or three adjacent towns of the province. Hence, the members of this association can be roughly clustered into two or three groups of relatives. Cardo immigrated from Western Samar to Marikina in 1972. After graduating from college, he undertook various menial jobs such as a driver and school jan-itor. He also went to the Middle East to work as a driver from 1994 to 1996.

The core members of the association are engaged in various jobs, such as fruit vendors, temporary employees of private companies, craftsmen, mechanics, sweepers, taxi drivers, policemen, farmers, public schoolteachers, and employees of Marikina City government. Unlike the core members of the Santa Maria Homeowners Association in Case 2.2, there are no transna-tional networks from which the members can secure ready access to resources unavailable in the Philippines. Among the 15 officers of the association, 11 are close relatives of Cardo. This core group, characterised by closely-knit kinship ties, has faced accusations of unaccountable management and the misuse of common funds for the past several years. Such accusations have resulted in a deepening distrust of the residents towards these officers.

In 2005, the treasurer of the association suddenly resigned and went back to her province, Western Samar. At that time, allegations of misuse of funds, embezzlement, and questionable bookkeeping by the treasurer and some other core members of the association were prevalently emanating from among the residents. Because of this, the treasurer could not keep her posi-tion and subsequently left Marikina. Since then, the doubt and distrust seen among the ordinary members towards the officers of the association have not been wiped clean, and eventually, the process of the CMP was suspended. Criticisms of the officers of the association can often be heard from the residents. One member, for example, says "We totally don't know where the money we paid has gone". Another says, "The treasurer of the association didn't care to produce even an inauthentic receipt", referring to an alleged utter lack of proper accounting. Further, full of sarcasm, "The fund of the association had wings, it freely flew somewhere else". Under such a situation, a resident concluded that "mutual trust among the residents had deeply waned" and any "spirit of cooperation had vanished".

Further, the residents are critical of core members who allow the association to be utilised as a political machine by local politicians, and who, in return for their loyalty and support, have been given certain rewards. According to some residents, when the local election approaches, the officers of the association usually call a meeting and ask the residents to vote for specific local politicians they support. They say that the officers are coddled by these local politicians, acting as patrons, and their misappropriation of the association's funds is tacitly permitted as long as they remain loyal to these patrons. In this way, according to an ordinary member, "While the houses of the officers are getting bigger and bigger, ours remain tiny shanties". This situation has eventually led to criticism about local politicians who mobilise the officers and the association for partisan purposes and personal interests. "The politicians are controlling our community through the president of the association. If the president fails to garner enough votes for the politician to win, he will be forced to resign from his post", explains one member. The other residents further speak critically of the local politicians, complaining, "During the election campaign, the politicians eagerly support the CMP, and even promise that soon the residents can secure land titles. However, by the end of the election period, they would have totally forgotten what they have promised... We are just being used as a stopgap measure by the politicians for their own self-interest (*Panakip butas lang kami*)... The CMP has become part and parcel of partisan politics (*Inangkin, sinarili ng mga politiko ang programa*)".

In response to the residents' criticism, Cardo, the president of the association, said, "The residents also benefit from the association. Some of them even rent out their houses and live off the rent. But they still don't want to cooperate with the association. They are stubborn (*matigas*), uncooperative (*pasaway*), and selfish (*makasarili*)". Thus, the views of the chairman and other board members are in direct conflict with those of the residents, and the distrust between them seems to have only deepened.

The case of the San Jose Homeowners Association presents quite a contrast to the former two cases presented above. It appears that the core members of the association may be appropriating the association and its funds for their own personal use, and that these unlawful deeds are tacitly permitted by local politicians who are trying to co-opt the officers. As a result, deep-seated distrust has arisen between the association's core members and its ordinary members, who have been left bereft of any benefits from the CMP and, as shown in the next section, quite marginalised in the periphery of the community. Relatedly, even in Cases 2.2 and 2.3, where the process of the CMP has been rather successful and some residents have actually completed repayment of their loan and secured individual land titles, there are still more than a few members who are incapable of paying, or who refuse to pay, the amortisation. Those members in default will be replaced, sooner or later, by what is deemed a more "appropriate (*karapat-dapat*)" member, that is, one who has the capacity to repay the loan.

These cases suggest that, rather than the direct intervention of the state into the community, which sometimes leads to coercive demolition and the eviction of residents, what has been observed in the communities of Barangay Malanday is an indirect intervention through making visible the boundary between disciplined, responsive "citizens" and "noncitizens". The latter, who are undeserving as members of an "orderly community", are hence marginalised and finally excluded. This point coincides with the conclusion made by Berner, who also conducted research on the CMP in urban poor communities in Metro Manila (Berner 1997). According to him, "the program always excludes a substantial part of the residents, among them the dire poor. In other words: success in the struggle for land jeopardizes the association's claim to represent all residents and, consequently, leads to internal struggles" (Berner 1997: 188). Further, in such a process of the CMP, a characteristic dynamism in the composition of the residents can be observed. "The outcome will most probably be a new dedifferentiation. While the marginal segments of the population have to move on to find shelter in other squatter settlements, the former slum becomes a middle-class area; not by invasion or gentrification, but because most residents, or at least those who have the capacity to organize are the middle class anyway" (Berner 1997: 188).

The following part of the chapter, focusing again on the case of the San Jose Homeowners Association, closely examines how such a "marginal segment" of the settlements, and particularly how the livelihood of those residents, are categorised as "uncivil" and thus excluded from the "orderly community".

Now, while in a state of deep distrust and conflict with the association, how are the residents, particularly those who are categorised as a "marginal segment" of the community, and who are made visible in contrast to "citizens", trying to maintain and improve their livelihoods, which are again marginalised as "uncivil" and "unproductive" jobs that, according to the core members of successful associations, should be excluded from the "orderly community"? The following case sheds light on this aspect.

Case 2.5: Street Vendors' Association and its failure

Throughout the 20th century, Marikina City has been known for its household industry of shoemaking, which used to provide a source of income for many local residents of urban poor communities. However, trade liberalisation since the 1990s has brought cheap shoes imported from China, leading to the decline of the shoemaking industry in Marikina. In Barangay Malanday, many former shoemakers are trying to make ends meet by the itinerant vending of fruits and other foods in the streets of Marikina and its vicinity using bicycles with sidecars (Picture 2.6). Table 2.2 indicates the number of such street vendors according to the commodities sold and the costs and profits of each commodity in Barangay Malanday.

It can be seen that the average profit per day for street vendors is barely enough to ensure the survival of a family of five, the average size of a Filipino family.[14] It should be noted that a substantial number of the 200 fruit vendors indicated in the table are members of the San Jose Homeowners Association examined in Case 2.4 above. In the area covered by the association, there are four persons who own trucks that deliver fruits purchased from the wholesale market. The

Picture 2.6 A street vendor who sells local snacks using the bicycle with sidecar

vendors usually pay a commission to the truck owners every day for the delivery of the day's commodities. In the early morning, the vendors process the fruits by peeling the skin off or inserting a wooden skewer. At around 8:00 a.m., they set out to peddle having loaded their bicycles with sidecars filled with fruits. Each vendor has his or her own route and regular customers on the various streets in Malanday and the other barangays in Marikina City. Their itinerant vending continues during the morning, and they are usually home by just past noon (Picture 2.7).

Table 2.2 Street Vendors of Barangay Malanday according to Commodity, Number, Cost, and Profit

Commodities	Number	Cost/day (average)	Profits/day (average)
Fruits (mango, papaya, pineapple, etc.)	200	Mango: P200~700 Pineapple: P1,000	Mango: P100~300 Pineapple: P300~500
binatog (snack food made from steamed corn mixed with the coconut flesh)	40~80	P250	P200~400
Rice cakes (*puto, kuchinta,* etc.) and *taho* (bean curd with sago pearl)	230	P150~500	P150~500
Fishball (fried and skewered snack made of ground fish meat)	6*	P700	P200~300

* There were about 50 fishball vendors until 2000, but their numbers have drastically decreased since then owing to the increase in the cost of fuel.

Picture 2.7 The neighbourhood of street vendors who belong to the San Jose Homeowners Association

These street vendors always have to be mindful of their surroundings as they go about their business because Mayor Fernando has prohibited the selling of goods in the streets of Marikina, and the monitoring and restrictions in this regard have increasingly tightened recently. According to the city administration, the reason for prohibiting street vending is to prevent traffic congestion, secure the smooth flow of public transportation, and maintain the safety and sanitation of public spaces, such as pedestrian lanes. In 1993, a city ordinance entitled "Ordinance Regulating the Use of Streets and Sidewalks in the Municipality of Marikina" was issued, in which the creation of the "Office of Public Safety and Security (OPSS)" was stipulated to monitor and restrict merchandising activities in the streets and other public spaces in the city (Table 2.1). Particularly, the vending of food is described as a "public nuisance" and an "eyesore" in the ordinance, and has become a target for strict penalties. Furthermore, the "Marikina Peace, Order, Public Safety and Security Code" promulgated in 2006 stipulates more comprehensive restrictions regarding itinerant street vending. According to the ordinance and code, if the vendors are caught in the prohibited act in the streets, their goods, bicycles, and sidecars can be confiscated. Although the vendors can redeem their confiscated bicycles and sidecars by paying 1,000 pesos, the perishable food and fruits are not redeemable in any case. Interestingly, if the vendors are unable to pay in cash, they are provided the option of donating 500 ml of blood in exchange for their confiscated items. A vendor complains about this policy, speaking not figuratively but literally, "OPSS is extremely cruel and strict. Our blood for our goods... for the things we need for our work, if we don't have enough money".

Under such hardships, the vendors express their feelings of helplessness: "With every pedal of our bicycles, we have to be wary, we have to be very careful... We feel pain not in our legs or thighs, but on our necks (while constantly watching for the OPSS, which polices us)... Our business is like carrying fresh eggs, always requiring we be careful not to drop them". At the same time, they are critical about, and express their mistrust toward, the mayor and city administration as a whole: "Marides is trying to clean up the whole of Marikina, up to the inside guts of people and all (*Gusto niyang linisin ang Marikina, pati bituka at tiyan ng tao*)... A white-skinned fish yet full of mud inside (*Isang kapak, laman ay burak*)... The city government is getting rich because of the money we pay for redeeming our bicycles... Once the city government legalises our business, they cannot anymore collect our money as penalty. They will lose the bulk of their revenue. That's why they won't permit our business... The city administration is obviously turning a profit from us".

The case of street vendors who are members of the San Jose Homeowners Association indicates clearly who are incorporated into an "orderly community", which is sought after by Bayani and Marides Fernando, and, on the other hand, who are excluded from it. The entrepreneurial residents with high marketability and employability are welcomed into the public space of the "orderly community" as "citizens" who are suitable to constitute such space. By contrast, such a public space marginalises, penalises, and excludes "noncitizens", whose livelihoods are considered unsuitable, or even "unworthy", to be a part of such an "orderly community". Under this process of marginalisation and exclusion, the vendors themselves engage in a counter-hegemonic practice, which is examined in the following part.

The Malanday Vendors' Association: Government of Self or Reproduction of Difference?

This section examines the case of the Malanday Vendor's Association and its attempt to propose a new ordinance intended to legalise the vendor's activities in the streets under certain conditions. The Malanday Vendor's Association was organised in 2005 for the purpose of "securing the freedom of street vending activity". In 2007, the association, with encouragement and technical help from the city councillors who were opposed to the Fernando administration, drafted the "Ordinance Regulating the Peddling Activities of Ambulant Vendors in the City of Marikina" and submitted it to the city council of Marikina for deliberation.[15] According to the proposed draft of the ordinance, the street vendors could be legalised after due registration coupled with the submission of a Community Tax Certificate, Barangay Clearance, and Police Clearance. Additionally, a registration fee of 600 pesos would have to be paid annually.

Further, in order for the vendors to be legalised, they would have to undergo annual medical and health examinations at the City Health Office of Marikina. An identification card issued by the City Market Office indicating not only the vendor's name and address, but also "two (2) kinds of items or wares he or she is selling", would have to be worn by the vendor at all times during his or her vending activities. There were also restrictions on the manner of dress of the vendors and the containers and weighing scales to be used: "Ambulant and transient vendors shall be required to wear uniforms or attire, which shall be colour-coded as designated by the City Market Office. The use of shoes is a must and wearing slippers shall be strictly prohibited"; " Containers of wares, goods, or merchandise of ambulant and transient vendors, whether hand-carried or wheeled, shall be prescribed and designed by the City Market Office, considering, above all, the sanitation and hygienic concern thereof"; "The weighing scale used for vending should be registered by the City Treasury Office. The said weighing scale shall be subjected to regular inspection by the Weight & Measures Office. Any weighing scale found being used, but is defective and/or tampered shall be confiscated and destroyed, and the corresponding penalty shall be imposed to any apprehended violator".

Further, hygienic measures for the foodstuffs and perishable goods were well covered: "The sale of fresh sea foods, fruits, vegetables and other foodstuffs shall be contained in covered containers and be placed in separate sealed plastic bags to protect them from pollution, and other germ-carrying pests and insects".

There were also several restrictions on acts and prohibited activities of street vendors: a) staying over a long period of time and permanently occupying any space on any street sidewalk or public or private place where vending or peddling is prohibited; b) peddling or vending within a 50 m radius of any school or educational institution, church or religious establishment, and public or private markets; c) storing or leaving his or her wares, goods, or merchandise on any sidewalk, street, or area where it is a public obstruction; d) strewing and/or throwing litter, garbage, and leftovers of his or her wares, goods, or merchandise in a public place or such other acts that create rubbish or unsanitary conditions in any place; e) selling or vending stale, rotten, or contaminated foodstuffs; f) selling or vending illegal wares, goods, or merchandise; and g) carrying or transporting wares, goods, or merchandise that can create harm or injury to pedestrians.

While the proposed ordinance examined in Case 2.5 above has not yet been passed by the city council because of Mayor Marides Fernando's objection to signing the draft, it is worthy of note and quite essential in the sense that the ordinance can be considered an attempt by the vendors themselves to legalise their trade through appropriating the logic of the city administration in illegalising them, and translating it into their own benefit. This aspect of the ordinance is suggested in the intentional and frequent use of such terms as "public space", "hygienic concerns", and "sanitary conditions", which were originally used by the administration in its justification for penalising the vendors. In this sense, the act of having proposed the ordinance can be considered a counter-hegemonic practice through acts of self-regulation or self-government.

However, what must be examined further is the possibility that the drafting and proposal of this ordinance have been motivated by some local politicians to advance their own political interests. There are several versions of the explanation regarding how the ordinance was drafted and who initiated the plan to draft it. Even among the city councillors who sponsored this ordinance, the explanation somehow varies. One councillor, who is the primary sponsor of the ordinance, said that the leader and other members of the vendor's association approached him and complained about the plight of street vendors. Thus, according to this councillor, the ordinance is truly a people's initiative. Another councillor, who is a cosponsor of the ordinance, explained that some councillors, including the primary sponsor mentioned above, and the congressman representing the local district, approached the members of vendor's association and brought up the idea of proposing the draft of the ordinance. Still, a leader and some of the core members of the vendor's association said that it was a collaboration between local politicians and vendors, and remained ambiguous as to who actually initiated the plan.

These various and conflicting explanations suggest a need to further inquire into who benefitted and whose interests were served through the proposal of this ordinance, the primary purpose of which should have been to alleviate the hardships of the street vendors. To discuss this, it is important to note that according to many of the ordinary rank-and-file members of the vendor's association, the plan of drafting the ordinance was originally brought up by some city councillors and the congressman of the district, who oppose Mayor Fernando and her allies in the city administration, just before the local and national elections of May 2007. Hence, as these members discuss, it cannot be denied that these local politicians were keen on garnering the support of local vendors for the coming election by way of dangling a carrot in the form of a proposed ordinance legalising vending activities. As such, there are more than a few vendors who are suspicious about the proposal of this ordinance: "We are always just used by the politicians (*Ginagamit lang kami ng mga pulitiko*)... What the politicians say is always a mere promise. Nothing is actually realized. They are just playing politics (*Puro pangako, walang nangyayari, puro pulitika, namumulitika lang*)". Accordingly, there is a substantial gap of concern for this ordinance between the core members of the vendor's association, who have actively cooperated with local politicians in drafting the ordinance on the one hand, and the other ordinary members who have not actually participated in the process of drafting the ordinance on the other. There are vendors who admit that they have never seen the ordinance and say that "the proposal of the ordinance is a concern for only the core members of the association".

The case of the counterproposal of a new ordinance aimed at legalising the street vendors' activities indicates a practice of regulating and governing the self through internalising a certain norm and rationality required to be a member of the "orderly community". In other words, it shows how self-disciplining subjectivity is born in interaction with the governmental effect working through the urban community. However, such a proposal, even after it successfully passes the city council, has the possibility of creating a new differentiation between vendors who are willing and capable of observing all the requirements and regulations stipulated in the draft and others who are resistant to, are not capable of, or simply ignore observing them. Hence, it might reproduce the process of inclusion and exclusion: while the law-abiding vendors, who are governed as self-disciplining subjectivity, are incorporated into the "orderly community", and the others who fail or refuse to be governed are excluded.

What can be understood from the cases of the homeowners associations promoting the CMP in Barangay Malanday examined so far? The first two cases, the Santa Maria Association (Case 2.2) and the San Pedro Association (Case 2.3), and the third, the San Jose Association (Case 2.4) presented sharply contrasting situations. As for the Santa Maria Association and the San Pedro Association, the values of discipline, diligence, transparency, and accountability were extolled by the officers and actively promoted among the members, and the programme was developed based on these values. No particular criticisms or complaints were heard from members about how the programme was implemented, and as a result, the two associations were largely successful in taking out loans and making subsequent repayments. On the other hand, the San Jose Association was unable to proceed with its programme due to a breakdown in trust between board members and resident members. To make matters worse, as Case 2.5 illustrated, the residents' subsistence activity of street vending was placed in an extremely precarious and uncertain situation because of restrictions imposed by the city authority, and attempts to form a vendors' association and draft an alternative ordinance to relieve the constraints on their livelihoods were also driven into a corner because of the suspicion of corruption entertained by the vendors against the association officers, who were linked to local politicians. Such being the case, it was not easy for the peddlers to both secure land tenure and stabilise their livelihoods. While one board member of the Santa Maria Association (Case 2.2) mentioned, "to be a beneficiary of the CMP, you have to work, whatever kind it is", the case of the street vendors of the San Jose Association showed that the reality was not so simple. Rather, Marikina's urban governance was enabled by making visible a clear distinction between the occupations of citizens who were regarded as legitimate members of the "orderly community" and "public space" on the one hand and occupations that were an "obstacle" or "eyesore" to publicity on the other, and by marginalising and excluding the latter while at the same time welcoming the former as part of the mainstream community.

Although these cases of associations suggest contrasting outcomes of the CMP, in the homeowners associations examined thus far, personal and intimate ties are commonly observed between association officers and local politicians, namely, the mayor and city councillors. Association presidents in particular were expected to play a role in organising the votes of community residents at election time. In return, the officers expected to be provided with various favours and resources from those politicians. Then, what were the factors that influenced the programme's success or failure implemented by the associations that share this commonality? The answer lies in the narrative of the resident members of the San Jose Association, who stated, "While the houses of the officers are getting bigger and bigger, ours remain tiny shanties", which indicates that the benefits and resources from the local politicians were monopolised by the officers without being redistributed among the members. To clarify this point further, I would like to refer to the case of another association. This case was observed during the campaign period of the association officers' election held in September 2015. The elections for the association board members are held every two years, and the following case indicates that these elections are often fiercely contested by rival camps, with the conflict being over how resources obtained by the board members through personal connections with politicians should be properly and fairly redistributed among the resident members.

Case 2.6: The association as a site of everyday conflict: Election of the Santa Clara Association board members (September 2015)

According to the by-laws of the homeowners associations, it is stipulated that the election of officers shall be held every two years. The biennial election for the officers of the Santa Clara Homeowners Association was set for

September 20, 2015. The election campaign started on September 12 with 20 candidates who had filed their candidacy to compete for 15 board member posts. Soon thereafter, it became clear that these candidates belonged to two opposing camps: the camp led by the incumbent president, Maria, fielded a total of eight candidates, whereas the camp of the incumbent secretary, Gracia, fielded 12.

The candidates visited the houses of association members, handing out fliers and cards with their names and photos, chatting with them, and encouraging them to vote for them and their camp's candidate. Throughout the campaign, the opposing camps made separate visits, seemingly on guard against bumping into each other on the streets along the way. Gracia, who led one camp, was concerned that his fellow candidates might be turned by sweet-talk from the other camp. A few days after the campaign began, Gracia began claiming that the master list of legitimate voters had allegedly been tampered with by Maria, the leader of the opposing camp. According to Gracia's claim, the master list drafted by Maria excluded residents who did not support her and candidates under her slate from the list of voters, and instead added new names of supporters who were not members of the association, and thus ineligible to vote. Despite these allegations, the vote was held as scheduled on September 20, and after a close race, all eight candidates in Maria's camp were elected, barely making up the majority of the board. Meanwhile, 5 of the 12 candidates from Gracia's camp lost.

A few days after the vote, Gracia and the candidates in her camp filed an official complaint to the COMELEC (Commission of Election) of both the local and national governments claiming that the election had been rigged. Their complaint raised two specific issues. The first was that the master list of legitimate voters may have been tampered with by the incumbent president, Maria, and that the elections should therefore be declared null and void. The second was that Maria should be disqualified as a candidate for this election because of numerous irregularities during her term as president. Gracia cited the following incidents as examples of such irregularities.

The first incident happened during Christmastime in 2014. Christmas parties are one of the most anticipated events for neighbourhood communities in the Philippines. For the Christmas party of 2014, Maria requested various local politicians, such as barangay councillors (*Barangay Kagawad*), city councillors, and the vice-mayor, among others, to donate prizes to be given to the residents through raffle draws. According to Gracia, it was never known to her or the officers of her camp that such a request was made by Maria in the name of the association. Further, they were not informed of whether any prizes were actually offered. While some raffle prizes were certainly given away at the actual Christmas party, it remains to be seen whether all of the items provided by the politicians mentioned above were properly distributed.

The second irregularity that Gracia pointed out was the following incident. In May 2015, Maria made a request for financial assistance to the office of the vice-mayor and received 10,000 pesos. Again, despite the fact that the request had been made in the name of the association, Gracia and her fellow officers remained unaware of why such a request had been made and how the money provided had been used. The third allegation relates to the distribution of relief goods provided by the government for the victims of heavy flooding caused by a typhoon that hit the entire city of Marikina in 2014. As a result of the typhoon, many of the houses of association members and officers were flooded; these members and officers were then forced to live in an evacuation centre. At the time, the distribution of relief supplies from the government and aid agencies to the residents was centralised with Maria as the president of the association. However, according to Gracia, although she and her fellow board members were equally affected by the disaster, no relief supplies were given to them, and she had no idea how the supplies channelled through Maria were distributed among the resident members.

Regarding those incidents, Gracia said in jest that, "the officers of the associations are like 'Solicitor Generals'", by which she meant that they are very good at approaching politicians and soliciting various favours, in cash or in kind. According to Gracia, "the officers are aware that the politicians cannot refuse their demands, as they have a lot of votes behind them. Just before local and national elections, for example, the candidates invariably ask the officers to hold a general assembly of the association and host a big party. On such occasions, the candidates do not overtly ask for votes, but their intentions are clear".

The associations we have examined thus far are small, consisting of, at most, about 200 households, and have no administrative functions. However, as the case of the Santa Clara Association above indicates, the election of officers is often very hotly contested, and associations are often the site where daily conflicts between residents in a community manifest. The association is a venue where claims and contestation regarding how resources from outside should be redistributed can be observed at the most grassroots, everyday level. Further, it is noteworthy that the complaint made by Gracia was not actually a criticism against improper personalised relationships per se that Maria entered into with local politicians, nor was it against the particular favours received from the politicians. In fact, Gracia, while condemning Maria, presumably approved of the gifts by repeatedly saying, "while support was given for the association as a whole, we never knew or saw what had actually been given". Thus, the problem instead lies in the fact that the resources received from outside were not fairly redistributed among the members of the association.

The cases we have examined so far show that the factors that undermine collaboration and trust among the association members are not personal exchanges per se, such as patronage and clientelism between officers and politicians, but rather the monopolisation of these exchanges by a few members such as the president or officers, or suspicion of such among residents. The cases in which such suspicion clearly manifested are those between the officers and members of the San Jose Association (Case 2.4), and between the officers of the vendors' association and its ordinary members. On the other hand, the cases of the Santa Maria Association (Case 2.2) and San Pedro Association (Case 2.3) show that the officers and local politicians appear to have been associated in a similar kind of personal connection. They were always loyal "allies" and supporters of the mayor and his camp. But what was emphasised and practiced by those officers was "discipline" and "diligence" as a work ethic, and "accountability" among the association members. Remarkably, no complaints or criticisms of these officers' attitudes were heard from the members; rather, a certain level of trust had formed between officers and members, resulting in good progress in the programme. These examples suggest that the perspective viewing patronage and clientelism only negatively, as private relationships that erode public policy,

Picture 2.8 Awarding of the original title to the CMP beneficiaries. Sitting in front of the beneficiaries are then-mayor and vice-mayor of Marikina City, an official of the SHFC, and the president of homeowners association

is insufficient. Rather, such informal connections can be reimagined as part of network that redistributes external resources within the community. While it is indeed true that the association is infiltrated with the logic of clientelism, it does not necessarily mean that it failed to make any tangible achievements. For example, on March 4, 2016, a ceremony was held to award original land titles to 26 CMP beneficiaries in Barangay Malanday who had successfully repaid their loans in advance. The awardees were smiling happily and holding their titles together with the key figures involved in the CMP—the city mayor, vice-mayor, MSO staff, and a representative from SHFC, which is the government agency that lends money to the association. Although the title is still under the association's name, and it would take further bureaucratic procedures and cash payments to individualise the titles, this episode indicates that the CMP is making tangible, albeit incremental, progress in achieving its purpose of land tenure security.

Discussion

During the development dictatorship of President Marcos in the 1970s and 1980s, various social policies were implemented through top-down interventions by the centralised state. By contrast, the democratisation process since the late 1980s has foregrounded "participatory democracy", under which, the state implements its policies in collaboration with a wide range of non-state actors, including NGOs and civil society. To realize this principle, decentralisation and the strengthening of local government were enshrined in the 1987 Constitution (especially Article 10), and specific and comprehensive provisions for its institutionalisation were made in the Local Government Code that came into effect in 1991. In addition, since the 1990s, various laws have been enacted to promote the idea that economic development, social justice, and national welfare can only be achieved through the "empowerment", "self-help", and "self-reliance" of cooperatives, associations, and grassroots community organisations. The idea had been institutionalised by, for example, Republic Act No. 6938 of 1990 (commonly known as the Cooperative Code of the Philippines), Republic Act No. 7279 of 1992 (commonly known as the Urban Development and Housing Act, or UDHA), and Republic Act No. 8425 of 1997 (commonly known as the Social Reform and Poverty Alleviation Act). Especially important in the context of this chapter is Republic Act No. 9904 of 2010 (commonly known as the Magna Carta for Homeowners and Homeowners Associations), which specifies the need to organise homeowners associations to alleviate poverty in urban squatter settlements and informal settlement areas. The use of homeowners associations was considered essential to promote government social policies targeting urban poverty, including reforms aimed at guaranteeing low-cost social housing, resettlement, and land use rights, such as the CMP.

Set in the context of the idea and institution of social policy in the democratisation period of the Philippines, the homeowners association examined in this chapter, I argue, has played a key role in implementing social policy based on neoliberal governmentality. In particular, in the process of CMP implementation, homeowners associations were the very mechanism that facilitated "governing at a distance" (Miller & Rose 2008), enabled through an activated community. This chapter presented some cases of such governance working effectively on one level; yet, some cases showed that the associations have become a forum for serious conflict and division among residents over how resources should be distributed. Here, we can identify a certain contradiction. The homeowners association, as a formal institution, is supposed to be run by the neoliberal norms of transparency, accountability, and self-reliant individuals. What actually drove the association, however, was clientelism as an exchange of individual benefits based on personal and intimate relationships and interdependence between superiors and subordinates.

However, this chapter avoids the blanket argument that such clientelism suggests the erosion of public social policies by spoiling the associations, which are expected to be a tool for achieving "participatory democracy". As the barangay captain of Barangay Malanday put it: "Thanks to the CMP, we now have very few squatters". Of course, this does not mean that most of the residents have become full-fledged owners of private property. On the contrary, as the examples in this chapter show, some residents are in the process of repaying their loans, and many are still not at the stage of taking out loans. However, their participation in a government programme of the CMP will at least grant them the right to legitimate land use and they will no longer be deemed "squatters". This would ensure stable land tenure for residents, even where the programme's progress appears to have stalled, as in the example of the San Jose Association in Case 2.4, without fear of their houses to be demolished and themselves being forced to vacate the land outright or relocate to a resettlement site.

During the field research conducted in 2010, only 4 out of 27 associations were successful in taking out loans from the SHFC, and more than a few associations were unable to make any progress amid the deep distrust and doubt held by members against the association officers who allegedly misappropriated resources provided by local politicians. In my follow-up research in 2016, however, it is noteworthy that 11 out of 29 associations in total were able to secure a loan from the SHFC. Even though most of them do not yet have individual land titles, once they have entered into the CMP scheme, they are officially considered formal settlers and are able to avoid the dangers of demolition and relocation.

Furthermore, as the examination of Cases 2.4 and 2.6 revealed, the associations were perceived by residents as a medium through which hard-to-get resources from outside the community were provided. When the goods provided were privatised, or monopolised, by only the closed-off officers, the residents heavily criticised such practices and their trust in the association was severely eroded. However, people were not criticising the exchange relationship itself, which was based on intimate ties between officers and politicians; instead, they perceived such ties as part of the informal networks maintained by the urban poor to access external resources. Associations were a formal institution that newly emerged in the 1990s to achieve "participatory democracy" and social inclusion by non-state actors. However, in the process of implementing the CMP, residents interpreted this institution through their own familiar logic of patronage and clientelism, taming it, so to speak, as another route for access to resources. Social policies aiming to grant land ownership to slum dwellers, such as those examined in this chapter, would be frustrated by formal, abstract logic alone, such as "participatory democracy" and "citizen's associations". Rather, the articulation of formal logics and institutions with informal ties based on clientelism has enabled the urban poor to access resources that enable them to make do in their daily lives. In this sense, informal networks are not a remnant to be peripheralised and eradicated in the predominance of the formal and modern institutions of democracy and neoliberalism, but rather are further activated in their mutual negotiation with such formal institutions. It is at this juncture of entanglement of formal institution, which is deeply penetrated by neoliberal logic, and informal mutuality that the vernacular public sphere for securing the life of urban poor would emerge.

Notes

1. This chapter is reprinted in a revised form from *Japanese Review of Cultural Anthropology*, Vol 11 (2011): 67–101, by permission of the Japanese Society of Cultural Anthropology.

2. The data of this chapter has been mostly gathered during the fieldwork on February 2008, February, March, and October of 2009, February 2010, and, additionally, on March 2016 in Barangay Malanday, Marikina City. Interviews were conducted in Tagalog (Filipino).
3. The barangay is the most basic administrative unit in the Philippines. The size of the population ranges from a few hundred in rural areas to tens of thousands in urban areas, such as the Barangay Malanday in this chapter.
4. Fukuda (2012) analysed the shoe industry in Marikina from the perspective of survival strategies of local industries facing globalisation. According to the study, the Marikina shoe industry is characterised by the typical characteristics of Philippine local industries, such as small-scale, labour-intensive technologies, and use of indigenous technologies based mainly on manual processing (Fukuda 2012: 73–74).
5. The basic principles of the CMP were stipulated in Republic Act No. 7279 of 1992, commonly known as the "Urban Development and Housing Act of 1992" or "UDHA". The National Home Mortgage Finance Corporation and the Social Housing Finance Corporation are the governmental financial institutions that are designated as implementing bodies by the law, and actual rules and regulations of the Program are decided by those organisations.
6. In the CMP, only the household heads are registered as beneficiary members. In reality, the maximum membership of 200 households is not always strictly observed. It is not unusual that several associations exceed this limit of membership. The officers of the association, including the president, are elected every three years by a vote among the resident-members. The association president can be elected and re-elected for a total of three terms, that is, a maximum term of office of nine years. However, these stipulations are not complied with by the members in actual practice, as shown in the cases of the associations.
7. The original English words for "delinquent" and "recalcitrant" are thought to imply the negative nuance that policy enforcers have towards residents who do not comply with the program. Therefore, in the following, these words are written in parentheses.
8. The local city council of Marikina is composed of 16 councillors, or local legislators, who are tasked with drafting and proposing various ordinances that directly regulate various aspects of the local society.
9. This kind of "banquet", called "boodle fight", which is done without spoons, forks, or plates (banana leaves instead), but eaten with bare hands (locally called *kamayan*) is often held by politicians during an election campaign to create a sense of closeness and familiarity with the people, and also to impress the "down-to-earth" image to the voters.
10. The names of the homeowners associations and members are pseudonyms.
11. At the time of this fieldwork, securing a nursing license had become a popular strategy for Filipinos planning to work or immigrate abroad to countries such as the United States, the United Kingdom, and some in the Middle East. A nursing license is, in a sense, a "second passport" to expedite the transnational migration of middle-class Filipinos (see Chapter 8).
12. The significance of overseas labor/residence relates to not only financial stability via remittances, but also the introduction of new values, which have a strong inclination towards middle-class citizenship, such as "discipline", "diligence", and "hard work", which have been nourished within expanding transnational social fields. In other words, what they bring into their home country are "new forms of consciousness", "new values, new expectations about the role of the government, and new notions about the basic entitlements of ordinary citizens", which will further lead to "greater democracy, more transparency in government, and more accountability in public life" (David 2005). Another public comment suggests that overseas labor/residence contributes to bringing "a vigorous, consensual and informed public sphere" into Philippine society (Pertierra 2005).

13. However, in reality, as shown in the latter case, it is not entirely correct to say that a member can do "any kind of work". Apparently, there are distinctions between the jobs appropriate for the "public space" of "orderly community" and those that are not. Accordingly, the jobs deemed inappropriate for the public space, such as itinerant vendors, are marginalized and excluded from the community.

14. As of 2010, the legal minimum daily wage in Metro Manila is 404 pesos, which is higher than that in other parts of the Philippines.

15. The author was provided a copy of this ordinance, which was still pending at the Marikina City Council at the time of the research, by one of the city councillors who was its sponsor.

3 "Investments in Human Capital" Adrift
Conditional Cash Transfers and the Clientelistic Connection

This chapter deals with conditional cash transfers (CCTs) based on the observation in the same urban community of Barangay Malanday in Marikina City introduced in the previous chapter.[1] CCTs are one of the social policies being enthusiastically pursued by the administrations of President Benigno Aquino (2010–2016) and incumbent President Duterte to alleviate poverty.

CCTs have been actively introduced as a targeted poverty reduction measure expected to efficiently alleviate poverty, even under severe fiscal conditions, in Latin American countries that have undergone neoliberal economic reforms since the 1990s (Fiszbein & Schady 2009). CCTs are based on a global trend in development policy that emphasises investment in human capital, particularly through enhancing support for children's education. Situated within the ideological framework of the so-called "Third Way" (Giddens 1998), which promotes the provision of goods and services, but not through state redistribution or the liberal market, such policies, with some modifications, have spread widely since the 2000s in not only Latin America, but also African and Asian countries.

Learning from these precedents, the CCTs in the Philippines were launched in February 2008 during President Arroyo's term (2001–2010) on a pilot basis with loans from the World Bank and the Asian Development Bank, targeting 6,000 families in pilot districts. By the end of 2009, the programme was expanded to cover about 1 million families. The Philippine version of CCTs is called the 4Ps (pronounced as "for peace") stemming from the acronym for the policy: *Pantawid Pamilyang Pilipino Program* (Program for the Filipino Family to Cross Over). The implementation of the 4Ps has been remarkably scaled up as a major policy for poverty alleviation during the administration of President Aquino. For example, out of the total national budget of 1.64 trillion pesos for FY 2011, a total of 29 billion pesos was spent on the 4Ps, with 2.3 million families reportedly benefiting from the programme by the end of 2011. In addition, of the total national budget of 1.816 trillion pesos for FY 2012, a total of 39.5 billion pesos was spent on the 4Ps, which was targeted to benefit 4.6 million families by 2016, when President Aquino's term of office was set to expire.

The Department of Social Welfare and Development (hereinafter referred to as "the DSWD"), the government office in charge of implementing the 4Ps, emphasises that the goal of the programme is "investment in human capital". In

DOI: 10.4324/9781003224273-4

other words, the programme is not just a safety net, but rather, as suggested by *"Pantawid"* ("crossover" or "bridging") in its name, a springboard for improving livelihoods. In particular, it is emphasised that the 4Ps encourage parents to invest in their children's human capital through enhancing their health and hygiene, monitoring their school attendance, and encouraging their participation in community activities (Vigilia 2010). What is emphasised further is that, while the programme provides cash, it does not intend to foster people's dependence on patronage from the state; instead, residents and communities are expected to activate their human capital voluntarily with cash provision as an inducement.

The ethnography of the 4Ps in Barangay Malanday, Marikina City, shows how undoubtedly neoliberal ideology and policies often coexist with seemingly contrary principles such as social welfare, redistribution, planning, and state intervention into the intimate sphere of the family. It suggests how the "art of government" originally developed within post-welfare states in the West "might take on new life in other contexts" and be adopted for other "usages" (Ferguson 2009)— particularly in a country that has never experienced a strong welfare state but is instead characterised by a weak state, deep divides among the social classes, clientelism and patronage politics, and a predominance of informal institutions. At the same time, this ethnography reveals that the 4Ps, which intend to achieve the social inclusion of the poor through a neoliberal logic, have unexpectedly resulted in various modes of exclusion. In this way, the chapter deals squarely with the interplay, one fraught with tension, between "neoliberalism as exception" and "exceptions to neoliberalism" (Ong 2006) in a concrete ethnographic setting of social development in the Philippines.

The next section provides an overview of the design of the 4Ps in the Philippines and a discussion of the mode of social inclusion that the programme seeks to achieve through targeting the urban poor. It argues that the neoliberal mode of social inclusion is necessary because of the deep-seated social divide between the middle and lower classes in the country. While presenting some successful cases of beneficiaries who experienced a certain degree of improvement in their living situations, it mainly focuses on cases that suggest the forms of exclusion brought about by the programme and on counterclaims made by beneficiaries who resist its logic. Finally, the chapter discusses that, while elaborating on the implications of these counterclaims, in the process of neoliberal restructuring of the social policy, the popular notions of patronage and clientelism is reinterpreted and reactivated as resources for the people to imagine the vernacular public sphere for more inclusive protection of their lives.

The 4Ps in the Philippines

The beneficiaries of the 4Ps—households with children up to 14 years of age— are selected through a means test, community investigation, and interviews conducted by social workers sent by the DSWD of the Philippine government.

Eligible beneficiaries are organised into neighbourhood groups comprising 25–30 members that function as basic units to ensure that the conditions for receiving the cash grant are met. Each group selects a representative, called a parent leader, who acts as an intermediary between the beneficiaries and City Link (a social worker dispatched by the DSWD) and plays a variety of roles, such as relaying information from the government, collecting complaints and grievances from members, and calling meetings (see Figure 3.1).

While the programme includes both mothers and fathers, in practice, it is almost always the mothers who participate most actively. Fathers might participate minimally, for instance, attending meetings if their wives are not available. Further, the government encourages mothers to be involved in the implementation of the programme more strongly than fathers, believing that women are more likely to spend money according to the real needs of the household than men, who tend to waste cash on alcohol and gambling.

There are two categories of cash grants that determine the conditions applied: the Health and Nutrition Grant, and the Education Grant. The Health and Nutrition Grant amounts to 500 pesos (equivalent to 12.50 USD) per month per household.[2] This grant is provided to households that include pregnant women and/or children of preschool age (0–5 years) on condition that the pregnant women visit their local health centre for pre- and post-natal care and use appropriate childbirth services provided by a professional obstetrics and gynaecology health worker. Childbirth with a traditional birth attendant, which is still common among the poor in the Philippines, is prohibited under this scheme. Preschool children must be taken to the health centre for health checkups,

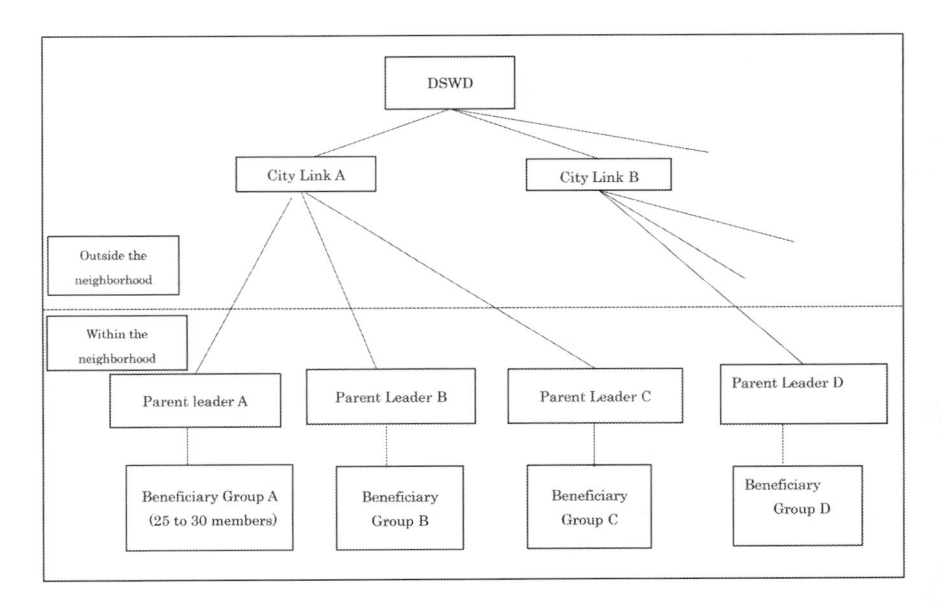

Figure 3.1 Organisation of 4Ps

immunisations, monthly weight monitoring, and nutrition advice. All these data related to the health conditions of mothers and children are recorded by the health workers and reported to City Link. Cash is allocated to purchase milk for the children and medicine and supplementary vitamins for both children and pregnant women.

The Education Grant provides 300 pesos (about 7.50 USD) per month per child to a maximum of three children per household. These children must be between 6 and 14 years of age. To receive the grant, in addition to monitoring the health conditions explained above and taking the vermicide twice a month, the children have to maintain a school attendance rate of at least 85 per cent per month, which means that if they are absent from school more than three times a month, they will not receive the grant for that particular month. Cash can be used for school uniforms and shoes, and for expenses for school projects. Combining these two categories, a family with three school-aged children and a pregnant woman or preschool-aged child can receive a maximum amount of 1,400 pesos (35 USD) a month. Supposing the poverty line of an average household with five members is 7,000 pesos (about 190 USD) per month, the grant covers about 20 per cent of the monthly income of poor households.

It can be argued that, under the current 4Ps scheme, the cash grant itself is not meant to achieve poverty alleviation and social inclusion. The amounts involved are actually too small and unreliable to bring about any substantial enhancements in the beneficiaries' lives. Rather, the cash grant should be considered an inducement for the beneficiaries to engage in various practices of "investing in human capital"—for themselves and their children—through education, enhanced health and hygiene, and self-development.

One of the key elements of these activities is the Family Development Session (hereinafter referred to as "the FDS"), attendance at which is considered the most important condition that the beneficiaries should observe. Several cases involving the FDS that reflect the basic principles of the programme are delineated in detail later.

A Mode of Inclusion through the 4Ps: Seen from Barangay Malanday, Marikina City

This section examines the ways in which the 4Ps are attempting to achieve social inclusion of the poor based on the case of Barangay Malanday, the same community introduced in the previous chapter. In Barangay Malanday, a means test by the DSWD and interviews for the selection of beneficiaries were conducted in October 2009. As discussed in Chapter 2, about 6,000 of the approximately 11,000 households in Malanday are informal settlers without legal land ownership, many of whom work as street vendors or in miscellaneous jobs in the urban informal sector, such as jeepney and tricycle drivers, the incomes from which are usually small and irregular. As of 2013, a total of 81 groups (2,444 households) were beneficiaries in Barangay Malanday.[3]

Profile of Households in Beneficiary Group A

The discussion of the 4Ps in this chapter is mainly based on one group of beneficiaries in Malanday. This group (Group A) is composed of 24 members (i.e., households). Based on the interviews conducted with all the 24 members belonging to Group A, some common features can be delineated below.

First, regarding the age of the beneficiaries, most mothers are in their 30s to 40s because of the requirement that they are raising children between the ages of 0 and 14 years. The next common feature is low educational attainment. In the Philippines, free public education covers six years of compulsory elementary school and four years of non-compulsory middle school.[4] Among the 24 beneficiaries and their husbands in Group A, just one couple had graduated from college; 14 had graduated from middle school, 29 had completed elementary school only, either not started, or dropped out of middle school, and 5 had not completed elementary school.

Now, let us look at the occupations of the members. In the Philippines, it is generally extremely difficult for those with only secondary school education to find work in formal sector jobs, such as clerical jobs. Therefore, the beneficiaries, many of whom are elementary school graduates or high school dropouts, work miscellaneous jobs in the urban informal sector, which is characterised by not only its accessibility for those with little education, but also its irregularity, low wages, and insecurity caused by the undocumented and/or illegal status of some occupations. These jobs include itinerant street vendors selling fruits and snacks, sidewalk vendors selling vegetables and cooked foods, garbage collectors, temporary construction workers, small grocery shop workers in front of the owners' houses (locally called *sari-sari* stores), tricycle drivers, and laundrywomen. Those people who are engaging in garbage collection are employed by a Taiwanese-based NGO that operates a recycling business in Metro Manila, paying 250 pesos per day to the collectors. A few of the beneficiaries are also engaged in the shoe industry. Although it has become an industry in decline, shoemaking continues to be a local industry in Marikina today, with a small number of residents doing contracted work by hand in their homes and earning wages on a piece-rate basis. The income from these miscellaneous jobs in the urban informal sector is insignificant and below the legal minimum wage of 430 pesos per day in the metropolitan area (as of 2011).

Next, daily expenditures are mainly made up of a child's "*baon*" (pocket money), rice, and side dishes. In the Philippines, whether a child receives a sufficient amount of *baon* has a significant impact on the school attendance rate. This is because schools in the Philippines do not provide school lunches, so each child must purchase his or her own snack or lunch with his or her own *baon*, and if there is little or no *baon*, the child goes hungry and consequently loses his or her urge to go to school. Normally, about 20 pesos per child for elementary school and 30 pesos for high school would be considered sufficient *baon*. If there are three children in a household who attend primary school or high school, the *baon* alone covers as much as about a third of their daily expenses. On the other hand, the average daily consumption of rice per household in Group A averaged 2–3 kg per day, which costs about 100 pesos.

Other monthly expenses include utilities, which average around 1,000–1,500 pesos per household, 500 pesos for water, and about 1,500 to 2,000 pesos for rent. In most cases, beneficiaries pay some cash to neighbours for an illegal electricity connection. Still, there are a few households that are unable to pay their bills and thus live without electricity.

The most explicit indication of poverty among residents is whether they can afford to have three meals a day. Among the 24 households interviewed in Group A, only 8 answered that they could afford three meals a day; another 8 households answered that they could not afford three meals a day and described their situation in a self-deprecating way as "one day, one eat". The remaining households answered that there were days when they could not have three meals a day. Understandably, the households that experience difficulty in having three meals a day usually send their children to school without breakfast and/or without *baon* for lunch. It is notable that even the households that can afford three meals a day sometimes have to make do with porridge when they lack enough rice. When they cannot afford a more substantial meal, the family members share rice mixed with instant coffee, a few pieces of dried fish, canned sardines, *bagoong* (fish and shrimp paste), or fried eggs. It can thus be said that the beneficiaries of Group A are experiencing difficulty in securing sufficient food with their meagre daily income. Lacking relatives or friends nearby who can help out, they often have to rely on informal loan sharks called "Five-Six", or "Bombay"—immigrants from India who target the poor for non-collateralised credit with high interest rates[5]. Thus, the popular local expression describing dire poverty, *Isang kahig, isang tuka* ("one scratch, one peck"), can be applied to most of the beneficiaries in this group.[6]

Now, how far can cash grants through the 4Ps contribute to alleviating this situation? Although members in Group A have been receiving cash payments since December 2010, we examine the latest situation, which is the amount paid since January 2012. Interviews with the beneficiaries of Group A suggest that the amount of cash grants tends to be quite irregular and unpredictable, and sometimes, some beneficiaries find no stipend in their bank account. While a beneficiary with three children can expect a full monthly amount of 1,400 pesos, as mentioned earlier, these beneficiaries seldom receive this much; on average, they receive only about 500 pesos monthly. Given the day-to-day expenditures of the beneficiary households explained above, the amount of cash payments under the 4Ps is unlikely to make a significant contribution to the beneficiaries' livelihoods. While it is often criticised that the 4Ps encourage mendicancy and laziness among the poor, the beneficiaries counter such comments by saying, "how can we live a lazy life if we only receive about 500 pesos a month?" Nevertheless, this does not mean that cash payments mean nothing to them. Rather, many beneficiaries talk in unison about "*malaking tulong* (big help)" or "*kahit papaano, nakakakatulong din* (even a little, it helps)". That the people wait impatiently for the cash grant is evident in the long queues that begin early in the morning when beneficiaries rush to the ATM in government banks to receive their cash. The cash remains in their accounts and can be withdrawn at any time after the disbursement date, but the beneficiaries continue to wait for hours in the scorching heat to get their cash as soon as possible.

What then is the reason for this irregularity of cash grants that the beneficiaries usually experience? It lies mainly in the incomplete information and records about the beneficiaries reported to the schools and government offices, which form the basis for calculating the amount of the cash transfer. Records such as the children's school attendance kept by each school, attendance at regular health checkups by mothers and children kept by local health centres, and official birth and marriage certificates kept by national offices are often incomplete, and individual names may be spelled incorrectly.[7] Although the mothers are partly responsible for such failures (see below), the schools, health centres, and government offices are also to blame for their inefficient maintenance of records and information.

Narratives about Changes in Life

Based on interviews with beneficiaries, this section presents their narratives of changes in their lives before and after the 4Ps cash transfers began. First, the most frequently mentioned change in their lives was in their children's education. The requirement to maintain a monthly school attendance rate of 85% means that if a child is absent more than three times a month, he or she will no longer receive cash benefits. Thus, mothers encourage, or often even force their children to attend school. One mother, for example, stated, "Before, if a child had a toothache or a slight fever, it was easy to let him or her miss school. But now I make them go to school as much as possible. If they have no choice but to take a day off, I will make sure to submit a certificate from the doctor to the school". According to another mother, "My child now forces himself to come to school even if he is not feeling well. If I don't wake them up in the morning, they cry because they are late for school". Growing concern for children's hygiene along with their education can be observed in the following narrative: "Before, we didn't pay much attention to children's cleanliness. Now we visit the health center more often and we pay more attention to children's cleanliness, hygiene, and health than before".

In addition to sending their children to school, mothers also monitor their children's activities, as shown in the following narrative: "Sometimes we have to watch them. I now go to their schools from time to time to make sure they are attending... I've learned the importance of constantly monitoring my children's schooling and health". At the same time, the children themselves have taken the initiative in going to school. In particular, children who were previously absent from school because they could not afford school uniforms or school supplies and felt turned away from their classmates may now be more active in coming to school because they can afford these things. According to one mother, "Since the children started to receive cash benefits, they are not forced by their parents to go to school, but they try to attend school as much as possible. Especially after they got their school uniforms, they started coming to school more enthusiastically. Before, I was often unable to pay for textbooks and other expenses for homework, but now I am able to buy them, and, as a result, my child's grades have improved. My child can now attend school events that he couldn't before because I couldn't afford to pay for those events. Now that cash transfers have started, I don't have to worry about school expenses (e.g., non-tuition fees, *baon* to buy snacks, lunch)".

Similarly, a frequently heard life change among the beneficiaries was that new relationships with neighbours had been created and bonds with other members had deepened. The deepening of such relationships is thought to come about as neighbours help each other comply with the various conditions imposed on them for cash transfers. For example, it was said that "Since the 4Ps started, my relationships have expanded... I wasn't very friendly before, and I didn't smile very often. I didn't volunteer to talk to people I didn't know very well, but now I am able to chat and mingle (*nakipaghalobilo*) with people I don't know well. I'm not shy about speaking in public... We used to get together with our neighbors and just engage in gossip (*tismis*). But now we share our concerns with each other about our children's health and education... Our concern (*makikisalamuha*) and care (*malasakit*) for our neighbors has deepened... A sense of brotherhood (*paki-kipag-kapwa*) developed with group members". Furthermore, as will be discussed later in this section, the FDS for the beneficiaries is a venue to discuss a variety of everyday issues, such as the economic deprivation of the people and their relationships with their families. As the following narrative shows, these interactions between neighbours also seem to have had an impact on the formation of new relationships in the community: "I appreciate the opportunity to share with my group members about daily life issues at the FDS seminars. We don't think each other as strangers; instead, we are interested in and concerned (*nakipagsalamuha*) about each other... To be able to continue attending the meetings, we need to invite and encourage each other. In this way, a new kind of bond was formed. There were a lot of people we didn't know before, but now we know each other... We try to help each other and encourage each other to continue attending meetings and having regular weigh-ins and health checks at the health center".

It can be argued that among the beneficiaries, the 4Ps, and in particular, continued participation in the FDS seminars, have nurtured a more introspective gaze toward, and a new awareness of, the self, as suggested in the following narratives. "In the FDS seminar I learned to know myself... In the TV news and elsewhere, there is criticism that the 4Ps promotes a begging mentality. But that's wrong. The beneficiaries receive cash in exchange for adhering to various conditions. This fosters awareness as a mother". Furthermore, the narratives indicate a new attitude towards the management of money and time and their planned use for future purposes: "I have learned to cherish even the smallest amount of money and to plan and spend it frugally... I don't feel comfortable gambling with my neighbors as much as I used to... When I shop, I make sure to keep a list of purchases and receipts and present them to City Link, if necessary. This is how I learned to be frugal... It takes a lot of planning and setting aside time to meet various obligations of the program, such as attending the meetings regularly".

Some Cases of the FDS Seminar

The most important condition that the beneficiaries should observe is to attend FDS seminars, which are facilitated monthly by government social workers or NGOs accredited by the government. Discussions focus on topics such as "To know myself", "Who am I?", "Parental responsibility", "What is the value and importance of family?", and "What is an ideal Filipino family?", as well as on practical issues such as the management of household finances, care for disabled children, prevention of infectious diseases, and improvement of hygiene.[8] One FDS seminar lasts for two hours. Generally, the participating members are the mothers, but a few fathers and teenage daughters sometimes attend as substitutes for their wives and mothers. In the following, three cases (Cases 3.1–3.3) of FDS seminars attended by the members of Group A are presented.

Case 3.1: "To know myself": FDS seminar held on September 14, 2011

Applying the "Johari Window" method, a technique often used in self-help seminars, the topic for this session was "To know myself" (*Kilalanin natin ang ating sarili*). In total, 27 members of Group A attended. A social worker sent by the DSWD gave a sheet of paper to each participant and instructed them to fold it into four equal parts. The participants were then told to write the following in the quadrants: "Your personality (*ugali*)[9] and a strong point (*katangian*) that you and others are aware of" in the first quadrant; "Your personality and a strong point that only you are aware of" in the second; "Your personality and a strong point that you were not aware of but which you realized after being told about it by others" in the third; and "Your ultimate desire in life" in the fourth. The participants were then instructed to separate into four groups and encouraged to share what they had written in each quadrant. After about 15 minutes of sharing, one member from each group was selected and called up in front of everyone to present what she had written, her self-analysis of her personality, the reactions of other members, and the discussion that was carried out in the group.

As indicated above, the FDS is not a kind of spoon-fed, unidirectional, lecture seminar provided by the social worker to the beneficiaries; rather, interactions among the participants are emphasised through group discussions, debates, and presentations (Pictures 3.1, 3.2, and 3.3). The participants are encouraged to engage in self-analysis, reflection, and introspection. Asked about the purpose of this FDS meeting, the social worker said that through group activities during the session, the beneficiaries are encouraged to become "good neighbors who help each other". When the City Link and NGO staff found that the participants were reluctant to speak up, they often encouraged them to ask questions and hold discussions by saying, "Don't be ashamed of

Picture 3.1 The beneficiaries engaging in a group discussion during the Family Development Session

Picture 3.2 The beneficiaries engaging in a group discussion during the FDS

Picture 3.3 The beneficiaries making a presentation in front of the participants

yourself, but let us exercise our right to ask questions" or "Stop gossiping and start thinking for yourselves". In this way, with the aim of making them accustomed to, and confident in, speaking publicly about themselves and their opinions, the members were encouraged to speak and make presentations in front of the whole group.

Case 3.2: "The Filipino family and me": FDS held on September 12, 2012

A total of 24 participants attended this FDS seminar. Prior to the start of the seminar, the facilitator, a staff member from the NGO, checked that all participants were carrying their beneficiary IDs and ATM cards for withdrawing cash grants from the bank. The facilitator reminded the participants that "You must bring your IDs and ATM cards to the seminar every time". The facilitator then announced that the topic for the day would be "The Filipino family and me (*Ako at ang Pamilyang Pilipino*)". She explained the purpose of the session by showing a board on which the following sentences were written: "As parents, our family is the highest priority in life. Everything that we hope for our children hinges on the family. Valuing our obligation as parents is, at the same time, valuing our family. It is of the highest importance to take time to know our families and to understand the true value of family".

The facilitator proceeded to explain the specific objectives of the session, such as understanding the values, duties, and obligations of the family.

Next, the participants were divided into six groups, and the following questions were assigned for each group to discuss and note the results on a sheet of paper:

1 What is the significance (*kahulugan*) of family?
2 What is the value (*kahalagahan*) of family?
3 What do you think of the present situation of the Filipino family?
4 What is your duty to your family?
5 What are the immediate problems that your family is facing?
6 How can you make your family stronger and more solid?

After the group discussion, all the participants were called together and asked to present their own answers. After making brief comments about each presentation, the facilitator created an impromptu script based on the presentations by the members and let them act out a scene in which the members performed the roles of the children, mother, and father. Finally, as a summary of the FDS, the participants were asked to write an essay on "What positive aspect (*positibong katangian*) does your family have?" in a notebook titled, "Everyday Records of the Whole Family (*Tala-arawang ng Sambahayan*)". Along with a beneficiary ID and an ATM card for receiving the cash grants, the beneficiaries are required to bring this notebook every time they attended the FDS. After spending about 20 minutes writing their essays, the facilitator signed each member's notebook as a proof of attendance and the session was concluded.

At the beginning of the session presented above, the facilitator asked the participants to present their IDs and ATM cards. This is intended to discourage the often widespread practice among the beneficiaries of secretly using their ATM cards as collateral to borrow money informally from their friends. Also of interest is the presence of a notebook called *Tala-arawan ng sambahayan* ("Everyday Records of the Whole Family"). Participants were asked to record in detail in the notes what the facilitator spoke about in the seminar and what was discussed among the members. At the end of the seminar, the notes were checked, and signed, by the facilitator as proof of their participation in the seminar. Often, with participants diligently writing down the lessons they learn, the seminar looks like a school classroom (Picture 3.4). Apparently, it is not customary in the everyday lives of the poor in the slums to carry their IDs and ATM cards at all times, or to record and take detailed and accurate notes of instructions from others. Surely, the internalisation of these new practices as embodied *habitus* is considered an essential part of "empowerment" that the 4Ps aim to achieve.

Case 3.3: "Preparation for a disaster": FDS in August 2012

The theme of this FDS was "Preparation for a disaster". It was timely because the session was held only a few days after Metro Manila had experienced extraordinarily heavy and continuous monsoon rain for more than a week. While many parts of the city were flooded, the most severe inundation was experienced by the slum communities clustered along the rivers and canals, including Barangay Malanday.

In the FDS meeting, the members were asked to reflect on their experiences during the disaster, to have a discussion with the group, and to share their

Picture 3.4 The beneficiaries eagerly listen to the instruction by the facilitator during the FDS

experiences in front of everyone. Specific topics for discussion were provided by the facilitator, including the following:

1 Share what happened during the flood.
2 What was your feeling (*narandaman*) during the flood?
3 What was the first thing that you thought about when the flood started, and what was the thing that you kept thinking about during the heavy rain?
4 What was the thing that worried (*nakakabahala*) you the most, or what affected you the most during the disaster?
5 Were there any changes in you either physically or emotionally before and after the disaster? What is your feeling now that you are alive and sharing your experiences in front of everyone?
6 What do we have to do and improve to tackle this kind of disaster? What were our failures and faults for such a disaster to have happened?

It is worth noting that this FDS on "Preparation for a disaster" did not deal with practical "how-to" measures for disaster prevention. Rather, the seminar urged the participants to reflect on their inner status during and after a disaster. It encouraged them to examine closely their experiences, emotions, and psychological states during the flood.

Some features of the FDS and 4Ps can be gleaned from the examples above. First, the purpose of the sessions was to promote people's "empowerment" by developing their reflectiveness and introspectiveness. Through nurturing such reflective and introspective views, the beneficiaries are encouraged to become responsible for their family and their community. Second, the FDS and 4Ps can be considered a "citizenship project" (Lazar 2004) that induces people to change their habits and relationships with their neighbours. It is also the "technology of citizenship" (Cruikshank 1999) to produce citizens who are conscious of political engagement and social participation. The beneficiaries are required to not only attend the meeting, but also participate actively in it through critical thinking, sharing, presenting, and taking careful notes. Furthermore, habits such as *tambay* (gathering for no particular reason), *tsismis* (gossiping and idle conversation), and *sugal* (gambling) are deemed to be unproductive activities that the beneficiaries should avoid (Pictures 3.5 and 3.6).[10] Instead, they are encouraged to shift into relationships based on *makikisalamuha* (fellowship) and *malasakit* (deep concern) for their children, family, and neighbours, which should be the foundation of a "productive community".[11]

Other attitudes and habits that the 4Ps try to inculcate into the beneficiaries are being careful about their time and expenses, properly managing and continuously updating their personal data kept in schools and government offices, and maintaining hygiene in one's family and community. Promoting these habits are as central to the programme as providing cash grants, and are aimed at allowing the beneficiaries to become empowered citizens capable of self-governing.

Picture 3.5 A family during *tambay*

Picture 3.6 Everyday *sugal* (gambling) at the street corner

The story of one member of Group A illustrates the type of empowerment and self-government that the programme seeks to achieve.

Case 3.4: "My only hope is to make my kids graduate": Teresa's case

Teresa was born in 1968 in Marikina City. She got married at the age of 19 years after dropping out of middle school. Her husband was a tricycle driver and used to earn about 300 pesos a day. However, he contracted tuberculosis (TB) and had to stop working. Teresa then started working as a shoemaker earning 500 pesos a week. Additionally, she earned about 900 pesos a week working as a laundrywoman.

When Teresa's husband was diagnosed with TB, the doctor explained that the infiltration of the lungs was already at an advanced stage and, according to Teresa, "his lung was almost eaten up" (*wala nang baga*). Her husband gave up further treatment, deciding that it was better to spend money on schooling for the children than on hospital fees and medicine. At that time, Teresa had seven children, from a young baby to a 14-year-old son. The couple was able to give only 3 pesos to each child as an allowance for school. Teresa used to feel pity for her children, who must have been going hungry at school. On most days, the family could eat only one meal. In 2005, Teresa's husband passed away. After his death, Teresa started to live with a new partner, who is currently employed as a private driver and earns 900 pesos a week. Teresa earns 500 pesos per week from collecting garbage for recycling, and continues her laundry work for supplementary income in addition to the cash she receives from the 4Ps, which averages 550–950 pesos per month.

Teresa still has three children going to school and has to allocate more than 100 pesos for school allowance every day. Although her life is difficult, she tries to secure this allowance for her children by any means to send them to school. Teresa is determined for her children to get an education: "[Now that I am receiving cash from the government for the children's education] I am wholly concentrating on making sure my children finish their schooling. I don't want my kids to become vendors of *sampagita* in the streets or dancers in a beer house.* My only hope is to make sure my kids graduate at least from middle school".

*sampagita (Jasminum sambac), or sampaguita, is a national flower of the Philippines. Wreaths made of sampagita flowers are sold on the street by children for a few pesos.

Teresa's case suggests that the 4Ps cannot alleviate the poverty of beneficiaries through the cash grant itself; the cash component is too small to bring any real change to Teresa's life, and she is as poor as she was several years ago when her husband had to abandon his TB treatment to save money for his children's *baon*. Yet, what defines her current life is a strong desire for her children's education. Although unable to provide a lot of cash, the 4Ps programme has sought to advance the inclusion of the poor through creating, nurturing, and strengthening such desires among beneficiaries. Under neoliberal social policy, the state avoids providing a comprehensive safety net or intervening through state regulations, but seeks instead to achieve its purpose by creating specific subjectivity and structuring the field of its conduct. Li argues that such a neoliberal subject is made through "educating desires and configuring habits, aspirations and beliefs" (Li 2007a: 5). The current 4Ps scheme seeks to achieve its purpose through capitalizing on the desires of the beneficiaries.

"Investment in Human Capital" Adrift?: Marginalisation, Unintended Consequences, and Counterclaims

As has been explained, the 4Ps as a social redistribution programme is premised on the neoliberal rationale of "investment in human capital". This section argues that, while this logic provides an effective justification for the implementation of the programme in a country defined by a deep-seated social divide, it also invites various unintended consequences.

Since it began, the 4Ps has been criticised, particularly by those in the middle class, as a handout policy that works only as a temporary "Band-Aid solution", without fiscal sustainability (Vigilia 2010). The programme has been further denounced for entrenching a "culture of mendicancy" and encouraging the "patronage politics" that is deeply rooted in the Philippine political culture (Salaverria 2010). As a backdrop to this criticism of the programme, there has been deepening distrust in the government, particularly since the administration of President Estrada (1998–2001); the middle classes complain that there is too much reliance on populist policies and handouts, without any clear long-range plan, and their distrust of politicians and the system of government has become entrenched. The hostility of the middle class towards the lower-class poor, whom they refer to derogatorily as *masa*, or the mass, is equally deep-seated. They see the poor as relentlessly demanding pity and compassion for their miserable situation to secure what they want from populist-style politicians. This distrust and hostility among the middle class is based on a common perception that the tax they pay is not being fairly redistributed through efficient government services, while the poor, who are engaged in untaxed informal-sector jobs, are courted by, and benefit from, populist policies.

The middle-class view of the poor leads to a distinction between those who are "citizens", or the tax-paying middle class, and those who are "noncitizens", or the untaxed poor.[12] The neoliberal rationale at the centre of the 4Ps is mobilised to justify and defend the programme against the critical view adopted by the middle class. However, as an unintended and ironic consequence of this rationale, which encourages beneficiaries to be self-activating citizens, various forms of exclusion have emerged; these include people who need help but are disqualified as a beneficiary because of the programme's system of selection, beneficiaries who have fallen into further poverty and marginalisation even after the implementation of the programme, beneficiaries for whom the programme has failed to produce the expected outcomes, and beneficiaries who make counterclaims against the logic of the programme, conjuring a popular notion of "help" and an alternative mode of social inclusion. Some examples are considered in this section.

People Who are Disqualified because of the Selection System

Case 3.5: "I cannot help but feel sorry for my children": Ana's case

Ana, a member of Group A, was born in 1964 in Camarines Sur, southern Luzon, and moved to Marikina City with her mother when she was four years old. She attended school up to primary school and was married in 1984, after which, the couple made a meagre living by growing vegetables on vacant land near Barangay Malanday and peddling them in nearby markets and on the street. Today, both she and her husband are employed by a Taiwanese NGO working in the area to collect and recycle waste products, earning 250 pesos per person per day. However, after deducting transportation and other expenses, they are left with only 200 pesos. Much of their daily income goes to pay off their debts. Ana and her family frequently cannot eat three times a day, and breakfast is sometimes just rice with coffee; if they do not have enough rice, they eat porridge.

Ana has a total of eight children, the eldest of whom is 26 years old and the youngest of whom is 8 years old. The eldest son, a primary school graduate, earns 250 pesos a day from the same NGO as his parents. The second son (23 years old), eldest daughter (20 years old), third son (17 years old), and second daughter (16 years old) are all primary school graduates and unemployed. The third daughter, aged 13 years, is currently in the third year of primary school, and the fourth daughter, aged 11 years, is in the second year of primary school. However, in respect to these two daughters, no official birth certificates exist, which is why they were ineligible for the 4Ps. On the other hand, the youngest child, the fourth son, who is eight years old and in the first year of primary school, is the only child eligible for the 4Ps education benefit award. According to Ana, her children are frail and sick and often miss school; this is the reason why the three children currently in school are significantly behind in their progress. Some days, they are forced to send their children to school without breakfast and others, without *baon*. Ana laments, "I cannot help but feel sorry for my children when I think of them being hungry at school".

Case 3.6: "I was bypassed": Ruth's case

Ruth was born in 1976 in Barangay Malanday. After graduating from high school, she got married at the age of 18 years. She then started working in the local shoe industry, and her current income is about 400–500 pesos per week. Her husband, a primary school dropout, is a local shoemaker (*sapatero*) who earns about 800 pesos per week. However, there are many days when there are no shoe orders, and when this happens, he works as a temporary construction worker and earns about 250 pesos a day. Ruth's 72-year-old mother works as a laundress and earns about 500 pesos every two weeks to help support her family. Ruth's father died of TB about ten years previously. At the same time, her brother died at the age of 24 years. Her brother had a preexisting heart condition, but he was so concerned about the family's struggling finances that he held off going to the doctor until it was too late.

Ruth also has a 14-year-old boy. Under normal circumstances, he would be a freshman in high school, but he was forced to abandon his education because the family could not afford to pay for the schooling. Ruth is also raising the child of her deceased brother. Her nephew, now 11 years old, is a late entrant to school and still in the second grade, and there are days when she cannot even give him 15 pesos of *baon* a day, so he often misses school. The family does not eat breakfast most of the time, and usually they have only two meals a day. They cannot pay the electricity bill and hence, they have to live without electricity in the house. Ruth considered the option of going abroad for work, but she could not bear to leave her children behind. Staff from the government visited several times to conduct interviews and surveys for the selection of 4Ps beneficiaries, but, according to Ruth, "I was bypassed (*iniwasan ako*)".

In these two cases, the continued enrolment of children in school was a serious difficulty, or was expected to become difficult in the near future. Nonetheless, owing to the programme's selection system, more than a few families are "bypassed" and considered ineligible for support. In Ana's case, struggling family finances have affected her child's nutrition and health, and her child is often absent from school. Although support is needed to continue their studies, the children are not able to receive cash payments because of a lack of necessary administrative documents such as a birth certificate. In Ana's case, older children who did not make it to secondary school remain in their households unemployed with no possibility of employment in the near future. However, since they are already over the age of 14 years, they are above the programme's recipient age limit and thereby ineligible for cash payments. Thus, the likelihood that they will again pursue education or training and gain some work qualifications is also very small. In addition, as the two cases show, many children from poor families are delayed in progression for a variety of reasons and often do not correspond to the standard age and grade level. For these children, the programme's age limits leave them ineligible for benefits, or if they are eligible, they have very little time left to receive them. Even if they do qualify, the vulnerability of poor people to sickness and disaster makes the programme's provision "a drop of water on a hot stone". Despite the progress of the programme, the poverty and marginalisation of the population have deepened. The following section examines such cases.

Further Impoverishment and Marginalisation

Case 3.7: Informal work of widows: Maria's case

Maria, a member of Group A, was born in 1977 in Barangay Malanday. After graduating from high school, she married in 1995. Her husband was a temporary electrical maintenance worker in several hotels and schools, earning a daily wage of 380 pesos. But later, he was found to have TB. Although taking medicine and undergoing treatment, due to his working environment, where he was breathing in a lot of dust and polluted air every day, his condition gradually worsened, accelerated by diabetes. He passed away in May 2012 at the young age of 36 years. Currently, Maria sells food at a food court in a nearby shopping mall and earns 125 pesos a day. However, it is difficult for her to earn enough money from this informal job, as she only works three days a week. She borrows money from her sister, who lives nearby, to try to tide herself over, and sometimes subsists a day by salt and water. She has five children, from the eldest, who is in the third year of high school, to the youngest, who is in the second year of elementary school. At the moment, her children are attending school, but their *baon* alone totals 250 pesos a day for five kids, which puts a big strain on the family budget.

Case 3.8: "What we really need is capital": Rose's case

Rose, who was born in 1970, used to earn approximately 5,000 pesos a month from itinerant vegetable peddling. Her husband sometimes works as a labourer at construction sites, but is unemployed most of the time. Rose often finds him drunk, even during the daytime. In September 2009, the lives of Rose and her family completely changed after they were hit by the super typhoon known locally as Ondoy and internationally as Ketsana. This powerful typhoon caused a deluge in the expansive slum areas along the Marikina River, including the community where Rose lived (Picture 3.7). Her house was totally submerged, and the equipment for her business was washed away. Fortunately, Rose and her family survived, but after the disaster, they could barely subsist on Rose's street vending earnings of 100–250 pesos a day. Her family frequently experiences days when they cannot have three meals. On some days, they have to make do with rice mixed with coffee or share a small amount of *bagoong* or fried eggs.

Rose has five children, three of whom still go to elementary school and could be beneficiaries of the 4Ps. However, two of these children were unable to receive any educational grant money for several months because of a discrepancy between school and government (DSWD) records in the spelling of their names. To rectify this, Rose has to go to the National Statistics Office to apply for a correction of the spelling of the registered names. However, she has not begun this process and seems to have given up because of a lack of knowledge, money, and, perhaps, the necessary motivation. Now, her children

Picture 3.7 Houses in Barangay Malanday submerged into water during the super typhoon Ondoy (September 2009)

are frequently absent from school because they often feel weak and hungry, and they do not have *baon* to buy food while they are in school.

In August 2012, heavy monsoon rains again caused the inundation of Rose's house and neighbourhood. She and her family had to spend a month in an evacuation centre, and then, because their house had been washed away, had to start renting a house. The monthly rent of 2,000 pesos is too burdensome for her, and her family is in danger of being evicted. This situation prevents her from foreseeing anything but a bleak future. When she receives the small grant amount from the 4Ps, she hides it from her husband to stop him from using it to buy alcohol, which she says frequently makes him violent. Faced with everyday uncertainty and the prospect of a bleak future, Rose says, "The provision of the 4Ps does help. But what we really need is capital (*puhunan*) to peddle on a regular and steady basis".

The cases of Maria and Rose demonstrate that the 4Ps programme has failed to alleviate the risks, such as disease and disaster, posed by the vulnerability inherent in urban slum living. Squatters, who occupy vacant land along river-banks, bear the brunt of natural disasters, especially typhoons and heavy mon-soon rains, which have become more frequent in recent years. The disasters that Rose experienced are not exceptional misfortunes, but rather constitutive elements of life in urban squatter settlements. The 4Ps grant is far from suf-ficient to alleviate her condition. Furthermore, the precariousness that Rose experiences deters her from engaging in the practices of "empowerment" that the programme regards as important. For beneficiaries to receive a cash grant, there is a procedural requirement for them to maintain updated personal information in various government offices, such as the National Statistics Office, health centres, and schools. That beneficiaries are able to manage their own official information is considered a prerequisite for the empowerment targets of the 4Ps. Rose—and many others in a similar situation—fail to meet this requirement and are consequently excluded from the poverty alleviation aspect of the 4Ps. In other words, for Rose, the "empowerment" envisioned by the programme is ineffective for her; rather, she requests a direct distribution of tangible resources, known as a *"puhunan"* (capital, or seed money). This suggests a discrepancy between the expectations of the programme implementers and those of beneficiaries. The following cases of the FDS seminars, which serve as the main mechanism for transmitting the logic and rationale of the programme, clearly indicate such discrepancies, as they often fail to achieve their intended effects among the beneficiaries.

FDS and Unintended Consequences

Case 3.9: FDS turned into a mere formality: FDS held on September 11, 2013

The topic of one FDS meeting was "financial literacy". In this meeting, a social worker from the DSWD explained how to manage household budgets properly and wisely using a table showing an example of household income and expenses, such as rent, electricity, water, and mobile phone service. One member standing at the back started to grumble in a low voice and could not be heard by the social worker at the front. According to the member: "The actual expenses of the household are not so simple. There are more items that we have to allow for. It is not easy to cut down on these necessary expenses, even though we try. For rich people like him [the social worker] who come from the government office, it might be easy to cut expenses. But for the poor like us, it is not. We have to cut down on expenses for rice, sugar, or allowance (*baon*) for the children. If not, we have to borrow money from someone".

The themes, contents, and format of the FDS are decided by the central office of the DSWD, and do not necessarily reflect the reality of urban poor communities. However, the social workers do not usually take on the task of adjusting and rephrasing these formats in line with the concrete realities of local communities; rather, the social workers sometimes complain about the attitudes of the beneficiaries. On one occasion, for instance, the social worker said, "No matter how hard we encourage the members, they don't like to grab the opportunity [to improve their lives]. Why? Because they don't like to change their habits [*nakasanayan*]. It is hard to change the customs [*kustombre*] that they are familiar with, such as how to spend money and how to spend their time".

This case reveals the existence of a gap between the reality envisioned by the seminar and facilitating social workers, on the one hand, and the reality of everyday life in the slums on the other. The existence of such a gap does not motivate the participants, and the seminar often becomes a place dominated only by formalities. When this happens, the participants' main concern is only to get the facilitator's signature on the notebook (i.e., *Tala-arawan*, mentioned before) that they bring as proof of their attendance to meet the requirements of the programme. Thus, the "empowerment" envisioned by social workers and the government is left behind, and the seminars continue to produce unintended consequences. Likewise, the intention of the social workers at the FDS to facilitate self-analysis and introspection by the participants often fails, and the meeting, as shown on other occasions of the FDS below, is appropriated by the people's own needs.

Case 3.10: FDS turned into an entreaty for help and emotional catharsis: FDS held on September 14, 2011

During the session mentioned above on "To know myself" (Case 3.1), the participants were asked to share the results of a group discussion about their personalities. Initially, the women were mostly shy and hesitant to speak in front of the group, but after being urged on by the social worker, they gradually began to talk. However, none of them actually spoke about, let alone analysed, their personalities. Instead, they focused on what they had written in the fourth quadrant, "Your ultimate desire in life", and started to talk about the hardships of their everyday life, their lack of income and a regular job, and family problems caused, for instance, by adolescent children and unemployed or underemployed husbands. Everyone mentioned being able to eat three times a day as their ultimate desire in life. Some of them even burst into tears while sharing the hardships that they endure every day. Many of the participants who were listening were also moved to tears in sympathy. The social worker, on the other hand, encouraged the participants by saying, "Follow the terms and conditions of the program and keep up with the information about yourself and your family, so that you will get 1,400 pesos per month".

An opportunity formally intended to inculcate citizens' values such as careful planning for the future based on detached self-analysis turned into the sharing of everyday difficulties, achieving emotional catharsis, and requesting help and compassion from neighbours. Thus, the intended aim of "empowerment" by the FDS was in a sense appropriated by the participants according to their specific needs. A criticism of "conditioned" help, with requests for "unconditioned" help instead, can be observed in the cases below.

Counterclaims against the Programme

The implementation of the 4Ps has not only produced an excluded population and unintended consequences among the beneficiaries, but also yielded counterclaims from people who do not agree with the programme's form of social inclusion or its mode of governing poverty, and those who would prefer to be dealt with differently. The following cases suggest this aspect.

Case 3.11: It is like requiring people to jump high to reach fruits on tall trees: Lisa's case

Lisa withdrew from schooling in her first year of college and currently manages a *sari-sari* store (a small-scale neighbourhood grocery shop). Her husband is a college graduate and licensed architect, but he is currently unemployed. Lisa used to be a member of Group A, and was one of the beneficiaries of the 4Ps programme. She was often unable to attend FDS meetings and failed to update the personal information for her family in school and government offices because she was busy attending to her small business. Although the social worker and group leader exhorted her to put more effort into fulfilling the conditions of the programme, it was hard for her to do so because of her business. Finally, she left the group and waived her rights as a beneficiary. Lisa's opinion on the programme is reflected in the following narrative: "The program requires numerous conditions in order to receive the cash payment. It is too burdensome.... The program just gives you a small amount of 300 or 500 pesos. Why it is necessary to require you to attend the meetings and to observe many conditions just to receive that amount? It is like asking people to be down on their knees to show gratitude for such a small amount of help received. It is like requiring people to jump high to reach fruits on tall trees. If the government wants to help us, why do they need to burden the people?"

Complaints such as "too many conditions for payment and very annoying" are often made by parent leaders who act as intermediaries between City Link and beneficiaries. The following case illustrates such a situation.

Case 3.12: Burden on parent leaders

City Link, that is, social workers dispatched by the government, makes regular visits to the community to check on beneficiaries' living conditions, compliance with the terms and conditions of their payments, and complaints about the programme. When such visits occur, the parent leaders of each beneficiary group are busy. According to one parent leader, when the time of the regular visit by City Link is approaching, they are busy going around to each member and asking them to update and correct their information on the Beneficiary Update Form (see note 7). Sometimes, if someone does not listen to the parent leader, she has no choice but to update the information by herself on behalf of that member. Lamenting the situation, she said, "Many members fail to update the information they need to receive cash payments, such as correcting their children's school attendance and spelling errors in their names on their birth certificates. We always tell our members to get together before a visit by City Link to update their personal information and complete and submit an Update Form. However, many of the members do not comply. They complain to me when they don't get paid or their benefits are reduced because they didn't make the update".

Danica, a former parent leader, offered to waive her benefits and has dropped out of the programme. Regarding her reason for quitting the programme, she said that she was often accused by members who discovered on the day of remittance that the amount received was zero or greatly reduced compared with the amount expected. On such occasions, the members suspected that the parent leader, who was the intermediary with the government, was embezzling the money that had been given to them or taking unfair advantage. After experiencing such misunderstandings with the beneficiaries, Danica said, "I became so annoyed by these things that I thought, let's stop this nonsense and abandon it". Danica goes on to say harshly that the programme is just a "consolation prize (*kunswelo de bobo*)" for the poor, referring to a situation where payments are not made on a regular basis, and when they are made, they are not paid in fixed or full amounts, sometimes even zero.

Case 3.12 suggests a situation in which parent leaders are put under tremendous stress to enable the beneficiaries to continue to receive cash payments. In the previous section in this chapter, positive changes in people's practices, such as child education and hygiene or the management of administrative information, were mentioned. With reference to the cases reviewed here, however, it is highly possible that these new attitudes among the beneficiaries are not so much spontaneous acts by "empowered" members as they are forced by the power relations and hierarchies that exist between them on the one hand, and City Link and the government on the other (see Figure 3.1). For example, one resident said, "Before, I used to leave my kids alone, even if they kept untidy. But now I make sure that my kids are tidy and well-dressed in case the DSWD might find them".

Furthermore, residents' sentiments suggesting power relations and hierarchies between them, City Link, and the administration are evident in the narrative by Danica, the parent leader in Case 3.12, who states, "City Link criticizes us for gambling all the time. But it's up to us what we do with our husband's money, isn't it? Is City Link going to give us money every day or every week? They think they've got us by the neck. We play bingo for a pittance of cash, it's just a way to pass the time (*libangan*), not gambling". Taking narratives such as these into account, the positive changes in the attitudes and behaviours of the beneficiaries mentioned in the previous section cannot be considered to indicate only their "inclusion" into mainstream civil society; here, too, the programme's intended "empowerment" seems to have come up empty. In the next case, the counterclaims made by the beneficiaries are more clearly expressed.

Case 3.13: *"Genuine help should come without conditions":* Melanie's case *(Interview on September 20, 2012)*

Melanie was born in 1979. She has a son in third grade and a 4-year-old daughter, and is currently expecting a third child. She got married after graduating from middle school, but they did not have a wedding because of a lack of money. Her husband is a street vendor who sells snack foods, earning about 300 pesos a day.

As a group leader, Melanie used to be an active member of the programme; however, she subsequently left the group and gave up her rights as a beneficiary. She said, "The 4Ps only caused us damage [*perhuwisyo*]". She was referring to her obligation as a parent leader to monitor whether the members were properly observing the conditions of the programme, which caused her to be out of the house so often that it affected her family's livelihood. Melanie's street vendor husband sells *binatog*, a popular snack food made of coconut flesh and corn that requires extra labour to process. Whenever Melanie was absent from home, her husband had to pay someone else to do the processing. Hence, he did not appreciate her joining the group and used to say, "Quit the program. I can earn more than the program provides you".

One night, Melanie was attending a funeral wake for an in-law, which usually lasts for up to a week, and playing cards, an activity very common in the Philippines during a wake. By chance, she was seen by the social worker and given a warning that she might lose her beneficiary status if she continued gambling. Regarding the incident, she said, "What's wrong with gambling with your own money? I am making sure that I send my child to school, even though I gamble. Even without the 4Ps I can secure allowance for my child so that he can go to school. We are burdened with so many conditions for just a small cash grant". She complained that the programme requires too many documents and too much information regarding the beneficiaries: "Submit a birth certificate, a baptismal certificate, and barangay clearance, etc. The really poor people, such as those sleeping inside a *kariton* [pushcart], do not have those kinds of documents. Without the documents, can't our government help these poor people? If it is genuine help from the government, it should come without conditions".

She also complained about the regulations on how to use the cash provided by the programme: "There are so many things that we have been prohibited from buying when using the cash grant from the 4Ps. For example, we are instructed not to buy rice with the health grant. Instead, we are allowed only to purchase milk and supplements for the children. When people are hungry, how can we not buy rice?... I used to attend the FDS even though I was busy. It was disappointing that you were asked to do meaningless things such as skits. They were just repeating the same thing. The meetings should deal with more important things since we attend the meetings instead of doing chores around the house and other things we have to do.... We are also required to go regularly to the health centre. But all they actually do is just weigh our children. That's it. It is meaningless. There should be more valuable things such as a regular and more comprehensive health checkup and the distribution of free medicine".

The above narratives suggest the popular notion of "help (*tulong*)", which implies that the social payments should be provided without any conditions or actions expected from the poor. Such a notion contrasts sharply with the citizenship project underlying the 4Ps, which aims, through cash grants, to induce people to empower themselves and become active and self-regulating citizen subjects who voluntarily engage in the practices of "investing in human capital". To that end, the programme sets up various systems of conditioning and selection, but the cases of residents who are disqualified as, or excluded from being, beneficiaries in the selection process suggest a wide range of people who are not able to engage in the envisaged "investment in human capital" (Cases 3.5 and 3.6). Meanwhile, the cases of further impoverishment and marginalisation showed that aid through "investment in human capital" was not at all effective in the face of slum vulnerability (Cases 3.7 and 3.8). In addition, the cases of unintended consequences showed that the production of civic subjects often came up empty (Cases 3.9 and 3.10). By contrast, the cases of critical narratives

(Cases 3.11–3.13) showed that what people are looking for is direct, unconditional assistance for tangible goods such as "capital" (Case 3.8), "jobs" (Case 3.10), and "three meals a day" (Case 3.10). The final case below (Case 3.14) is about the tragic end of Melanie, who appeared in Case 3.13, which suggests the other dark side of the "citizenship project". Her case suggests that "investment in human capital" can turn into an explicit and violent power of exclusion for those with less or no "capital value".

Case 3.14: The war on drugs and Melanie's tragic end (February 2017)[13]

After leaving the 4Ps, Melanie helped her husband peddle and support their five children, including their eldest son, now aged 13 years, and an 8-month-old baby. However, her income from the unstable peddling business was meagre and her life was difficult. The small piece of land and dwelling she had inherited from her parents had to be mortgaged in order to borrow money to live on. After that, she and her family moved from one small room to another. When they did not have the money to rent a room, they built a hut on the bank of the Marikina River to live in. In the midst of this difficult life, Melanie's husband gradually turned to drugs. Soon after, Melanie joined her husband in his drug use. Melanie's husband was not only a drug user, but also a prolific trafficker, and according to the Malanday Anti-Narcotics Committee, he was suspected of running a hangout for drug addicts.

Meanwhile, in Philippine national politics, a new president, Rodrigo Duterte, was elected in June 2016. His first pledge was to restore security in the country, and to that end, he set out to eradicate drugs and allowed drug dealers and users to be killed without a trial. Less than a year after President Duterte took office, more than 7,000 people had been killed in such "extrajudicial killings". The damage was widespread as the killings were carried out by not only the police, but also local killers and vigilantes sometimes hired by the police, and these killings targeted not only those who dealt or used drugs, but also those suspected of doing so.

The incident in this case took place on February 20, 2017. Melanie and her children, who were living in a rented part of her husband's sister's house, were suddenly confronted by masked men with guns. Seeing the danger, her husband quickly climbed onto the roof and escaped the danger. The masked men first took the 8-month-old baby in Melanie's arms and threw her to the floor. As the men pointed a gun at the mother, the 8-year-old daughter pleaded, "Don't shoot my mother! Who's going to take care of us when my mother dies?" Immediately afterwards, Melanie was shot four times, killing her instantly. The first shot entered the corner of her left eye and exited through the back of her head, the second hit her right cheek, the third her right armpit, and the last went through the right palm of her hand, which Melanie had reflexively held up. After the men left, it was the eldest son of 13 years and the eldest daughter of 8 years who wiped up their mother's blood, which had been splattered across the small, rented room. The two children found two of their mother's teeth on the floor where the blood had been spattered.

Days after the incident, the eldest son and daughter were still stunned. Even the 8-month-old baby, who used to be happy and laugh when he was picked up, became reluctant to be carried by others and seldom laughed. Melanie's husband is still missing, having fled after the incident. The five remaining children were taken in separately by several relatives.

About the incident, Melanie's mother said, "I know for sure that Melanie took drugs, but she's more of a victim (unlike her husband, who was even trafficking). Look at the house she was living in. She lived in a small room with no furniture and household utensils whatsoever. The government only targets small, poor people like Melanie, not big-time traffickers. The police demanded an autopsy of Melanie's corpse, for which we had to pay 12,000 pesos, even though it was obvious that she had been shot to death. How far are the police willing to go to squeeze us?"

The 4Ps continue to grow in size under the current Duterte administration. However, the war on drugs suggests a situation in which the government is encouraging the poor to "invest in human capital" while forcibly eliminating drug users, who are seen as having no "capital value", so to speak. In this context, the life of Melanie, who pleaded for the direct and unconditional provision of concrete goods, became even more peripheral, ultimately leading to disastrous consequences.

Discussion

Today, "the social" in the Philippines, reflected in social policies and programmes such as the 4Ps, is increasingly intermingled with the neoliberal rationality of "governing through freedom" (Rose 1999), which creates incentives and disincentives, rather than repression or constraints, for specific actions related to the administration and management of a population. Based on the same logic, the government of poverty examined in this study seeks to realise the social inclusion of the poor through the nurturing of desires, habits, and dispositions that are conducive to "investment in human capital". It is noteworthy, however, that the case of the 4Ps examined here suggests that such neoliberal governmentality coexists with the rather classical social intervention of "policing the family" (Donzelot 1979), as clearly observed in the FDS sessions. It is a main argument of this chapter that such an amalgam of different technologies, or "neoliberalism as exception" (Ong 2006), produces modes of exclusion as well as inclusion of specific populations in the process of its deployment.

The intention of this chapter, however, does not lie in blaming the implementer or government for these exclusions or for any unintended consequences caused by the programme. Shore and Wright (2011: 10–11) claim that anthropological studies on social policy avoid identifying the "agent" or the "authoritative will" behind the policy, the process of which is usually "messy", "ambiguous", and therefore "faceless". Rather, this study tries to delineate how power works in the field structured by neoliberal social policies and the way in which the actors, including the poor beneficiaries, social workers, and other implementers of the government, are equally entangled within this power configuration; it is at such configuration that the emergence of vernacular public sphere among the people can be observed. With this in mind, this section discusses the implications of the counterclaims presented above, which are voiced from the zone of "exception to neoliberalism" (Ong 2006).

As the counterclaims made by Lisa (Case 3.11) and Melanie (Case 3.13) in the previous section suggest, the popular concept of "help (*tulong*)" is deeply rooted in the notions of patronage and clientelism, which have been said to define the social relationships of the Philippines (Kerkvliet 1991). In the discourses of the middle class and civil society in the country, patronage and clientelism—seen as the particularised and personalised exchange of votes and support for goods, favours, and services between the poor and elites or politicians—have been sharply criticised as a source of corruption that hinders the development of a rights-based public sphere of citizenship. Still, I would argue that the counterclaims, and the notions of patronage and clientelism inflected in it, can be considered part of a "regime of living" (Collier & Lakoff 2005) among the poor. This is a situated configuration of techniques, subjects, and norms through which the ethical question of "how to live" is posed in relation to problematic and uncertain situations. Inherent in such a regime are the notions of what a socially just redistribution of resources should be and how people with differentiated resources should coexist.

There are now classic studies on Philippine society that argue that patronage and personalised patron–client relationships have nurtured a tacit norm of reciprocity that underpins a "right to survive" and a "subsistence ethic" shared by resource-poor farmers and fishers that resource-rich capitalists and local politicians are required to follow (Szanton 1972; Szanton 1981). This enables the "everyday politics" of the weak in Philippine rural villages, which influences interactions among subordinate and superordinate people regarding the control, allocation, and use of resources, including land, credit, interest rates, work opportunities, wages, livelihoods, and arrangements for selling or buying rice (Kerkvliet 1991). Cannell (1999) discusses patronage in the rural Philippines in relation to the indigenous notion of power, which results not in a static and rigid social hierarchy, but in a more malleable and flexible relationship between the "people who have nothing" and the patrons with economic power and spiritual potency. Under such a fluid hierarchy, the poor negotiate and manipulate their relationships with patrons by putting themselves in a highly subordinate position that paradoxically induces intimacy with, and concessions from, the patrons.

In the context of contemporary electoral politics, it is argued that patronage and the personalised distribution of resources contribute to the construction of "good" and "bad" politicians in the eyes of the poor (Schaffer 2005; Garrido 2008). Based on the case of the urban poor community in Metro Manila, Schaffer argues that such views reflect their "moral calculus [which] leads many voters to choose candidates whom they perceive to be caring, kind, and helpful; candidates who respect their *kapwa*—their fellow human beings, especially those who are poor" (Schaffer 2005: 15). Elaborating on the difference in this view of politics between the poor and the upper and middle classes, Schaffer (ibid.) further argues:

> Politics, then, for many among the poor... is a politics of dignity. "Bad" politics is a politics of callousness and insult, while "good" politics is a politics

of consideration and kindness. In contrast, many in the upper and middle classes tend to view "bad" politics as a dirty politics of patronage and corruption, while they see "good" politics as a clean politics of issues, accountability, transparency.

In a recent study on local and village politics in the Batangas Province in the Philippines, Soon (2015) demonstrated that patron–client relationships should not be viewed simply as a political machine embedded within the hierarchy existing between the poor and the elite that is instrumentally maneuvered by local politicians to elicit political support. Rather, these relationships are indicative of a negotiation of power flowing from "above" as well as "below", through which individuals' "moral politics" emerge (Soon 2015: 128). Village residents, who are the clients, constantly "scrutinize (*kilatis*)" acts of "assistance (*tulong*)" and "gift-giving (*paghahandog*)" made by superiors, or patrons, regarding whether these acts are based on their "good inner being (*magandang loob*)". In return, the superiors attempt to portray themselves as individuals having "compassion (*malasakit*)" and demonstrating "sincerity (*matuwid*)" towards their "fellow human beings (*kapwa*)". Therefore, patron–client relationships cannot simply be interpreted as a personalised exchange of votes and assistance. What should be understood instead is the moral politics derived from such informal relationships between the poor and elites, and how balance and equilibrium, rather than hierarchy, between them will be elicited from such moral politics.

When the case of the 4Ps is contextualised in these discussions of clientelism and reciprocity in the Philippines, it becomes apparent that denouncing patronage and clientelism as a hindrance to democracy, the civil public sphere, and the modern political system would result in, at best, a lopsided interpretation of reality. Rather, we should consider them, particularly the counterclaims made by the people against the 4Ps, ethical notions of the poor that indicate an appropriate relationship between the haves and have-nots about how the two should coexist, and what should constitute a just (re)distribution of resources between them. Asking for "help (*tulong*)" and narrative of patronage by the people in this chapter should not be considered as retrogressive nostalgia for the pre-capitalist past. Rather, those counterclaims made by the people experienced further exclusion and marginalisation under the neoliberal restructuring of "the social" should be taken as serious envisioning for the vernacular public sphere, where another mode of redistribution amid the overwhelming imbalance and disparity of wealth, goods, and power could still be possible.

Notes

1. This chapter is reprinted in a revised form from *Development and Change* 46.6 (2015): 1253–1276, by permission of the International Institute of Social Studies.
2. At the time of the fieldwork, 1 Philippine peso was equivalent to about 0.025 USD.

3. The data for this chapter had been gathered during the fieldwork mainly in Barangay Malanday on August, September, and November 2011, August and September 2012, and intermittent follow-up researches thereafter. Interviews were conducted in Tagalog (Filipino).

4. There was a reform of the school education system in 2012 that extended middle school education for two additional years. As a result, the current primary and middle school education period is 12 years in total.

5. They are called "Five-Six" because of the high interest rate of 20 percent, which means that if you borrow 500 pesos, you must pay back 600 pesos. The immigrants from India called "Bombay" not only lend money at high interest rates but also sell daily necessities such as blankets and sheets to borrowers at high prices.

6. While this expression in Filipino can be translated plainly as a "hand-to-mouth existence", it implies a sense of self-pity among the poor, who are comparing themselves with chickens restlessly scratching the ground and pecking for food. Group A's situation can be considered more or less common to other beneficiary groups existing currently in Malanday, of which there are about 80.

7. Aside from these records, the documents that need to be submitted include the following: 1) Beneficiary Update Form: this must be updated every time there is a change in a family member's status (e.g., birth, death, higher education). In case of some changes, verifying documents such as birth, barangay captain, school attendance, death, or nursing certificates must be attached; 2) Compliance Verification System: this document is made by the schoolteachers and health workers at the local health centre to certify the child's school attendance and health screening rate at the health centre. The information on this form is used to determine the amount of each cash payment; and 3) Grievance Redress System Form: this is a form for beneficiaries to file a grievance against the program. The beneficiaries can file complaints with the Department of Social Welfare and Development about disbursement delays or shortfalls, health centres, and schools and teachers.

8. The themes of each FDS seminar are selected and formulated by the central office of the DSWD based on the principles of the programme provided in the guidebook (titled *Gabay ng Pamilya para sa Pagtupad ng Kanilang Tungkulin sa Programa*, or *The Guide for Accomplishing Program Obligations for the Family*) published by the DSWD, which all beneficiaries are required to keep and bring to every FDS. This guidebook carefully explains the basic principles of the program, such as parental responsibility for their children's education, awareness of the importance of hygiene, nutrition, and the health of the children and family, discipline in every aspect of daily life, particularly in the management of time and cash expenses, and continuous updating of personal data registered at schools, health centres, and government offices. These principles can be summarized in the foremost objective of the program: "investment in human capital".

9. The Filipino word *ugali* not only means personality, but also refers to collective traits such as "culture" and "custom", or even personal "habits" and "idiosyncrasies". Thus, it can be argued that the FDS, and the 4Ps programme itself, intends to accomplish a more comprehensive and thorough transformation of the beneficiaries' self, the nuance of which is somewhat lost in translation from *ugali* to merely "personality".

10. *Tambay* is a Filipino word derived from the English word standby, which means "to stand ready for a turn" or "to wait".

11. Of course, these values of fellowship and concern for the neighbours have long been appreciated among the slum dwellers in the Philippines. Jocano, for example, discussed such norms among neighbours from his research in slums in the 1960s (Jocano 1975, especially Chapter 6). In this chapter, however, I re-focus on such values because of the novelty of considering social relationship as a resource for "investment in human capital", "productivity", "health", and "self-help".

12. See Kusaka (2017) for a discussion of the "dual public sphere" resulting from the cultural politics between "citizens" and "noncitizens".
13. This case is reconstructed based on interviews with Melanie's mother, aunt, and other family members and neighbours after the incident, as well as an article in the Philippine Daily Inquirer that reported on the incident (Agoncillo 2017).

Prologue to Part II

Conservation and Emergent Community

In Part I, I examined how neoliberal governmentality affected the relationship between cities and people. In Part II, I examine this with a focus on the relationship between nature and people.

Neoliberalism is essentially, and necessarily, an environmental project (McCarthy & Prudham 2004; Heynen & Robbins 2005; Heynen, McCarthy, Prudham, & Robbins 2007). Classical liberalism, on which contemporary neoliberalism fundamentally draws, centrally and explicitly turned on restructuring social relations with nature. Liberalism, which had developed concomitantly with the enclosure of commons in 18th-century England, is associated with reconfigurations of property relationships that amounted to "freeing" up nature, that is, "detaching it from complex social constraints and placing it under the auspices of the self-regulating market" (McCarthy & Prudham 2004: 277). As Polanyi argued, the modern market society has emerged through the creation of a self-regulating market that commodifies "land", "money", and "labour" (Polanyi 1944). In a similar vein, classical liberal thought was present in the background of the process of the "disembedding" of nature, which used to be embedded in a concrete relationship with humans and communities. Thus, the discussion of contemporary neoliberalism should necessarily lead to an examination of power relationships between people and nature.

In the following, various studies on natural resource management regimes based on neoliberal environmental governance are reviewed to clarify the theoretical perspective of the chapters in Part II. First, I identify the general feature of neoliberal environmental governance. Second, I summarize studies that discuss themes such as nature conservation, "conservation elites", ecotourism, and "environmentality" as the main research interests. Finally, I clarify the theoretical position of this part.

Neoliberalising Nature

A neoliberal regime of environmental governance requires people to internalize a specific rationality as to how nature should be dealt with. It is realised through "the restructuring and capitalization of nature-society relations that exist as uncommodified or underutilized by capital markets" (Goldman 2005:7).

DOI: 10.4324/9781003224273-5

Castree summarises the characteristic aspects of neoliberalisation of nature using the following concepts: "privatization", that is, "the assignment of clear private property rights to social or environmental phenomena that were previously state-owned, unowned, or communally owned"[1]; "marketisation", that is, "the assignment of prices to phenomena that were previously shielded from market exchange or for various reasons unpriced"; "deregulation", that is, "the 'roll back' of state 'interference' in numerous areas of social and environmental life"; "reregulation", that is, "the development of state policies to facilitate privatization and marketization of (...) social and environmental life"; "market proxies in the residual public sector", that is, "the state-led attempt to run remaining public services along private sector lines as 'efficient' and 'competitive' business"; and "the construction of flanking mechanism in civil society", that is, "the state-led encouragement of civil society groups (charities, NGOs, 'communities', etc.) to provide services that interventionist state did, or could potentially, provide for citizens" (Castree 2008: 142–143).

One aspect of neoliberal environmental governance dealt with in a growing number of studies is the process involving the enclosure and privatisation of nature. These studies examine the re-working of the property relations governing the access to and control of nature under neoliberal governance and how it results in greater individuation, exclusivity, private control, and marketisation (McCarthy 2004, 2005; Mansfield 2004a, 2004b; Robbins and Luginbuhl 2005; St. Martin 2005; Swyngedouw 2005; Bridge 2007). Another aspect dealt with by various studies is the process of "commodification and marketization". These studies discuss the political-economic processes through which the environment and particular ecosystems are reduced to commodities through pricing mechanisms that open them up to free-market profiteering and, oftentimes, their destruction (McAfee 1999, 2003; Robertson 2004; Bakker 2005; Correia 2005; Hollander 2007; Young and Keil 2007). Still another aspect often discussed is the effect of the devolution of environmental governance and its negative effects in localities caused by the increased influence over local resource use by multinational corporations and international agencies through decentralised governance structures (Holifield 2004; Prudham 2004; Heynen & Perkins 2005).

Neoliberal Mode of Conservation

With the neoliberal regime of environmental governance delineated above as a background, increasing numbers of studies have discussed the conservation of protected areas and its effect on local people. Particularly, the anthropological approach views protected areas not only as sites that are rich in biological diversity, but also as sites that work to "restructure how people understand, use, and interact with their surroundings" (West & Brockington 2006: 609, see also West 2005). People's understanding, use, and interaction with nature have necessarily been transformed under neoliberal regimes, which aim to commodify nature and turn land, flora, and fauna into natural resources whereby "their principle value and right to existence lies in what the market is willing to pay for them in monetary terms" (Büscher & Dressler 2007: 597). Under this neoliberal conservation agenda, it is not only nature, but also "natives" that are commodified to be efficient labour to protect and maximize the market value of nature (West, Igoe, & Brockington 2006). A process concomitant with the commodification of nature is a restriction on the community's use of resources, which often results in deprivation of people's livelihoods and displacement from the protected area (Brockington 2004; Igoe 2004, Adams and Hutton 2007; Igoe and Croucher 2007; Dressler 2009).

Emergence of the "Conservation Elites"

The literature on biodiversity conservation has increasingly dealt with the aspect of partnerships between state and non-state actors, such as the private corporate sector and non-government organisations (NGOs). Such private support has increasingly been crucial in the context of the declining financial capacity of the state to fund the management of protected areas. It is observed, however, that such partnership results in an "inequitable structural relationships in which local people find themselves and their value disregarded" (Fortwangler 2007: 504). These studies argue that the benefits of biodiversity conservation are disproportionately appropriated by the "conservation elites" in a capitalist society and that the economic value produced from certain ecosystems works to entrench capitalist class power (Brockington & Dyffy 2010; Igoe, Neves, and Brockington 2010). These studies particularly focus on the integral role played by "philanthropists" (Fortwangler 2007; Spierenburg and Wels 2010), "celebrities" (Brockington 2008, 2009), the "for-profit sector" such as big business and corporations (Holmes 2010; MacDonald 2010), and "BINGOs (Big International NGOs)" (Grandia 2007; Levine 2007; Brockington & Scholfield 2010; Sachedina 2010; Wilshusen 2010) in promoting biodiversity and the conservation of protected areas. Through active partnerships and endorsements given by these actors, it is argued that conservation and capitalism are thoroughly integrated to become "two core complementary and mutually enforcing processes in the contemporary production of nature" (Brockington and Scholfield 2010: 552). A significant implication of this process is that the private support of protected areas can disenfranchise those outside the circle of the conservation elites, such as indigenous people and local resource users (Fortwangler 2007).

Ecotourism and the Consumption of Nature

Studies on neoliberalizing nature have also focused on the commodification of nature, and subsequently people, in the context of ecotourism. These studies discuss how "wilderness" is produced and nature is reconfigured and redesigned for the consumption of global tourists (Brockington 2004; West and Carrier 2004; Carrier and Macleod 2005; Duffy and Moore 2010; Neves 2010). In this process, not only nature, but also animals are trained, repackaged, and developed for consumption by the tourism industry (Duffy and Moore 2010). In ecotourism, nature, animals, and sometimes "natives", are reconfigured into a "new type of commodity", which, while no longer consumed directly as a material commodity, provides ecological services such as entertainment, amusement, catharsis, and even therapeutic healing (Neves 2010). The primary beneficiaries of this ecotourism venture are actors with economic power, such as the commercial tour agencies, "eco-real estate developers", and hotel owners, who are supported and endorsed by the government of the host countries, global NGOs, and business and corporate sectors (Berlanga & Faust 2007). In this process, the human–nature relationship embedded in the social relationships of local societies, the identities of the local people constructed through their interactions with nature, as well as local livelihoods utilising natural resources in the community, are marginalised and dislocated, which leads to the "generification" and "decomplexification" (West, Igoe, & Brockington 2006) of people's social practices, causing them to adapt to the expectations and desires of global tourists and the tourism industry[2]. In sum, the critique of neoliberal conservation made by the political ecology literature centres on "a deep-seated uneasiness with the relationship between conservation and inequality" (Fletcher 2010: 172), which results in exclusion and the further marginalisation of local resource users.

Environmentality and Eco-rational Subjectivity

Another set of studies discussing neoliberal conservation in a contrastive vein with the political ecology critique reviewed above deals with the subjectivity of resource users constructed by the neoliberal power relationship and ideology, which is called "environmentality" (Luke 1999, 2005). Generally, these studies advance understanding of "changes in human subjectivities, as these occur concomitantly with changes in institutionalized governance of the environment" (Agrawal 2003: 258). Focusing particularly on institutional and regulatory strategies to govern the environment, Agrawal argues that "it is important to recognize how these strategies and their effects on flows of power shape human subjects, their interests, and their agency" (Agrawal 2003: 258)[3]. Specifically, under contemporary neoliberal environmental governance, what is crucially important is to understand the aspect of decentralised governance, which mobilises the rhetoric of capacity building, local knowledge, and individual rationality, and leads to the "alteration of the subjective relationships of people with each other and with the environment as part of changing relationships of power and governance" (Lemos & Agrawal 2006: 304–305).

As one of the major studies that squarely tackled the problem of human subjectivities and environmental governance under the neoliberal restructuring of human–nature relationships, Goldman, for instance, focuses on the subjectivities shaped under "green neoliberalism" through a discussion stating that "the current neoliberal agenda is to compel us to reconsider the ways we govern each other, govern ourselves, and have our government govern us" (Goldman 2005: 183). Such subjectivities, he continues, are compelled to "take on the responsibility of government (themselves) and to do so in order to privilege above all the needs of the economy" (Goldman 2005: 183–184). These subjectivities, or "eco-rational" subjects, find environmental sustainability as well as human rights and justice only through the nourishment of markets and the economy. Goldman calls political rationality internalised by these subjectivities "eco-governmentality", which compels "state and citizens to improve their care of nature and their care of each other for the greater good of the economy" (Goldman 2005: 184).

Likewise, Agrawal proposed "environmentality" as a framework for analysing "when and for what reason do socially situated actors come to care about, act in relation to, and think about their actions in terms of something they identified as 'the environment'?" (Agrawal 2005a: 162). The framework of environmentality explores "the deep and durable relationship between government and subjecthood and shows how regulatory strategies associated with and resulting from community decision-making help transform those who participate in government" (Agrawal 2005a: 162). Particularly, he focuses on the "environmental subjects" shaped under environmentality, for whom the environment constitutes a conceptual category that organises some of their thinking and actions (Agrawal 2005b: 164–165). His discussion identifies the process of government that succeeded in gaining the participation of villagers in community forestry protection, the goal of which the villagers were made to regard as if it was their own, and through which they had been turned into environmental subjects (Agrawal 2005b: 199–200).

Li, on the other hand, focuses on the "assemblage" of environmental governance, which consists of heterogeneous elements, including "discourses, institutions, architectural forms, regulatory decisions, laws, administrative measures, scientific statements, philosophical, moral and philanthropic propositions" (Li 2007a: 264). The purpose of this assemblage is "the will to govern or, more specifically, the will to improve: the attempt to direct conduct and intervene in social processes to produce desired outcomes and avert undesired ones" (Li 2007b: 264). This will help to govern works by shaping the environmental subjects. Her study deals with the dual aspects of assemblage: one is the practice of government, that is, governmental interventions to improve the community and people through rendering their environment legible and "technical", so that such intervention will produce a beneficial result; the other is the practice of politics, that is, the expression, in word or deed, of a critical challenge to the governmental intervention made by the agency of people in the community or their environmental subjectivities (Li 2007b: 27).

The literature on neoliberal environmentality reviewed above expounds on an aspect of subjectification of resource users into a regime of conservation. In this sense, contrary to the literature discussing the exclusion and further marginalisation of resource users under neoliberal environmental governance, these studies focus on the process of inclusion of people into a mainstream conservation regime. Such inquiry into the formation of environmental subjectivities has significance not only in terms of the practical question of when and under what kind of governmental intervention eco-friendly subjects are created, but also, and more crucially, in terms of a theoretical query on the transformation and durability of subjectivity in the shifting boundaries between community, society, market, state, and transnational social fields in the age of neoliberal governmentality.

As summarised thus far, studies of "environmentality" discuss the process by which eco-rational subjects are constructed and integrated into resource management regimes as an "assemblage" of power, knowledge, and practice. However, studies of political ecology, which share a "deep-seated uneasiness with the relationship between conservation and inequality "(Fletcher 2010: 172), emphasise the marginalisation and exclusion of resource users. The chapters of Part II maintain, however, that the diversity and complexity of resource users' agential practices cannot be captured by such dichotomies as either integration versus exclusion or subjection versus resistance under resource management regimes. Rather, it is the complex interplay between subordination and resistance, freedom and constraint, articulation and disarticulation of various stakeholders in the process of negotiations over access, possession, and distribution of resources that needs attention. In the chapters of Part II, I discuss the "institutionalization process" of resource management (Chapter 3), in which people are constrained by the institutions that support a particular resource management regime and subjected to become rational resource managers. In Chapter 4, another process of the resource management regime, called the "contextualization process", is discussed. In this process, the institution is interpreted, manipulated, modified, and selectively incorporated by the resource users. As the ethnography of these chapters shows, the two processes—institutionalisation and contextualisation—are inextricably intertwined and proceed simultaneously in a mutually constitutive way.

Thus, Part II focuses both on the macro-level process of resource management with global environmentalism as its background, and the micro-level process of people's everyday resource use practices, which is embedded in the environments of local communities. Particularly in Chapter 6, I present the life history of a fisherman whose resource use practice does not fall into a simple dichotomy of conservation/resistance or integration/marginalisation. Rather, it indicates "the practices and thoughts of environmental subjects that may not always lead to environmental conservation" (Agrawal 2005: 164–165), but is still shaped and constituted, directly or indirectly, by the political rationality prevailing under the neoliberal environmental government regime. In this way, the chapters of Part II attempt to argue the diversity and complexity of environmental subjects. The community of resource users dealt with in these chapters is not a closely bounded homogenous intimate sphere; rather, it is open to various external actors such as NGOs and local and central governments. It is in this interface between the neoliberal restructuring of the conservation policy and localised mutuality, particularly community, that the following chapters seek to identify the emerging contours of the vernacular public sphere.

Notes

1. This "privatization" is the same process as "territorialization", under which "state-controlled territories are being made available to investors through rents and concessions" (Igoe & Brockington 2007: 437), as well as by the "enclosing" and "delimiting" of formerly open-access resources such as the ocean (Mansfield 2004a).
2. Related to this topic of commodification of nature in eco-tourism is a discussion on the consumption of products with fair trade certification, such as organic coffee, and its unintended consequence of the reproduction of inequity in global neoliberal economies (Carrier 2010; West 2010).
3. As one of the provocative theoretical reorientation of political ecology, Biersack argues that "today's political ecology inevitably engages to some degree with 'practice theory', a theory that attends to the constraints of structure but also to the indeterminacies of agency and events" (Biersack 2006: 5).

4 A Community Disciplined

The Institutionalisation Process of Coastal Resource Management

In the chapters of Part 2, including this chapter, the discussion is based on a case study of coastal resource management in a fishing village in Palawan Province in the southwestern Philippines. This chapter examines the "institutionalization process "(see the prologue of Part 2) of coastal resource management observed at a field site in the community.[1] In the following, an overview of the current coastal resource management system in the Philippines is presented. The subsequent section provides an overview of the current status of fisheries in the community. The final section discusses how the process of institutionalizing resource management has progressed at the field site through several case studies. Throughout this chapter, it becomes clear how the neoliberal resource management regime discussed in the prologue is actually realised in the coastal communities of the Philippines.

Institutions Supporting the Coastal Resource Management Regime

In the general trend of the democratisation and devolution in the Philippines during the 1990s, the institution of co-management, which involves various stakeholders such as the national and local governments, NGOs, and local resource users, had become mainstream.[2] Several national laws provide a basic institutional framework of current coastal resource co-management in the Philippines. First, Republic Act (RA) 7160, a local government code issued in 1991, regulates the devolution process of the national government and defines the scope of local government authority in regard to the use of local resources. Second, RA 7586, the National Integrated Protected Areas System or NIPAS Act issued in 1992, establishes sanctuaries and reserves for the country's natural resources. Third, RA 7611, the Strategic Environmental Plan for Palawan Act, also issued in 1992, pertains to the conservation and utilisation of resources endemic to Palawan, which is the field site for this study. Finally, RA 8550, the Fisheries Code of the Philippines (henceforth "Fisheries Code"), issued in 1998, is the law that has the most substantial effect on local coastal resource use.

The main features of current coastal resource co-management can be culled from the provisions of these laws. First, it defines the boundary of the resources that belong to the local government, as well as the control of access to such

DOI: 10.4324/9781003224273-6

resources. RA 7160 defines "municipal waters" as marine waters included within 15 km from the shoreline and stipulates that the municipal government has the authority and responsibility for the management, conservation, and utilisation of the fish and aquatic resources within their respective municipal waters. In turn, the Fisheries Code imposes various restrictions on the use of fishing methods and gears within municipal waters. Fishing vessels that weigh 3.1 gross tons or more are categorised as commercial and are deemed illegal for operation within municipal waters. Furthermore, the operation of active fishing gear, which involves any movement, such as pulling, encircling, driving, or chasing, is also prohibited within municipal waters. The fine mesh net, which is defined as a net with a mesh size of less than 3 cm, is also prohibited for use within municipal waters. The Fisheries Code further limits access to resources within municipal waters in favour of the residents of the municipality only. These residents need to secure a permit and ID from the municipal mayor, following a prescribed procedure and paying a required fee (Picture 4.1). In addition, the law stipulates that

Picture 4.1 Operation permit and ID issued by the Town Mayor attached even to the small fishing boat

15% of municipal waters must be designated as a Marine Protected Area (MPA) (Pictures 4.2 and 4.3).

The Fisheries Code also provides for the creation of a particular organisation that would play a pivotal role in the mechanism of the current co-management institution. This organisation is called the Municipal Fisheries and Aquatic Resources Management Council (MFARMC), which is constituted by an elected town councillor, particularly the chairman of the Committee on Agriculture and Fishery in the town council, the engineer of the Municipal Development Office, an officer in the local Department of Agriculture office, a representative of an NGO based in the municipality, and at least 11 representatives of the local fishermen. The main functions of the MFARMC are to recommend municipal fishery ordinances for discussion in the municipal council and to assist in their enforcement. The national fisheries laws are implemented and put into practice in the local fishing communities only after the municipal council has issued the corresponding municipal ordinances. To draft such ordinances, the MFARMC holds public hearings among local resource users. The MFARMC then submits various recommendations to the local government based on the interests of local resource users, which at times conflict with the centralised interests of the state, to be incorporated into the municipal ordinance. In this sense, the MFARMC is considered a venue where conflicts in the appropriation of, access to, and allocation of local resources are negotiated between the community and the state.

Picture 4.2 Sign indicating the no fishing and trespassing zone of the MPA

Picture 4.3 Guard house on the MPA

The Setting: A Stratified Fishing Community

The data presented in Part II of this book were gathered during fieldwork conducted in a coastal municipality of southern Palawan, a province in the southwestern Philippines.[3] The province of Palawan consists of the main island, which stretches 425 km in length and has a width of 40 km at its widest point, and numerous small islets. The province is bounded by the Sulu Sea on its southeast shore and the South China Sea on its northwest shore (Map 4.1). It is rich in resources and possesses vast arable land, timber, mineral, and marine products. These abundant resources have enticed a huge number of immigrants from other parts of the country since the mid-20th century. As a result, the competition to control, exploit, and, more recently, preserve these resources has increased, and "the politics of resource use" dominates the everyday lives of the residents (Eder & Fernandez 1996).

The fieldwork was conducted mainly in Barangay Panacan, one of the 22 barangays that compose the municipality of Narra, which lies about 90 km south of Puerto Princesa City, the capital of Palawan (Map 4.1). Barangay Panacan was established by Ilonggo migrant fishermen who, with their families, came to Palawan from Sicogon Island of the Municipality of Carles in Iloilo Province. The first batch of immigrants settled here beginning in the early 1950s. Even though the in-migration of the Ilonggo fishermen ceased in the 1970s, that of other Visayan fishermen from Cebu, Leyte, and Samar continued through the 1980s. Currently, the second-generation Ilonggo migrants who have remained actively engaged in fishing comprise the majority in this coastal

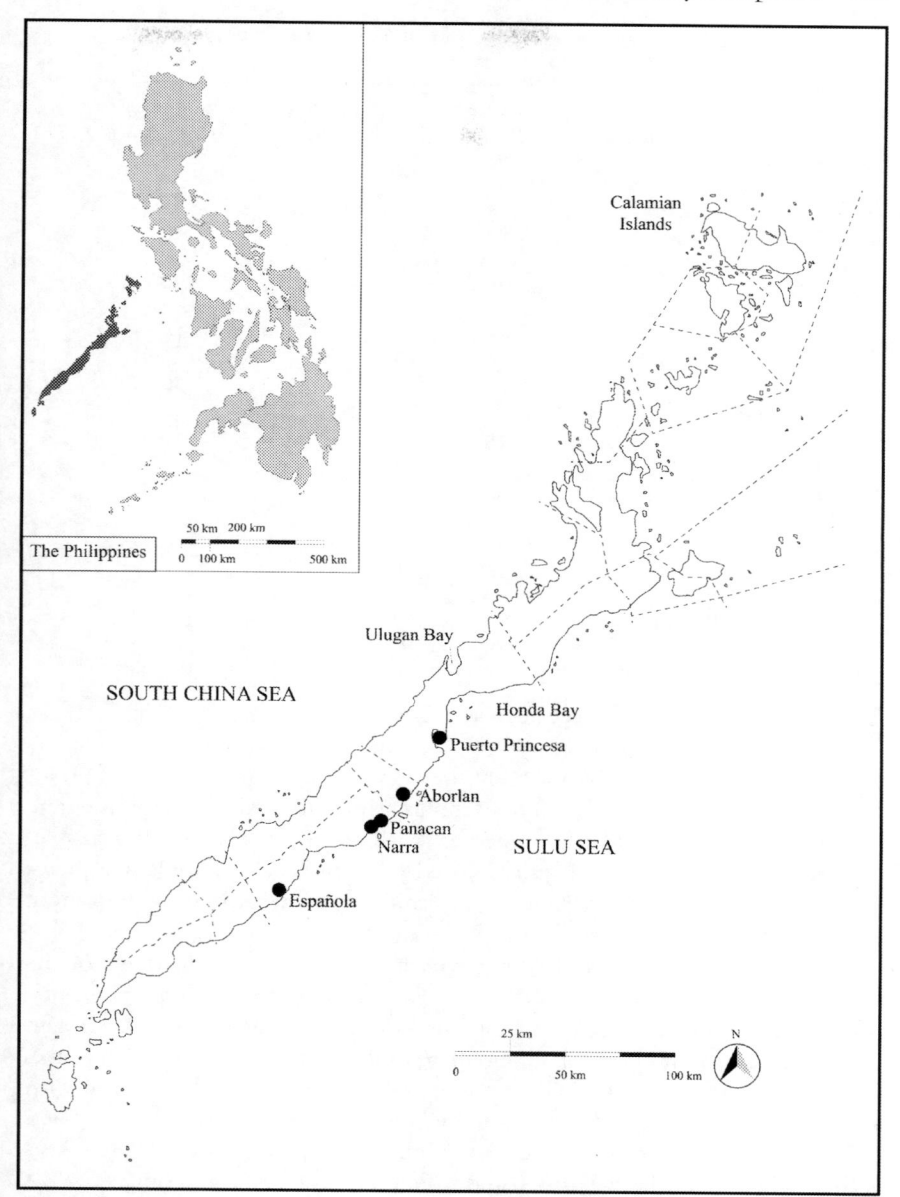

Map 4.1 Palawan Islands

settlement. Panacan had a total population of 8,656 and 1,768 households as of 2008.[4] Compared with the average barangay in the rural Philippines, a large number of residents of Panacan are engaged in various occupations aside from farming and fishing, particularly because of its proximity to the town proper of Narra. Barangay Panacan, in turn, consists of 14 *puroks* (neighbourhoods),

Table 4.1 Number of People, Household, and Fishing Boat according to Fishing Activities in Panacan

Fishing Activities		Number of People	Number of Households	Number of Fishing Boats
Likom	Owner	7	7	21
	Crew	146	109	–
Kulong	Owner	21	21	46
	Crew	145	68	–
Pangawil	Owner	108	108	155
	Crew	111	73	–
Likos	Owner	10	10	10
	Crew	6	3	–
Suwayan		4	4	4
Baklad		3	3	3
Pamanti		19	19	19
Pamana		3	3	3
Pamarongoy	Owner	5	5	5
	Crew	6	5	–
Dried Fish Dealer		30	30	–
Dried Fish Retailer		4	4	–
Dried Fish Worker		26	17	–
Fresh Fish Retailer		4	4	–
Total		657	507	240

seven of which are on the coast. The present study focuses mainly on these seven *puroks* of Panacan, where most of the fishermen, their families, and others engage in fishing-related livelihood reside. The research area has a total population of 4,464 persons and 880 households as of 2008. Although an accurate record of the population of fishermen and fishing households is not available, approximate numbers were acquired based on a field survey. Table 4.1 shows the number of people, households, and fishing boats according to the fishing methods and activities carried out in Panacan.

There are two mainstays of commercial fishing in Panacan in terms of the number of fishermen involved and the amount of fish caught: *likom* and *kulong*. *Likom* is nighttime purse seine for catching round scad (*Decapterus* sp.), Indian sardine (*Sardinella longiceps*), slipmouth (family *Leiognathidae*), and the like. A unit of a *likom* fishing group is composed of at least two boats, one with high-powered lights to attract fish at night, and another carrying the fishing net. One unit of *likom* costs around P1.2 million (P1 is approximately US$0.02, as of the fieldwork) for the two boats, and from P700,000 to P1 million for the net (Picture 4.4). This method of fishing requires a fishing crew of around 40 on average, and there are fine distinctions among the ranked officers on the basis of their designated roles and expertise. It is extremely difficult to know the exact number of members of the *likom* fishing crew because many crew members work on a casual basis. Unlike the regular members of the group, these casual labourers, called *bolero*, do not accompany the operation on a daily basis, and are considered a pool of floating manpower from which boats and community

Picture 4.4 Fishing boat for likom

draw services as needed. Thus, the total number of crew indicated in Table 4.1 increases substantially when the number of *bolero*, which fluctuates significantly depending on the season, is included.

Kulong, the other mainstay of commercial fishing in Panacan, is the daytime purse seine for catching mainly anchovies (*Engraulis japonicus*). *Kulong* fishing is carried out by one boat loaded with a net and, occasionally, by an accompanying boat with appropriate storage for carrying the catch to shore (Picture 4.5). The fishing boat for the *kulong* currently costs about P200,000, while the fishing net costs about P450,000. Although *kulong* is usually carried out by a crew of 15 to 20 men, the group is, similar to *likom*, a loosely structured organisation with flexible membership whose number will increase when the mobile, and hence elusive, *bolero* are considered.

Apart from "commercial fishing", various small- and medium-scale fishing activities, or what is officially categorised as "municipal fishing", can be found in Panacan. *Pangawil* (hook-and-line fishing) is one of the municipal fishing methods for catching various kinds of coral fishes such as grouper (*Cephalopholis sexmaculata*), bream (*Nemipterus bathybius*), and snapper (*Etelis coruscans*). *Pangawil* is quite popular in Panacan because it requires only a small amount of capital and simple gears. It is usually carried out by two to three persons, including the owner of the boat as the skipper. The recent phenomenon of the drastic increase of *pangawil* fishermen is discussed later in relation to the coastal resource management institutionalisation process in Panacan.

Picture 4.5 Fishing boat for kulong

There are several traditional fishing methods in Panacan. Although these methods have a rather subsistence character and cannot be said to be market-oriented, many village residents rely on these activities, particularly during the off-season of major fishing operations. One of the traditional activities is *suwayan*, a beach seine. *Suwayan*, a method that requires intensive labour for pulling the net towards the shore, provides an opportunity for daily sustenance for many villagers who would otherwise have no source of income (see Figure 5.2 of Chapter 5). However, as explained in detail later, in the process of coastal resource management, the operation of *suwayan* began to be restricted, and currently, only four owners of *suwayan* remain in the village. Another method is called *baklad*, an artificial fish corral made of bamboo that utilises the ebb and flow of the sea (Figure 4.1). Although there are still three persons who own this device at sea, building a *baklad* has become extremely difficult, as explained in a case to be shown later, owing to the coastal resource management process, particularly its general trend of establishing the MPA. There is also *pamanti*, or small-scale gill net fishing, which is carried out mostly by the owners themselves and occasionally with their wives.

In addition to the many who are engaged in actual fishing operations, a number of people in the community are also involved in fishing-related activities on shore, among whom, dried fish dealers make up the largest group. These dealers process dried fish using *kapils* (Pictures 4.6 and 4.7), split-bamboo trays or

Picture 4.6 Processers of dried fish in Barangay Panacan

Picture 4.7 Beach of Barangay Panacan filled with dried fish

bamboo thatched mats for drying, after having bought fresh fish mainly from the owners of *likom* and *kulong*. They then sell their product to buyers from the town proper, who, in turn, bring the tons of dried fish to Manila. These dried fish dealers employ workers to process the dried fish. Many women, particularly widows and unmarried youth, earn their subsistence or augment their household income as dried fish workers. It can be understood that Panacan today is not a community with a homogenous socioeconomic class, but rather, a highly stratified commercial fishing village. To simplify, it has a three-strata pyramidal structure where occupying the top stratum are the owners of commercial fishing such as *kulong* and *likom*, as well as the large-scale dried fish dealers; at the middle stratum are the owners of small-scale fishing, such as *pangawil* and *likos* (encircling gill net); and finally, at the bottom stratum are the numerous rank-and-file and casual crew of the commercial fishing operations and the dried fish processing workers.

Institutionalisation of Coastal Resources Management and Its Impact on the Community

This section focuses on the three aspects of the coastal resource management institutionalization process: (1) the enclosure of local resources, (2) the zoning and classification of municipal waters, and (3) the inclusion of a new notion of obligation and responsibility in the community. Each aspect is delineated in detail with specific cases in the following.

Enclosure of Local Resources

As explained above, the Fisheries Code reserves the right to utilise the resources within municipal waters exclusively to the fishermen residing in the same municipality. Owing to this provision, conflicts and disputes frequently arise when fishermen trespass into the municipal waters of other towns. In Panacan, the individuals most affected by the current situation are the fishermen of *kulong* and *likom*. These fishing groups were accustomed to operating in fishing grounds located in neighbouring towns, where the competition among the commercial fishers is lower than that in the municipal waters of Narra. Since the early 2000s, however, the *likom* and *kulong* fishers began to be apprehended frequently by local enforcement agencies in the neighbouring municipalities. When apprehended, they were fined the amount of P5,000–P10,000 and sometimes even jailed for a few days. Generally, and traditionally, small- and medium-scale fishermen of the Philippines are accustomed to a rather mobile way of life, migrating seasonally between several settlements depending on ecological factors such as monsoon winds, current flow, and migratory fish routes (Seki 2000). However, the current trend of enclosing local resources has placed substantial constraints on the conventional way of resource use, as demonstrated in the following cases (Cases 4.1–4.3).

Case 4.1: A conflict between the Municipalities of Narra and Aborlan

In the coastal villages of Aborlan (Map 4.1), a town just northeast of Narra, the dominant mode of fishery is small-scale hook-and-line fishing, and commercial fishery is absent. For this reason, the coastal waters of Aborlan have not been exploited much, and traditionally have been a good fishing ground for commercial fisheries such as the *kulong* and *likom* fisheries of Narra, particularly those from Panacan. In 2000, however, the fishery ordinance of Aborlan prohibited fishermen from other towns from operating in the waters under the jurisdiction of Aborlan. Since then, there have been many cases of fishermen from Narra being caught in the waters of Aborlan. They are fined between 5,000 and 12,500 pesos per incident and may even be detained for a short period inside the municipal jail.

Noel, born in 1965, is a fisherman who owns four *likom* fishing groups in Panacan. From 2001 to 2006, when this fieldwork was conducted, Noel and his *likom* fishing group had been apprehended by the *Bantay Dagat* ("guardians of the sea"; the coast patrol assigned by the town mayor) twice in the municipal waters of Española (Map 4.1), a neighbouring town southwest of Narra, and three times in the municipal waters of Aborlan. According to the captain of the fishing group, who was actually operating at sea at the time, when he was caught in Española in 2003, he was asked to pay a fine of 20,000 pesos, which he could not afford, but managed to get it reduced to 5,000 pesos by "begging for mercy (*nagpakaawa*)". However, in 2004, when he was caught in the waters of Aborlan, he was taken to the municipal jail by the town's fish warden. According to the captain of the operation, he was at sea at the time and was wearing only his underwear, but he was not allowed to put on clothes and was detained without being questioned. The captain was released the next day after Noel was able to quickly prepare and pay the fine of 5,000 pesos. According to Noel, "There are no buoys or other markers at the boundaries of the waters belonging to each town, so it is difficult to know where the waters of the neighbouring town begin. There should be markers at the boundaries of these waters".

Case 4.2: A dispute and conflict between the Municipality of Narra and the City of Puerto Princesa

Normally, the *likom* fishing groups in Panacan maintain several seasonal camps for their operation during certain months of the year. Particularly during the season of the northeast monsoon winds from October until March, some *likom* fishing outfits from Panacan transfer to the fishing grounds of Honda Bay and Ulogan Bay, which are at the northeastern side of Palawan island facing the South China Sea (Map 4.1). These bays, which abound in marine resources, are protected by the strong northeastern monsoon winds. These bays, however, were located within the waters belonging to Puerto Princesa City, the provincial capital. Therefore, for fishermen from the Panacan area to operate in these bays, an "agreement of reciprocal access" was required between the mayors of Narra and Puerto Princesa City. For this reason, the municipal fishery ordinance of Narra, which came into effect in 2001, stipulated that "no fishermen from any other town, *except those from Puerto Princesa City*, shall operate within the municipal waters of Narra (emphasis added)", expecting that the fishermen from Narra would be given the same privileged access to the waters of Puerto Princesa City. However, the Puerto Princesa City ordinance did not allow the same special measures for the fishermen from Narra town. As a countermeasure, in February 2006, the town of Narra amended its fisheries ordinance to abolish the privileged access to its waters that had been granted to fishermen from Puerto Princesa City. After that, there was a compromise between the two parties, and the mayors of Narra and Puerto Princesa City began talks for the "agreement of reciprocal access" to the waters of both sides. However, as of the time of the research in August 2006, no agreement had yet been reached. The meticulous regulations on access to the waters have prevented a final agreement from being reached, as the parties have been unable to agree on language such as "reciprocal access shall be limited to small-scale fishing only" or "reciprocal access shall be limited to a maximum of 24 fishing vessels, with a maximum of three crew fishermen per vessel". This indicates the heightened micro-politics of resource use between the local governments. The following incident took place in this context.

A resident of Panacan named Lito, who was born in 1960, had been a *likom* skipper for several years. As was usual in *likom* fishing, Lito carried out his operation in Ulogan Bay in January 2006. On the night of January 31, an enforcement team composed of the Philippine National Police, the Coast Guard, and a local environmental NGO apprehended him and his fishing group. Because the waters of those bays fell within the jurisdiction of Puerto Princesa City, the fishermen from Panacan were prohibited from operating in the area. As a result, Lito's fishing gear was confiscated, he was fined, and he had to face a criminal lawsuit in the provincial court. He was forced to stay in the provincial capital go through the legal proceedings. The owner of this *likom* fishing operation spent more than P70,000 on legal expenses and the retrieval of confiscated gear. The skipper Lito, even after being able to return to Panacan, was prohibited from operating the fishing group while his lawsuit was pending. Lito complained about the NGO that led to his arrest as follows: "I have been apprehended by the local Bantay Dagat in Narra and neighbouring towns many times. These people, some of whom I know personally, just ask me to pay an administrative fine of 5,000 pesos, then allow me to go fishing the next day. But if you are caught by an NGO, it's a different story altogether. The people of the NGO based in the capital are really strict!". This narrative suggests that the actors who enforce the coastal resource management regime are not monolithic, but rather, have variegated interests and concerns. As said by Lito, many of the *Bantay Dagat* are local residents of coastal communities, and hence, Lito and the people who work as *Bantay Dagat* know each other well, and most of the time, they are lenient enough to let the trespassing fishermen go, after having been asked for mercy and/or being paid some cash. However, the national environmental NGOs, the members of which are the outsiders to the community, who do not have any personal ties with the fishermen, do not allow such leniency or supplication from the fishermen. According to Lito, they are often stricter and more cold-hearted than the police in terms of controlling illegal fishing.

The enclosure of the municipal waters examined here suggests clear neoliberal trend in coastal resource management, in which formerly open-access waters will be "delimited", "territorialized", and sometimes "privatized" as discussed in the Prologue.

Zoning and Classification of Waters

Another aspect of the current regime of coastal resource management is the zoning and classification of municipal waters according to the distribution of resources and their market values. At times, this process conflicts with the traditional way of resource utilization. A case involving *baklad*, a fish corral that the local government had ordered to be relocated, illustrates one such conflict.

Case 4.3: Removal order of Rafael's fish coral

Rafael is a resident of Panacan who, since 1986, has owned a *baklad* near Rasa Island, which is about 20 minutes from the shore of Panacan by motorboat. A mangrove and coral reef surrounds Rasa Island, providing a rich fishing ground for the residents of Panacan. The *baklad*, a traditional device made of locally available materials such as bamboo, has been a means of subsistence for local fishermen (Figure 4.1). Rafael, however, was suddenly ordered by the Protected Area Management Board (PAMB) of Narra and the KATALA Foundation, an environmental NGO based in Narra town proper, to remove his *baklad* as soon as possible. Rafael found himself at a loss and could not understand why he had to remove the *baklad*, which he had been operating for more than 20 years.

Behind this order by the local government were two related laws, RA 7586 and RA 7611. The first establishes and manages the NIPAS, which encompasses biologically important public lands that are habitats of rare and endangered flora and fauna. It stipulates the creation of a PAMB composed of the mayor and other representatives from the municipal government, as well as representatives from the barangay, NGOs based in the locality, and departments and agencies of the national government. RA 7611 adopted a strategic environmental plan for rare natural resources and endangered flora and fauna endemic to Palawan. It conferred on the provincial and municipal

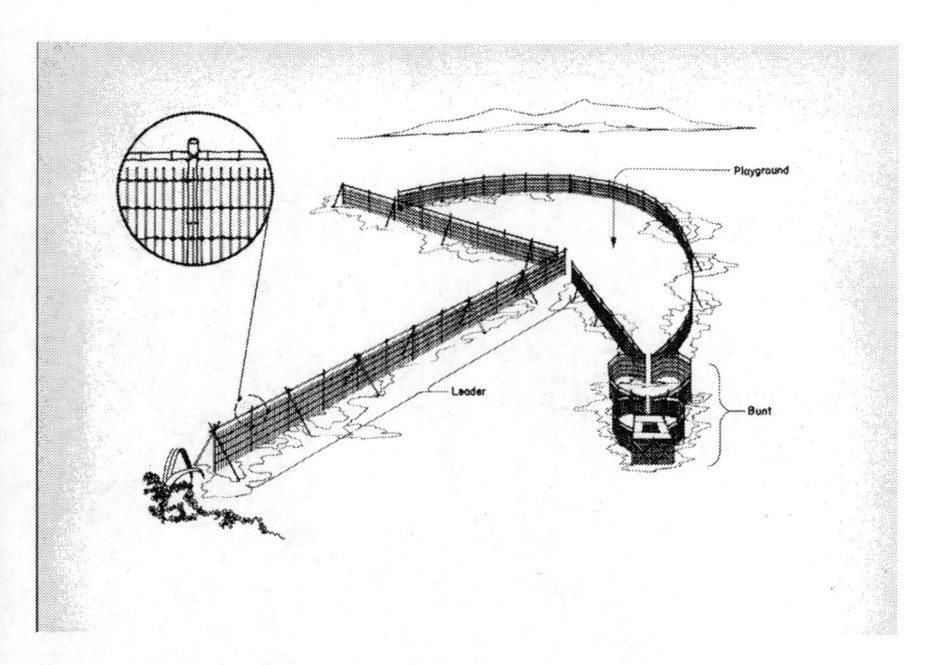

Figure 4.1 Fish coral (*baklad*)

Source: Umali (1950)

governments of Palawan the authority to manage, utilize, and conserve the natural resources existing in the territory of Palawan Province. Based on the authority bestowed by these two national acts, the local government of Narra declared Rasa Island a protected area.

Rasa Island was so declared because it is a habitat of a rare and endangered bird species called *katala*, or the Philippine cockatoo (*Cacatua haematuro-phygia*), which is endemic to only some places in southern Palawan (Picture 4.8). The local NGO, named the KATALA Foundation, which is funded by European environmental NGOs, has been conducting its operations in Narra town proper since 1998. It started an activity that combined the preservation of *katala* with ecotourism, the main attractions of which are *katala* bird watching and scuba diving in the coral reef around Rasa Island. As of 2006, there were about 150–200 Filipino and foreign tourists visiting the island annually. The municipal fishery ordinance of Narra issued in 2001 prohibits the building of a *baklad* within the protected area, and based on this regulation, the KATALA Foundation, in cooperation with the Narra municipal government, insisted strongly on the removal of the *baklad* owned by Rafael.

Furthermore, the same ordinance requires that the municipal waters should be classified and delineated into several zones according to specific activities such as aquaculture, communal fishing grounds, navigational lanes, tourism belt, recreational and sports fishing areas, fish and marine sanctuaries and reserves, and so on. The *baklad* of Rafael, according to a representative of the local government, was not properly located within the zone specifically allotted for this kind of activity. Therefore, several laws and ordinances, coupled with an NGO as a new actor with the power to implement legislation, lay behind the order to relocate Rafael's *baklad*.

Picture 4.8 Rasa Island surrounded by mangrove forests

It can be said that the primary purpose of such zoning and classification is to protect and nurture valuable resources in the marine area, such as seaweed, coral reefs, and rare fish, and to increase their market value. The case involving the removal of Rafael's fish coral suggests that resource use activities that have supported people's subsistence and livelihoods are being marginalised by conservation activities to increase the profitability of marine resources. This is exactly one of the consequences of the neoliberal conservation regime discussed in the prologue of Part 2.

Inculcation of the Ideas of "Obligation" and "Responsibility"

As a third aspect of institutionalization, it is worth noting that to implement new rules and regulations successfully, the ideas of obligation and responsibility, which particularly emphasise concepts such as empowerment, accountability, and a sense of audit, must be internalised by the people. These concepts can be said to fit well into the green neoliberal ideology, which lies behind the current regime of resource management and further encourages the formation of eco-rational subjectivities. The Fisheries Code states that the actors authorised to enforce these rules and regulations are national agencies such as the Philippine Navy, the Philippine National Police–Maritime Command, and the Philippine Coast Guard; community-based local representatives such as the *Bantay Dagat* and the fish wardens who are local residents that act by virtue of deputised authority after having undergone training in law enforcement.[5] One such training seminar for the enforcers is examined in the Case 4.4 case below.

Case 4.4: Training Seminars for the Fish Wardens

In the case of Narra, there are about 30 deputy fish wardens selected from each coastal barangay, including Panacan, who frequently patrol within municipal waters. They keep a close watch for fishermen engaged in illegal fishing activities, which include not only grave violations such as the use of dynamite and poisonous chemicals such as cyanide, but also light negligence such as the conduct of fishing operations without a valid license and ID. Officials of the Bureau of Fisheries and Aquatic Resources (BFAR) based in Puerto Princesa provide regular seminars aimed at "retooling" the skills and knowledge of local fish wardens. These seminars inculcate in fish wardens' various "duties" and "responsibilities" in the implementation of laws and administrative orders regarding coastal resource management. Wardens are taught that they are endowed with the "full power to enforce all fishery laws, rules, and regulations within an area of jurisdiction"; that they should "act as government witness in court for the speedy prosecution of criminal complaints against fishing violations"; that they are "authorized to make an arrest even without a warrant of arrest"; that they should "deliver the offender to competent authority within the prescribed period from the time of his arrest and file the proper complaint within the appropriate offices"; that they are to "assist in the dispositions of confiscated illegally caught fish"; that they are "to conduct fishing information campaign against all forms of illegal fishing"; and finally, that they are "to submit a monthly accomplishment report to BFAR field offices". Officials of the BFAR frequently emphasise those phrases, which are written in a textbook used during the seminar. To renew their status, fish wardens are required to pass the examination given at the end of the seminar (Picture 4.9).

Picture 4.9 Training seminar for the fish wardens. A scene from the final examination to be qualified

Through these seminars, local residents are certainly disciplined to be "responsible" wardens of their community resources. However, they often find themselves under pressure because of conflicting obligations as fish wardens, on the one hand, and as kin and peers of community members on the other. Another case below (Case 4.5) suggests such a dilemma entertained by the local enforcers under the current resource management regime.

Case 4.5: A balance between "responsibility" and "human consideration"

Dennis, a resident of Panacan who was born in 1966, was appointed as a member of the Bantay Dagat in Narra in 1990. He grew up with parents who fished in Panacan. He still often goes fishing with his brother on his fishing boat. From 1998, when the Fishery Act came into effect, until around 2000, Dennis used to patrol the waters of Narra daily. Today, he still patrols once or twice a week. He says that he tries to keep "human consideration" in mind when monitoring the illegal operations of the local fishermen. For example, if he witnesses illegal operations in the area, he will give a warning only the first and second times. However, if he sees the same fishing boat operating illegally for the third time, he has no choice but to impose a penalty. Even if the violating fishermen are his relatives or friends, he does not pardon them on the third offense. Although the municipal ordinance imposes confiscation of the catch as a penalty for such offenses, Dennis said that he allows boat owners to sell their catch first and then pay the fine with the proceeds. However, if the illegal operator is a fisherman from another town, he says he will not tolerate it, regardless of whether it is the first time. This suggests, rather than Dennis' partial treatment for his kins and friends, the emergence of an intense sense of boundary between local waters in the resource management regime institutionalization process. Dennis, who insists on the importance of "humanitarian considerations" for small-scale fishermen, narrates as follows: "If we apply the Fishery Code strictly word for word, I feel sorry for the fishermen. When it's windy, it's impossible to operate far out to sea, outside the municipal waters (where they are legally permitted to fish). In such cases, we have to close our eyes. We tolerate them, except when they are operating in shallow waters too close to the beach. If we were to enforce the ordinance really strictly, we would have to stop all the small fishing boats that do not carry the ID issued by the municipal government. How can we enforce the law so strictly when we know that hungry families are waiting for those fishermen to come home with even a small amount of catch?"

As indicated in this case, it is no easy task for fish wardens to intervene in an illegal fishing operation carried out by their peers within the same community, and all the more to impose a fine and confiscate their gear. It is particularly difficult when the violation is that of light negligence, such as operating without a valid license and ID, as fish wardens are aware that the probable reason for this offense is the processing fees that the fishermen could not afford to pay. In these situations, the wardens would call on other wardens from adjacent villages who are not directly related to the fishermen to be apprehended to do the job. On other occasions, they try to let the fishermen know in advance that the fish wardens will be patrolling the sea. In this way, they are able to avoid conflicts with their kin and peers within the community and maintain a balance between the public responsibility required of fish wardens and "human consideration" for their kinsmen and peers in the local community.

As discussed in this chapter, the institutionalization of marine resource management has been a process of enclosure and delineation, zoning and classification, and the inculcation of notions of obligation and responsibility. The case of Panacan shows that the apparatus of the neoliberal resource management regime has been translated into a number of laws and ordinances and works as a power that constrains and disciplines everyday livelihood activities and resource use at the community level. One fisherman said, "Unlike before, we are unable to move freely on the sea. It is like we are paralyzed". Indeed, the process of institutionalizing examined in this chapter is a form of governing power, or "environmentality", that operates at the most microscopic level of the body of the fishermen. Thus, to survive in the intensifying political environment of resource use and preservation, they have surely been trained and disciplined to be eco-rational subjects.

In a community disciplined under such a resource management regime, new differences and disparities among resource users are expected to emerge. In particular, the gap is expected to widen between those who are deprived of their means of livelihood, or have their opportunities of fishing drastically reduced, and those who have alternative means and resources to avoid the impact brought about by the institutionalization of the resource management regime. Is it an irreversible process caused by the penetrating effect of the resource management regime that accelerates differentiation and fragmentation among fishermen in the community, where there used to be a certain degree of cohesiveness and homogeneity despite a certain level of hierarchy? In the next chapter, I attempt to answer this question by focusing on the "process of contextualization", that is, the practice of resource users interpreting, manipulating, modifying, and selectively incorporating the institution of the coastal resource management regime.

Notes

1. A part of this chapter is reprinted in a revised form from *Philippine Studies* Vol. 57.4 (2009): 901–936, by permission of the Ateneo de Manila University.
2. For the major institutional transitions in coastal resource management in the Philippines, see Pomeroy and Carlos (1997). For case studies of natural resource co-management in the Philippines, see Snelder and Persoon (2005).
3. Since I first visited Barangay Panacan in March 1999, I have visited the place intermittently and continued to talk and interview with the people. The data of this chapter and the subsequent chapter had been gathered during the fieldwork on February, March, and August 2006, March 2007, and March and September 2008.
4. Data based on a survey carried out by *barangay* health workers in Panacan.
5. Although the Bantay Dagat are employees under the municipal mayor and thus members of the local government, the fish wardens referred to in this article are volunteers from among village residents. Hence, the two groups differ in terms of affiliation and function.

5 Emergent Community
The Process of Contextualising the Coastal Resource Management Regime

This chapter discusses the process by which the institutionalisation of coastal resource management examined in the previous chapter has been contextualised into a particular circumstance of local communities.[1] This process of contextualisation means that the resource management system, even though stipulated by state law, is subtly modified by the people and contextualised to the unique circumstances of the local community, thereby creating alternative forms of resource use. It suggests the agentive practices of resource users, through which access to the resources is secured and opportunities for subsistence are expanded. In the following section, I first describe the process of formulating the municipal fishery ordinance of Narra, which played a pivotal role in such contextualisation. I further delineate on how the ordinance has affected the community's resource use patterns. In the subsequent section, I examine the resulting restructuring of resource use patterns in the community. In the third section, I discuss the new fishery complex that has emerged as a result of such restructuring. Finally, I expand upon the implications of this contextualisation process in terms of the vernacular public sphere, which can emerge at the interface between the neoliberalised institution of coastal resource management and localised mutuality of the community.

Municipal Fisheries Ordinance and Its Effect on Local Resource Use

As explained in the previous chapter, the Fisheries Code prohibits the operation of commercial fishing and the use of active gears and fine mesh nets within municipal waters. Had those regulations been strictly implemented, most of the fishing methods in Panacan would have been banned and, accordingly, most of the people would have been deprived of their livelihoods. Instead of this bleak scenario, however, what actually transpired was the emergence of an alternative pattern of resource use that secured the means of subsistence even for fishermen who had experienced adverse effects from the regulation. This process was initiated by a municipal ordinance entitled "An Ordinance Regulating the Fishing and/or Fisheries in the Municipality of Narra, Palawan" (hereafter "municipal fisheries ordinance"), which was enacted in February 2001.

DOI: 10.4324/9781003224273-7

It is stipulated in the Fisheries Code that the MFARMC assists, recommends, and advises the municipal council to prepare and enact the municipal fishery ordinance. Therefore, the MFARMC plays a pivotal role in drafting municipal ordinances related to fishing activities. In August 2000, the MFARMC, for the purpose of drafting the recommendation to be incorporated in the municipal fisheries ordinance, initiated a series of public hearings in each coastal *barangay* in the municipality. The public hearing in Panacan was held in the schoolyard of Panacan National High School. It was packed with fisherfolk, particularly those who would have been greatly affected by the implementation of the Fisheries Code. There were heated discussions, and strong opposition against the code's implementation came from owners of fishing gear, such as trawls, *kulong*, and *likom*, which were supposed to be banned by the law. Furthermore, most members of the MFARMC, particularly representatives of the local fisherfolk, were sympathetic to the opposition because they themselves were owners of *kulong* or *likom*.[2] After a series of exhaustive discussions at those public hearings, the MFARMC drafted recommendations for a new fisheries ordinance. Although in most parts, the enacted fisheries ordinance apparently copied the detailed wording of the Fisheries Code, in some parts, it rephrased sentences found in the code and inserted others in a new section. The slight rephrasing and insertions actually had a substantial effect, as described below, in the coastal resource use of Panacan.

It can be gleaned that, although the Fisheries Code prohibits the operation of all kinds of commercial fishing within municipal waters, which is 15 km away from the shore, at the same time, it defines a particular buffer zone within it. The law stipulates that "the municipal government may, through its local chief executive, authorise, or permit small and medium commercial fishing vessels to operate within the ten point one (10.1) to fifteen (15) kilometer area from the shoreline in municipal waters provided that no commercial fishing can operate in the above mentioned zone with depth less than seven fathoms".[3] However, the municipal fisheries ordinance of Narra slightly rephrased this regulation and inserted a new sentence. The related part of the ordinance states that "The Municipal Chief Executive may authorize or permit the following: 1) small- and medium-scale commercial fishing vessels to operate within the 10.1–15 km area from the shoreline in the municipal waters at low tide; 2) small-scale commercial fishing vessels catching anchovies, *tabagak* (goldstripe sardinella), and salmon during the daytime and nighttime in not less than seven (7) fathoms at low tide".

These newly added sentences on the "permit" can be read to mean that "certain" types of commercial fishing can be conducted in the *entire* area of the municipal waters as long as the depth of water is more than 7 fathoms. Although the Fishery Code, which is a national law, allows special exceptions for commercial fishing in the buffer zone only (10.1–15 km from the shore *and* with a depth of more than 7 fathoms), the municipal ordinance reads the buffer zone as "10.1–15 km from the shore *or* the depth more than 7 fathoms". Through this "translation" of the Fishery Code, the municipal ordinance made it possible for certain small-scale commercial fishing outfits to operate throughout the coastal waters as long as the depth of the water was more than 7 fathoms.

The inserted sentence in the municipal fisheries ordinance is particularly relevant to *kulong* and *likom* fishing. The phrase "small-scale commercial fishing vessels catching anchovies" refers to *kulong* fishing, while fishing for *tabagak* and salmon refers to *likom*. *Kulong*, on the one hand, is for catching anchovies at the surface of the seawater; the fishing grounds should have a favourable depth of 7–12 fathoms. *Likom*, on the other hand, requires a favourable depth of about 20 fathoms to set the net. The local fishermen know that once outside the municipal waters of Narra, or even in the buffer zones, it is quite difficult for *kulong* and *likom* to find fishing grounds with favourable water depths. Therefore, the strict implementation of the Fisheries Code would have been fatal for both fishing methods. In effect, the municipal fisheries ordinance saved *kulong* and *likom* through the insertion of a new stipulation on the "special permit" granted by the mayor. According to the local fishermen, the seabed suddenly sinks in many spots in the municipal waters of Narra. As a result, fishing grounds with a depth greater than 7 fathoms can easily be found, even if the fishing operation is just a few kilometres offshore. The municipal fisheries ordinance of Narra has taken this ecological feature of its local waters into consideration, and, as a result, enabled the *kulong* and *likom* to operate within municipal waters, even just near the shore, as long as the spot is deeper than 7 fathoms. In this way, the owners of those fishing operations have avoided having their operations banned, enabling them to save fuel costs and time in delivering their catches to shore.

Now, how do the members of the MFARMC explain the reason behind their drafting and enactment of the fisheries ordinance, which might contradict the national law when it is interpreted strictly? The council's president in Narra, a woman in her 40s and an owner of several *kulong*, explains, "In order for the national laws such as the Fisheries Code to be accepted among the local people, it should be balanced so that no one will be disproportionately disenfranchised (*para walang maaagrabyado*)". Another member, a 40-year-old male, says, "The national laws are made by the politicians in Manila who don't know the local situation. Thus, the laws should be applied into the local context. We enact the municipal ordinance in order to implement the laws while applying it into the local context. Unless the municipal ordinance reflects the local context, the local fishermen cannot be protected". He says further, "Of course we have to abide by the law. However, sometimes the law is cruel to the people. There are times that we have to adjust the law a bit". Another female member, who also owns *kulong* in Panacan, further expresses her feeling that "the Fisheries Code will kill the small fisherfolk like us.... I was born and grew up here in Panacan and experienced every kind of fishing together with my father and my husband. I know how it is to live by fishing. I, as a person who understands the hardship of the fishermen, wanted to show my concern (*malasakit*) for my fellow fisherfolk".

On a cursory reading, the municipal fisheries ordinance appears to contradict the provisions of national laws, particularly the Fisheries Code. Whether it will stand if any challenge is made as to its legality remains to be seen. However, the members of the MFARMC believe that their act and the ordinance they helped pass are justified based on the "jurisdiction" and "responsibility" bestowed upon them by the same Fisheries Code regarding the protection and utilisation of coastal resources within municipal waters (cf. Philippine Fisheries Code of 1998, Art. 1, sec.16). As further discussed in the conclusion, this act of the members of the MFARMC cannot simply be considered resistance or a counter-legal activity. Rather, it is a revision, or "translation", that capitalises on a particular ambiguity in the national law (i.e., the Fisheries Code) and appropriates its authority, of whose power the members are fully aware.

In a sense, the process presented above suggests a familiar scenario in the Philippine setting. The owners of commercial fishing groups, who occupy the upper stratum of the socioeconomic hierarchy of the village, were elected as members of the MFARMC owing to the backing of a large number of their crew fishermen. Exploiting a lacuna in the national law, they were then able to recommend and have enacted an ordinance that serves to secure their own interests. Rather than simply focusing on this somehow mechanistic explanation of cause and effect, however, I explore the fishermen's social practices that accompanied the implementation of the municipal fisheries ordinance. Such practices made possible the shift in the pattern of resource use and further resulted in the emergence of a new fishing complex. Although this shift in the resource use pattern was initiated by the enactment of the local fisheries ordinance mentioned above, it was actually the agency of the resource users engaged in micro-level negotiation and cooperation that finally brought about this shift.

Changing Pattern of Resource Use

As the most conspicuous feature of the changing pattern of resource use in Panacan, the phasing out of trawl fishing and the consequent absorption of former trawl owners into various alternative opportunities should be examined. Before the Fisheries Code began to take effect around the turn of the millennium, the fishing method most commonly utilised by the fishermen in Panacan was small-scale trawl fishing, locally referred to as "baby trawl" fishing (Figure 5.1). However, the Fisheries Code banned this method because it utilises active gear, which causes great harm to sea grass. Field survey data showed that 45 fishermen, representing a majority of owners of fishing vessels in the village, used to engage in baby trawl fishing and that 55 fishing boats were used for its operation until the advent of the Fisheries Code. Aside from the fishermen who had specialised in baby trawl, others, such as *kulong* fishermen, utilised baby trawl as an alternative fishing method during the monsoon season. As mentioned earlier, *kulong* involves catching anchovies at the surface of the sea, so operations are greatly affected by strong northeastern monsoon winds from October to March. In contrast, trawl fishing is seabed fishing that catches fish, shrimp, and crab from the bottom of the sea and is thereby unaffected by the winds. Therefore, the fishermen occasionally shifted their fishing methods depending on the season, and small-scale trawl fishing contributed significantly to maintaining this pattern of resource utilisation in Panacan. Furthermore, because the owner of the baby trawl used to be accompanied by one or two crews during the operation, it can be estimated that there were

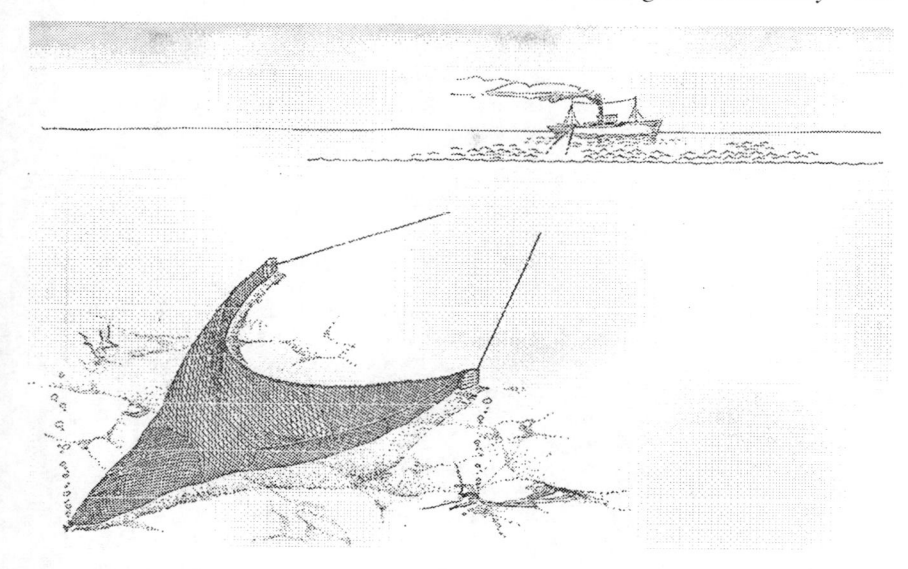

Figure 5.1 Trawl fishing

Source: Umali (1950)

around 100 fishermen, aside from the owners, who had lived by baby trawl operations. Clearly, the trawl occupied a vital part of the pattern of resource use before the Fisheries Code took effect. However, in 2002, the operation of baby trawl was restricted to the months of November through February only, when the northeastern monsoon is strong. When the baby trawl fishermen failed to follow this regulation, they were frequently warned and fined, and their gear was sometimes confiscated by the local government and its enforcing unit, such as the *Bantay Dagat*, fish wardens, and members of the MFARMC. Finally, after such seasonal regulation, baby trawl fishing was totally banned in 2004. What has happened to the former trawl owners since their livelihood was banned? Here, I present three cases of such trawl owners (Cases 5.1–5.3).

Case 5.1: "Alternative livelihoods are not given to the small fishermen who really need them"

Ben was forced to stop baby trawl fishing around 2003. With the 3,000 pesos provided by the mayor of Narra, he purchased a *palangre*, a small longline, and tried to operate it, but due to lack of familiarity with that fishing method, he could not obtain a good catch and thus continued to operate at a loss. He currently makes a living by buying fresh fish from the *likom* and *kulong* fisheries and selling them as dried fish. Ben noted, "They say that baby trawls destroy coral reefs, but this is not true. If you put a net in where there is a reef, it will tear it up. In fact, we avoided coral reefs in our operations". As for the Fishery Code, he said, "It is very strict for small fishermen like us, while the owners of big fishing boats (like *kulong* and *likom*) are overlooked". And as for the current situation, "alternative livelihoods are not given to the small fishermen who really need them".

Case 5.2: "We're too scared to go into debt now"

Rolando, who was born in 1954, has been operating a baby trawl since 1979. Around 2003, many crab fishermen who utilise crab traps set at the seabed, a legal form of fishing due to the use of inactive gear, began to complain that their traps were broken by the nets of the baby trawls. Since then, the *Bantay Dagat* has become stricter in its enforcement. Although Rolando was opposed to such restrictions in the beginning, after attending a series of seminars organised by the municipal government and learning about the damage that illegal fishing would cause to the marine environment, he "gradually came to resign myself to accept the law". Similar to the case of Ben, with the 3,000 pesos provided by the mayor of Narra, Rolando bought a small longline, but it did not go well because he was not used to it, and it soon got caught in the coral reef or swept away by the waves, which cost him a lot of money. At present, he earns a living by serving as a temporary crew member on other fishing boats, helping his parents-in-law grow coconut palm to produce a small amount of copra, and raising a few pigs.

Compared with the days when the baby trawlers could operate, life is now much tougher for Rolando. He says, "Before, I used to be able to borrow 10,000 pesos without difficulty, because with the baby trawls, I could earn about 16,000 pesos a half month. Thanks to the baby trawls, I was able to build a house and buy appliances. But now, I am too afraid to go into debt. My son had to drop out of high school".

Case 5.3: "Life used to be very good"

Rudy, who was born in 1951, has owned two baby trawlers since 1984. Around 2001, the *Bantay Dagat* began to tighten the restrictions for the illegal fishing methods. The first time Rudy was spotted by the *Bantay Dagat*, his nets were confiscated. The second time, he was fined, and the third, his fishing boat was confiscated. Later, using 3,000 pesos provided by the mayor, he bought a *pamangti* (a small gill net) and tried to operate it, but he could not catch enough fish to support his family. According to Rudy, when the baby trawl was operational, "life used to be very good (*maganda ang buhay*)". Even if he had a debt of 20,000 pesos, he could always pay it back little by little with a small amount every day. The house and land where he currently lives were acquired in 2000 with the proceeds from his baby trawl operation. Now that he is banned from fishing, he ekes out a living by buying fresh fish from other boats, drying them, and selling them in nearby towns.

As can be seen from these cases, the ban on baby trawl fishing has caused a severe situation for the baby trawlers who used to comprise the majority of the fishermen in Panacan. It was not easy for them to switch to other unfamiliar fishing methods. The 3,000 pesos offered by the mayor was not sufficient to help them shift their livelihoods. It is also true, however, that in today's Panacan, the former trawlers have found some alternative livelihood activities and are making a living. Table 5.1 shows the number of former trawl owners, 45 in all, according to their current alternative sources of income.

Table 5.1 suggests that conspicuously, many former trawlers are now engaged in dried fish processing. Among them, a sizeable total of 12 are living exclusively by this activity. A significant number of former trawlers have shifted to

Table 5.1 Number of Former Trawl Owners According
to the Current Source of Income

Current source of income	Number
Dried fish processing	12
Pangawil	8
Pangawil + dried fish processing	3
Pangawil + dried fish processing + *likos*	1
Pangawil + *pamanti* + *bolero*	1
Pamanti	3
Pamanti + *bolero* + boat carpentry	1
Kulong (owner)	5
Likom (owner)	1
Bolero	3
Bolero + beach seine (crew)	1
Baklad (owner)	1
Migrate to adjacent municipality	4
Tricycle driver	1
Total	45

the use of *pangawil*, that is, hook-and-line fishing. It can be understood that 25 of 45, or more than half of the former trawlers, have found an alternative source of income from either dried fish processing or *pangawil*, or a combination of both. It can also be seen from the table that several former trawlers utilise gill net fishing, locally referred to as *pamanti*. Although *pamanti* has more of a subsistence character, being carried out by husband and wife for fish meant for local consumption, it plays a significant role as a substitute for major commercial fishing during the monsoon season, as explained below. Some former trawlers who had succeeded in accumulating a good amount of capital have ventured into *kulong* or even *likom* fishing. Furthermore, some of the former trawlers have been absorbed into the *bolero*, the casual rank-and-file crew of *kulong* or *likom*. One fisherman shifted to *baklad* fishing. Four persons left Panacan and migrated to adjacent municipalities that seemed to offer better opportunities for fishing.

The other significant feature suggesting a new pattern of resource use in Panacan is the drastic increase in the number of fishermen who rely on *pangawil*, or hook-and-line fishing, in recent years. Table 5.2 shows the transitions in the numbers of fishermen and fishing boats engaged in *pangawil* fishing based on data collected during fieldwork. The data were gathered from 83 of the 108 *pangawil* fishermen in Panacan and information was obtained on 120 of the 155 fishing boats. According to Table 5.2, 40 fishermen started *pangawil* fishing after 2001. Furthermore, among the 12 fishermen under the column of 1996–2000, 8 started *pangawil* fishing in the year 2000. This means that more than half of the *pangawil* fishermen interviewed started their operation when the implementation of coastal resource management took effect in the local community and trawl fishing was banned. In the same way, 84 of 120 fishing

Table 5.2 Transition of the Number of *Pangawil* Fishermen and Their Fishing Boats

	~1975	1976~1980	1981~1985	1986~1990	1991~1995	1996~2000	2001~2005	2006~	Total
No. of fishermen	2	7	7	10	5	12	21	20	84
No. of boats	2	7	7	10	5	13	29	49	122

boats started to operate after 2000. This indicates that many fishermen made or bought additional boats when the restrictions on resource use started getting stricter. These fishermen, who have ventured into *pangawil* fishing since 2000, had been engaged in various activities; some used to work as *kulong* or *likom* crew, others had joined *pangawil* operations owned by someone else, and others had engaged in baby trawl fishing as either an owner or crew member. In any case, it is safe to say that, although a former main source of income among the village fishermen such as baby trawl was prohibited, many fishermen found an alternative livelihood in *pangawil* fishing.

Pangawil fishing is usually carried out by two to three persons and requires a relatively small amount of capital. During the 1990s, the fish caught by *pangawil* used to be bought by a local middleperson and sold at the local market. In early 2000, the situation changed when some locals with sufficient capital to buy fish in bulk started to bring them to the provincial market of Puerto Princesa, or even to Manila. The price of the fish caught by *pangawil* increased, making it a profitable business. This situation accelerated in 2004, when some buyers from adjacent municipalities started to buy live fish, particularly grouper, for the markets of Hong Kong and Taiwan.[4]

Clearly, the contextualisation of the institution of coastal resource management explained above has changed the pattern of coastal resource use, leading to the emergence of a new fishing complex. As explained in detail below, major commercial fishing, such as *kulong* and *likom*, is at the core of this newly emerging complex; this supports other common activities such as dried fish processing and *pangawil* and is complemented by alternative fishing activities such as *pamanti* and *suwayan*, during the monsoon season, when *kulong* and *likom* cannot operate. It is therefore a coordination of interdependent fishing activities minutely adjusting their operations by utilising specific seasons and space of the coastal environment.

Emergence of a "*Kulong–Likom* Complex" as an Alternative Fishing Complex

In the beginning, the core of an alternative fishing complex, *kulong* and *likom* fishing, worked as a pivot by providing an ample supply of fresh fish for the dried fish processors and also of bait for *pangawil*, or hook and line fishing. Dried fish processing and hook-and-line fishing, which can be said to be auxiliary, but indispensable, activities of the new fishing complex, are not sustainable without an ample, continuous, and cheap supply of fresh fish from *kulong* and *likom*.

Pangawil fishing requires 40–50 kg of fresh fish as bait during an ordinary trip, which lasts for two to three nights. While at sea, *pangawil* fishermen approach the *kulong* or *likom* from Panacan to ask for some fish as bait. When the *kulong* or *likom* have a bountiful catch, they give up to 5 kg of fish for free to the *pangawil* fishermen. On ordinary days, they sell the fish caught at a price much cheaper than market price. *Pangawil* fishermen, for example, can purchase their bait at a very low price, from P700 to P800 for 50 kg, when these can cost them from P2,000 to P2,500 (P40 to P50 per kilogram) on the local market. On other occasions, *pangawil* fishermen purchase their bait on the shore when the *kulong* and *likom* have just arrived from their operations. They can buy bait for P1,000 to P1,500 per 50 kg on the shore, which is still much cheaper than that on the local market. Therefore, a shift of baby trawlers into dried fish processing and a drastic increase in the numbers of *pangawil* fishermen in recent years have been realised through the steady and cheap supply of fresh fish from the *kulong* and *likom* operations.

This complex, however, should be complemented by alternative fishing activities during certain periods when the *kulong* and *likom* cannot operate. While the *kulong* operations cease when winds are strong, particularly during the northeastern monsoons, as groups of anchovies cannot be found at the surface of the sea, the *likom* operations cease during the full moon period, when lights to aggregate the fish at night do not work effectively. Accordingly, during these periods, the dried fish processors and *pangawil* fishermen bring their activities to a halt owing to the lack of fresh fish supply from the *kulong* and *likom*. Alternative livelihood opportunities are provided by simple fishing methods such as *pamanti* or gill netting on the nearby shore, *suwayan* or beach seine, and *pamisugo* or catching *bisugo* at the nearby coral reef protected by mangroves and the island. Although Table 4.1 in the previous chapter shows that *pamanti* is the main source of income for 19 persons in Panacan, this number does not include many fishermen who own *pamanti* but utilise it only as a substitute for their main fishing activities. Because *pamanti* and *kulong* utilise the same fishing grounds, conflicts may arise between the two; however, any such conflict is avoided because *pamanti* most frequently operate when the wind is strong and the seawater is turbid, when *kulong* cannot expect a productive operation. Regarding this interchanging utilisation of the fishing grounds, a *pamanti* fisherman explains, "If the water is turbid, the fish do not notice the net. That is why *pamanti* fishing can expect a bountiful catch during those times".

Suwayan, another alternative activity that complements the fishing complex, is a traditional beach seine (Figure 5.2). As indicated in Table 4.1, four persons own the net for *suwayan*, which provides subsistence opportunities for the village people. They say, "Most of the students in the village help to pull the net when school is out; in this way, they are supporting their parents". This activity has traditionally been a source of extra income for many residents. Usually, fishermen who could not fish because of bad weather or children who were on school vacation would join in to pull the nets, earning about 50–100 pesos per person. However, seine nets are defined by the Fishery Code as active

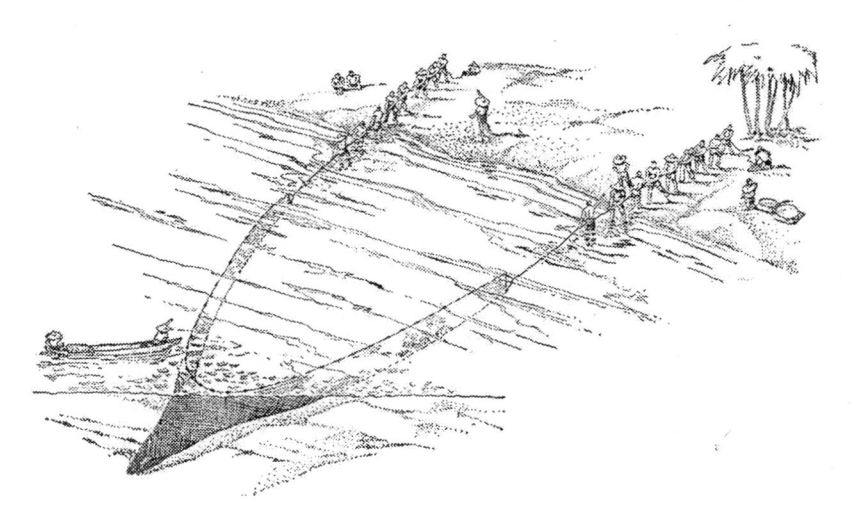

Figure 5.2 Beach seine (*suwayang*)
Source: Umali (1950)

gear because they use fine mesh nets and are pulled towards the beach; therefore, if the Fisheries Code were strictly applied, the operation would be illegal. However, the MFARMC of Narra negotiated with the mayor and the town council and succeeded in obtaining an "internal agreement" to allow the conditional operation of beach seine. The agreement was that *suwayan* would be permitted to operate only during the monsoon season, when the *kulong* cannot operate. *Suwayan* is for catching anchovy, the same species targeted by *kulong* fishing. As with gill nets, this could potentially lead to conflicts with the *kulong*. However, such conflicts are avoided because *suwayan* is used only during high winds, when *kulong* cannot operate. According to the fishermen, when it is windy and rainy and the water is muddy, the anchovies move from offshore to the shallows near the beach. In addition, anchovies usually stay offshore, but when the spawning season is near, they come to the mouth of the river near the beach, where they spawn and then die. It is impossible for *kulong* fishermen to catch anchovies that have migrated to these shallow waters, so *suwayan* is more effective in such cases. Furthermore, at those times, owing to the decrease of the catch of anchovy by the *kulong*, the market price of the same fish caught by *suwayan* soars and high profits can be expected. In this way, *suwayan*, which could have been banned from operating if the law were strictly applied, was allowed to continue by "informal consent" among local actors, which also enabled a balanced complementarity between commercial and traditional subsistence fishery.

It should be noted that the three activities, *pangawil, pamanti,* and *suwayan,* that complement the emergent fishing complex by providing alternative opportunities, particularly during the monsoon season, would have faced a conflict with the baby trawl had the latter's operations still been permitted. This is because the alternative fishing activities mentioned above utilise the same fishing grounds and catch the same kinds of fish as the baby trawl. Therefore, it can be said that the three activities are able to function as a safety net for the emergent fishing complex precisely because of the phasing out of the baby trawl.

As has been suggested so far, the people of Panacan have coped with the uncertainty of the maritime world through a multi-layered combination of several alternative livelihood options. However, they expanded their life chances by not only securing multiple livelihood activities available within one settlement, but also maintaining access to multiple places where the same livelihood activities were operational. To examine this point, I present another case (Case 5.4) in the following.

Case 5.4: Codel Island as a niche of the "Kulong–Likom Complex"

About 30 km off the shore south of Panacan, about two hours by ordinary pump boat, there is a small island locally called *Isla Codel* (Codel Island). *Isla Codel* (Picture 5.1) has played an important role in the livelihood strategies of the fishermen of Panacan, particularly after the implementation of the Fisheries Code. It offers a shelter for a safer operation during the monsoon winds and a spacious area along the shore to set a series of *kapils* for dried fish processing. Three fishermen from Panacan are called the "pioneers" of

Picture 5.1 Isla Codel seen from afar

Picture 5.2 A fisherman's hut and *kapil* in Codel island

Isla Codel because they "discovered" the island sometime during the 1970s. They built transitory huts along the shore that were utilised as spaces for processing dried fish and the seasonal mooring of their fishing boats (Pictures 5.2).

As can be seen below, the fishermen who have been affected by the implementation of the Fisheries Code and its related laws and ordinances started to utilise the niche offered by *Isla Codel* by activating kinship ties with the pioneers. Figure 5.3 indicates the kinship relationship of those utilising the *Isla Codel*.

One of the pioneers of *Isla Codel* is Dante Martinez (⑫ in Figure 5.3). During the 1970s, he conducted survey trips, together with his father (⑩) and uncle (①), to look for good fishing grounds and islands with wide shores that could accommodate the fishermen during the monsoon season. They found *Isla Codel* during one of these trips. Dante owns three units of *kulong*, a *suwayan*, and a fishing boat for *pangawil*. He used to own a baby trawl until it was banned in 2004. Currently, he maintains his house and a *kapil* in both Panacan and *Isla Codel*, and he plies between the two depending on the winds. Former baby trawl owners, who are relatives of Dante, have shifted to dried fish processing after baby trawl fishing was banned. While maintaining their houses in Panacan, they built *kapil* on the shore of *Isla Codel* and started to buy fresh fish from Dante. Shown on the kinship chart are Dante's younger brother (⑪) and other fishermen (②, ④, ⑦, ⑧, ㉑, ㉒, and ㉓) who were former baby trawlers that have shifted to dried fish processing on *Isla Codel*. They utilised their close kinship relationships with Dante to obtain permission to build huts and *kapil* along the shore of *Isla Codel*. Today, these new dried fish processors purchase fresh fish from not only Dante, but also other *kulong*, such as those mentioned below.

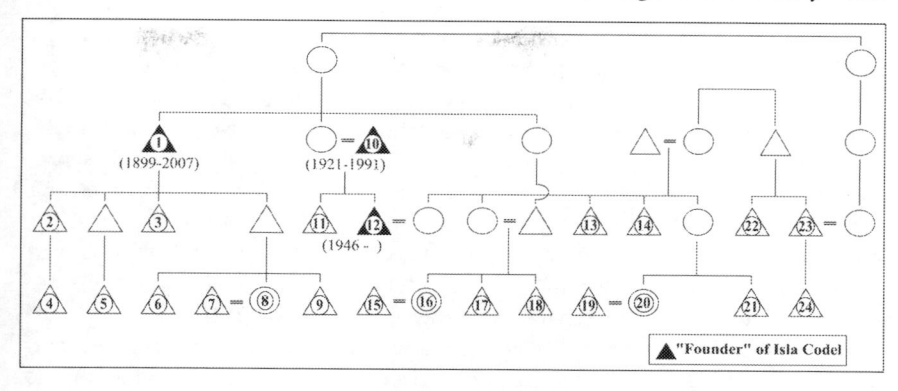

Figure 5.3 Kinship relationship of the fishermen utilising *Isla Codel*

Many *kulong* owners in today's Panacan used to combine their operations with trawl, as mentioned earlier. In times of strong winds, they shifted to trawl instead of *kulong*. However, this strategy had to be abandoned when trawl was banned. They had to look for alternative activities when the winds were strong. *Isla Codel* offered these fishermen shelter and a secure space for their *kulong* operation during the monsoon season. The fishermen numbered ③, ⑤, ⑨, ⑭, ⑲, and ⑳ are among the *kulong* owners who found a niche for operations during the monsoon season on *Isla Codel* and started to provide fresh fish for the dried fish processors mentioned above. Aside from these former trawlers and current *kulong* owners, *Isla Codel* offers an opportunity for additional income for the subsistence fishermen who live by *pamanti* (⑮ and ⑯), who help in dried fish processing (⑰, ⑱, and ㉔), and who accompany the *kulong* operation as *bolero* (⑥, ⑬).

One informant said, "Isla Codel is a big help for our clan" (*Malaking pakinabang ang Isla Codel sa angkan namin*). The case of *Isla Codel* indicates that the fishermen who have been negatively affected by the institutionalisation of the coastal resource management regime have utilised a newly found niche for their alternative livelihoods by activating kinship ties.

Discussion

In this chapter, I have examined the process of contextualisation in which the institution of resource management is adapted and embedded in the specific context of the local community. It should be noted that the process of institutionalisation discussed in the previous chapter and that of contextualisation discussed in this chapter are inextricably linked and proceed in a mutually constitutive manner. In other words, it is not appropriate to view institutionalisation and contextualisation as two separate processes, where the state regulates the local community in the former and, in return, the local community counteracts against the state in the latter. Rather, institutionalisation and contextualisation are, as both sides of the coin, always considered to develop with the other as part of the process.

In a similar vein, this dual process of institutionalisation and contextualisation cannot simply be considered as the power of the state, on the one hand,

and the resistance to such power by the local community on the other. As the municipal fisheries ordinance demonstrates, the rephrasing of laws and the insertion of a new sentence into the ordinance were not simply a rejection of the law or a counter-legal action meant to confront the regulation adversely; in fact, the people are fully aware of the power and constraints of the law. In this sense, agentive practices involve "not simply rejection but the creation of something new, as people articulate their critiques, find allies, and reposition themselves in relation to the various powers they must confront" (Li 2005: 391). The data suggest that power and resistance—or, in this case, regulation and practice—are intertwined and cannot be separated (Agrawal and Gibson 2001).

As discussed in Chapter 3, under the regime of global environmentalism and green neoliberalism, people are disciplined, physically and mentally, to be subjects internalising a certain rationality regarding their relationship with nature (Agrawal 2005a, 2005b). Being governed to be proper wardens of nature, the people in the coastal community in this chapter internalise the "eco-rational subjectivity" to live the tightened "politics of resource use" (Eder & Fernandez 1996). While living under the strong effect of eco-governmentality, however, people engage in agentive practices to create an alternative social order in the locality by rearranging their relationship with nature. The enactment of the municipal ordinance encouraged practices among the fishermen to realise a shift in the local resource use pattern aimed at avoiding a situation in which most of the local fishing activities would have been prohibited. This resulted in the emergence of a new fishing complex, the "*Kulong–Likom* Complex", in which even the fishermen who were severely affected by the implementation of laws, such as the trawlers, were provided an alternative livelihood opportunity. As Chatterjee (2004, 77) discusses, people are not simply governed; at the same time, they have the agency to devise "new ways in which they can choose how they should be governed".

I would now like to argue the characteristics of the emergent community discussed in this chapter. The emergent community, which includes various stakeholders, has achieved a certain kind of mutuality, even though it contains conflicting interests. The community presented in this study is not a homogenous entity that shares norms and identity; rather, it is composed of various stakeholders with multiple and sometimes conflicting interests. It is true that the interests of the actors who regulate and monitor resource management, such as national government entities (e.g., the Department of Environment and Resources, the Bureau of Fisheries and Aquatic Resources (BFAR)), the local government (e.g., municipal mayors, councillors), environmental NGOs, fish wardens, and the MFARMC, sometimes directly conflict with those of the resource users, such as the local fishermen. The point, however, is that such conflicting interests do not simply result in discord and divide among the various stakeholders who belong to different social classes; rather, such conflicts coexist with networks among the stakeholders, which can be utilised to bring about an alternative pattern of resource use. As mentioned earlier, the enactment of the municipal fisheries ordinance served to protect the interests of the commercial fishing own-ers, who at the same time, were members of the MFARMC. However, as stressed by two different informants, compassion, rather than self-interest, explains the motives behind the new ordinance. One says, "In order for the national laws such as the Fisheries Code to be accepted among the local people, it should be balanced so that no one will be disproportionately dis-enfranchised". Another asserts, "I wanted to show my concern (*malasakit*) for my fellow fisherfolk". As shown in this study, the alternative pattern of resource use and a new fishing complex would not have been realised had commercial fishing, such as *kulong* and *likom*, been banned altogether. Therefore, although the ordinance has surely protected the interests of own-ers of commercial fishing, it has also enabled the fishermen who had been deprived of their former means of subsistence to seek a niche for alternative livelihood opportunities. Thus, the community presented in this study is not a given, bounded unit, but rather a social space emerging from the practice of activating and utilising the networks of various stakeholders with multiple interests.

The last, but the most important, point that can be made from the ethnogra-phy presented in this chapter is that the emergent community observed requires a reexamination of the conventional binary that counterposes community as a bounded intimate sphere with civil society as a discursive public sphere.[5] Under such a binary, community is assumed to be bound by primordial attachment and the interdependence of the people, while civil society is assumed to be the asso-ciation of free citizens who share issues, interests, and rationality. However, the emergent community, and the mutuality realised by it, cannot be understood through such a conventional binary. It is true that the community examined in this chapter retains the characteristic of a traditional community bound by local and blood ties. As shown in the case of *Isla Codel*, the kinship ties in the locality contributed immensely and allowed many people to utilise the lim-ited niche, where an alternative resource use pattern can be made possible. Still, such intimate ties are interacting and actively negotiating with the regulations and constraints emanating from the public rationality of resource management. For example, as indicated in the previous chapter, the fish wardens are made to internalise rationality and are expected to belong transparently to a public sphere. However, they are doubly bound by, on the one hand, the obligations and expectations of the kinsmen and peers in the community, and, on the other, the responsibility required by the institution that should be unencumbered by those conventional constraints. To illustrate further, the MFARMC, which plays a pivotal role in the regulation and monitoring of the resource manage-ment process, can be said to be an actor that introduces public rationality to the community of resource users. However, the MFARMC initiated the enactment of the ordinance, which is motivated by the localised and intimate "concern for the small fishermen". Within the community indicated in this case, the intimate sphere of personalised interests and the public sphere of eco-rationality cannot be separated; rather, both are infiltrated by each other. The "balance", mentioned by the MFARMC member, which should be maintained "so that no one will be disproportionately disenfranchised", can be possible in this social space of emerging community.

This chapter maintains that the localised mutuality enabled by such an emerging community lies at the basis of the vernacular public sphere that is the focus of the whole book. The idea that only the discursive space of civil society, made up mainly of the middle class, has the capacity to stand up against the power of the state and market has been severely criticised by some scholars (e.g., Fraser 1992, 1995; Gupta 1995; Hann 1996; Comaroff & Comaroff 1999; Ferguson and Gupta 2002). The vernacular public sphere in this study shares an "indigenous public sphere" (Comaroff & Comaroff 1999) in which differential power relations infiltrate into the supposed equity of the public sphere, as well as a "subaltern counterpublics" (Fraser 1992, 1995), which is made up of the people marginalised by the bourgeois civil society of Western modernity. In other words, it is "the relatively unregulated negotiational domain of subaltern political society that is not centrally governed by elite civil society ideals of law, rights, citizenship, and equality" (Sharma 2006: 80). Also, it is this vernacular public sphere where people engage in the agentive practice of "governmentality from below" (Appadurai 2002) against centralised governance from above. This chapter, together with Chapter 3, suggests an unexpected consequence of neoliberal environmentality. The ethnography of this chapter described the conduct of various actors induced by the institution of resource management which is deeply restructured by neoliberalism, which interact, and articulate, with localised mutuality of emerging community. What is produced at such interface is not only the eco-rational subjects, but also the emergent vernacular public sphere that works to secure the lives of the people.

Notes

1. A part of this chapter is reprinted in a revised form from *Philippine Studies* Vol. 57.4 (2009): 901–936, by permission of the Ateneo de Manila University.
2. Among the members of the MFARMC, the representatives of the local fisherfolk are elected through votes cast by residents in each coastal barangay. Thus, the owners of the commercial fishing outfits, such as *kulong* and *likom*, are usually elected because of the large number of votes cast by their crew. It is difficult for small-scale fishermen who go fishing by themselves or only with a small number of companions to garner enough votes to be elected as representatives.
3. In the Fisheries Code, commercial fishing is categorized into three scales: small scale, which utilises fishing vessels from 3.1 to 20 gross tons; medium scale, which utilises fishing vessels from 20.1 to 150 gross tons; and large scale, which utilises vessels more than 150 gross tons. One fathom is 6 feet (about 1.8 m).
4. The rapid increase in fishing for live fish for export to Hong Kong and mainland China is a common trend in not only Narra, but also Palawan Province as a whole. See Fabinyi (2014) for the remarkable expansion of fishing for live fish in the Calamian Islands in the northern part of the province in the 1990s. According to the article, 55% of live fish exports from the Philippines came from Palawan as of 2003 (Fabinyi 2014: 152).

5. Under this binary, both community and civil society are essentialised and given a series of contrastive and distinctive characteristics. For major discussions on civil society in the Philippines, see Hedman (2006), Silliman and Noble (1998), and Ferrer (1997). In most of these studies, civil society is taken to be equivalent to "sectors" or "organizations" such as NGOs. This study, however, considers both community and civil society as networks and social spaces. Along the same line, Hilhorst (2003: 5) claims that "students of NGOs must shift their attention away from organizational features, structures and reports to the everyday practices of the social actors in and around the organization".

6 Crafting Livelihood under the Neoliberal Eco-governmentality

Life History of a Visayan Fisherman

This chapter presents the life history of a fisherman named Lito, who lives in Barangay Panacan, the same coastal village introduced in Chapters 4 and 5, under the Municipality of Narra, Province of Palawan.[1] Lito was born in the southern part of Cebu Island, the central Philippines, and later migrated to Panacan, where he has spent his entire life since his youth (Map 6.1). The development of the life history of Lito and the transition of the community in which he lives clearly indicate a shifting pattern of coastal resource use; that is, from the time of "the great fish race" (Butcher 2004), in which unlimited expansion of the frontiers of fishing grounds under an open-access regime as a background was possible, to the time of the enclosure of waters and restriction of access to resources. Such a transition is a characteristic feature of various communities in Palawan and the Philippines, in which people are increasingly entangled in the politics of resource use and conservation (Eder & Fernandez 1996; Dressler 2009). In this sense, the story of Lito and his community below contributes to an understanding of the particular position of a subject living under the neoliberal eco-governmentality explained in the Prologue to this part.

Lito's life history suggests that although he is heavily influenced and constrained by the neoliberal conservation regime analysed earlier, he himself has not become a so-called "eco-rational subject" (see prologue to Part II). Whereas Lito's livelihood strategies are often heavily limited by the governmentality of neoliberal resource management regimes, at times, Lito himself takes advantage of new opportunities created by such governmentality. As Agrawal argues, the practices and thoughts of "environmental subjects" are not always directly linked to environmental conservation. Nevertheless, the environment in which such subjects live is oriented and structured, directly and indirectly, by the political rationality that underpins neoliberal environmental governance regimes (Agrawal 2005a: 164–165). In the following, I examine the formation of such subjects through Lito's life history while focusing on the connections that subjects maintain with the community. What is revealed by this life history is the practice for securing livelihood, and life itself, through negotiating with the institutions that support the environmentality permeating deeply into the coastal communities in the Philippines. In other words, this chapter is an attempt to examine how the dual processes of "institutionalization" and "contextualization" of the resource

DOI: 10.4324/9781003224273-8

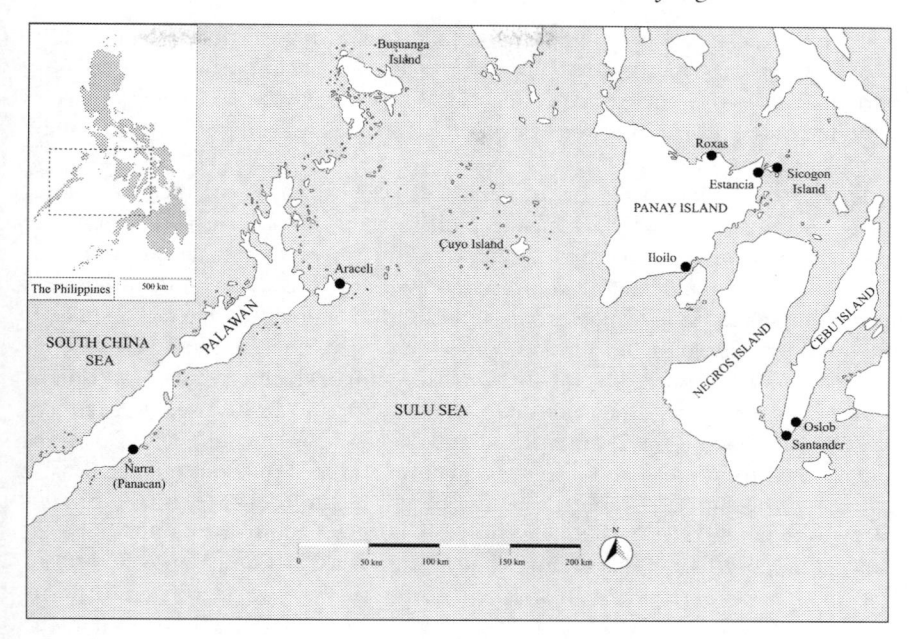

Map 6.1 Palawan and islands of the Visayas region

management regime discussed in the previous chapters are reflected in, and actually lived by, an individual fisherman. The practice of Lito indicates an active creation of "relatedness" (Carsten 1995) among kins and non-kins within and above the community. Such practice further clarifies the characteristic of the emergent community which is discussed in the previous chapter.

Childhood as a *Muro-ami* Diver in the Time of "the Great Fish Race"

Lito Navaro was born in Oslob, a southern town on Cebu Island, in 1960. In this part of Cebu, arable flat land is scarce and the people engaged in small-scale corn cultivation. During his childhood, political and economic life in southern Cebu, particularly in the towns of Santander and Oslob, was monopolised by the Abines family. Although the family patriarch, Apolonio Abines, Sr., who had started his career as an obscure fisherman during the 1920s, became a municipal councilor and rose to become town vice-mayor of Oslob, the power of the Abines family reached its zenith during the 1970s and 1980s, brought about especially by the political and economic savvy of Apolonio Abines, Jr. and his brother Crisologo.[2] The Abines, particularly Crisologo, exercised coercive power to defeat their political rivals and economic competitors. Crisologo's way of governance is frequently termed as "*bossism*," a characteristic feature in Philippine local politics, that "combined paternalistic pretensions with violence and intimidation to acquire wealth and property, exploit labor, and mobilize followers during elections" (Sidel 1999: 123). The Abines dynasty in southern Cebu relied on a transportation monopoly, particularly the bus line, which connects the southern towns of Cebu and Cebu City, and of the fishing industry, *muro-ami*, on which Lito and his family in Oslob were dependent for their survival.

Lito narrates that during his grade school years, most of the men in Oslob, including his father and elder brother, joined the *muro-ami* fishing operation. Lito remembers that at that time, there were 14 large *muro-ami* vessels in Oslob, another 14 in Santander, and two in Siquijor, with each vessel carrying 280 fishermen.[3] These *muro-ami* fishing groups in Oslob and Santander were managed and recruited by Crisologo and his family members, who entered into a partnership with the Frabal fishing company in Navotas, Manila, which provided the fishing vessels. The *muro-ami* expeditions during the 1970s and 1980s usually lasted for ten months straight and brought thousands of residents, including Lito's father and brother, from southern Cebu to the remote waters of the South China Sea.

During the entire 10-month expedition, which Lito recalls as usually occurring from January to November, the vessels from Oslob maintained a base, called *istasyunan*, on Talampulan Island, Busuanga, Palawan (Map 6.1). *Muro-ami*, which was introduced in southern Cebu by the Itoman fishermen from Okinawa, Japan, during the 1920s, is a highly productive method utilizing a large corn-shaped bag net set between coral reefs and a nylon scare-line held and jiggled by the swimmers, numbering almost 300 for each vessel, to drive a large volume of fish into the net. The scare-lines, attached to a stone weight, are repeatedly dropped to the sea bottom, and quite often on corals, by numerous swimmers. It also involves 20–40 divers who dive 12–24 m below the surface of the water to make sure that the net is securely set at the bottom. These swimmers and labourers were mostly teenage boys recruited from poor families in southern Cebu. The extremely severe conditions of *muro-ami* labour in the deep sea is a well-known fact in the Philippines. Quite often, the swimmers and divers were coerced to work by cruel managers on board, who were armed with pistols and firearms. Sometimes, during such expeditions, the heavy labour took a toll on the lives of young swimmers.

Lito joined the *muro-ami* operation just after finishing grade school at the age of 14 years. His reason for having joined *muro-ami*, Lito relates, is that he was so envious of his male friends who, after having come back from a 10-month expedition in the distant South China Sea, spent their money extravagantly in the village. Lito's envy of his peers can be more clearly understood by the following description of the young labourers of *muro-ami* fishing during the 1980s.

> Upon landing at the home port, the labourers are seen to be walking jauntily about with their bleached hair and goggles on their heads, status symbols perhaps, and are thought then to have a quantity of money which they sometimes throw away freely on drinking sprees, gambling, cockfighting, or consumer items, or, through their mothers, on fiestas.
>
> (Olofson, Cañizares, & de Jose 2000: 235)

At a young age, however, Lito apparently did not realise that the extravagant spending of his peers was firmly tied to "credit bondage" (Olofson & Tiukinhoy 1992: 46), which had been cunningly established by the Abines family. To entice poor young boys and their families to join *muro-ami* expeditions, the Abines offered a cash advance, called *bale*, of 300 pesos (one sack of corn grits, a staple food, cost 8 pesos during the late 1960s). Additionally, during the 10-month expeditions, the crew members' families who remained in southern Cebu were allowed to buy items such as rice, corn, and pig feed on credit from the store owned by the Abines. At the end of each expedition, the swimmers and divers were paid their wages that remained after deducting the value of the advances given to their families. In the event their wages could not fully cover these advances, which was usually the case, they were obliged to return to sea for another tour.

The period of thriving *muro-ami* expeditions during the 1970s and 1980s was the time of "the great fish race" (Butcher 2004) staged in the vast open-access oceans, during which fishers based in not only Cebu, but also the whole Philippines, extended their capture into ever deeper and more distant waters, or frontiers, by applying new techniques and updated versions of old methods (Butcher 2004: 193). Lito had been working as a swimmer for 2 years from the time he joined *muro-ami* at the age of 14 years when he was promoted to "official," a somewhat upper rank in the labourer hierarchy. He recollects that the work of a swimmer was bearable only if you were a good swimmer. Unfortunately, Lito had difficulty enduring the cold during labour at sea. In an expedition in 1978, when Lito was 18, he made a drastic decision in his life. During an expedition on the South China Sea, the vessel he joined stopped by a coastal settlement in southern Palawan to fetch water. While the vessel was moored at night, Lito decided to run away from the group and sought a place to stay among the residents in the nearest settlement. According to him, he was driven not by a desire to escape the hardships of labour in the *muro-ami* expedition, but rather, to answer a rather youthful yearning to try his luck in a new environment.[4]

After World War II up to the present, Palawan as a "last frontier" (Eder & Fernandez 1996), has been accepting many migrants from various parts of the Philippines, who have come for its rich natural resources, such as timber, minerals, arable land, and marine products. Palawan's abundant resources have enticed a huge number of immigrants from other parts of the country since the mid-twentieth century. The village where Lito settled in after leaving *muro-ami* was one of the many migrant communities formed along the coast of Palawan by the fishermen enticed by its rich marine resources.

Settling in a Bustling Fishing Community in Palawan

Lito settled in Barangay Panacan, a bustling fishing settlement in the municipality of Narra, 91 km south of Puerto Princesa City, the capital of Palawan Province. Through the 1970s until the mid-1980s, the mainstay of the fishing in Panacan was *basnig* (bag net) fishing. Lito was soon accepted by a *basnig* fishing outfit as a rank-and-file crew member. It should be noted, as background to Lito's seemingly easy accommodation in the community, that the core members of the community shared a common experience with Lito: they had run away from an extremely exploitative boss who monopolised the local politics and economy.

Some core members of the Panacan fishing community were originally from Sicogon Island, which is under the jurisdiction of the municipality of Carles, Iloilo, on the northwestern tip of Panay Island (Map 6.1). While they were in Sicogon, they used to work as crew members for *basnig* fishing outfits based in Estancia, Iloilo, a hub of the fishing industry and marine product distribution system in the Visayas. The owners of *basnig* outfits in Estancia, particularly during the pre-World War II period, had maintained "diffused social and political as well as economic leadership and responsibility toward, and feeling of interdependence with, (their) large number of crewmen and their families" (Szanton 1970: 118). However, the intensified capitalism and commercialization that encroached into rural society during the post-World War II period resulted in the deterioration of the traditional reciprocal relationship between social classes and further caused the "anarchic and exploitive state of labor-capital relations" (Szanton 1981: 53). Under this situation, the livelihood of the small fishermen in Sicogon increasingly became constricted, so they started to immigrate to Panacan, which used to be one of the seasonal camps of the *basnig* outfits from Estancia. Through the 1950s and 1960s, the families of these fishermen followed and began to migrate into Panacan. One woman recollects her exodus from Sicogon, "Entire families joined, and that was like the whole of Sicogon! Almost all of us were here [in Panacan]! The whole village joined. We gathered here!"

The bustling *basnig* fishing community formed by the fishermen from Sicogon has since enticed fishermen from various parts of the Visayas. In the late 1970s, migrants from Leyte introduced a new fishing method called *kulong* (daytime purse seine), which is still popular in Panacan today. During the 1980s, fishermen from Samar brought with them longline fishing with multiple hooks called *palangre*. Also in the mid-1980s, faced with the declining efficiency of *basnig*, the fishermen from Sicogon modified *lawag* (round haul seine) fishing, which they used to engage in Sicogon, into a new type of fishing method called *likom* (night-time purse seine). Furthermore, during the 1990s, fishermen from Roxas City, Capiz, brought two types of trawl fishing called *hulbot-hulbot* (Danish trawl) and baby trawl. Also in the mid-1990s, fishing for flying fish called *pamarongoy* was introduced by the Cebuano from Dalaguete. As such, the development of Panacan as a migrant fishing community has been facilitated by the successive introduction of new fishing methods by new migrants who had previous experience in such methods from their place of origin. Although these methods were later modified to make them more viable in the situation of the host community, old methods do not simply fade away to be replaced by newer ones. For example, most of the *kulong* owners in Panacan today, faced with the increasing cost of fuel and less productive catches, have revived their old method, *basnig*, since 2009. In this way, the fishermen in Panacan utilise various methods and gear interchangeably according to the contingencies that all fishing communities equally face.

In 1982, Lito married Marife, who was originally from Sicogon Island and settled in Panacan with her parents. She had many close relatives among the *basnig* owners and crew fishermen. One of those *basnig* owners was Dencio Danao, who, when still in Sicogon, used to work as skilful *piloto* (master fisherman) of *basnig* owned by the Reyes family, the leader of which was a prominent local politician cum landlord. Dencio, after having settled in Panacan, served as a long-term *barangay* captain of Panacan and also owned several outfits of *basnig* by himself. Lito was allowed to accompany one of the outfits of Dencio, who was an uncle of Marife. As explained above, *basnig* had been phased out in the mid-1980s and shifted into the more effective, but costly, fishing method called *likom*. That time, Lito approached another in-law originally from Sicogon, who owned the vessel for *likom*. During the 1990s, Lito was fully occupied by *likom* fishing as a *piloto*, a skipper, and ran operations in not only the waters near Panacan, but also various fishing grounds in Palawan. Various fishing methods in Panacan, such as *basnig*, *likom*, *kulong*, and *hulbot*, often had their operations in the waters under the jurisdiction of other municipalities. They also transferred seasonally to other coastal settlements according to the monsoon seasons. As such, ample opportunities became available to the fishermen, and this had been made possible by the existence of various fishing methods in Panacan realised through unrestricted access to the waters. By around the turn of the century, however, this open-access regime had substantially shifted to one of restricted access. Moreover, various activities, such as *hulbot* and baby trawl, which are deemed to cause heavy damage to corals and the seabed, had started to be prohibited. Lito's livelihood has been inevitably affected by this situation.

Encroaching Neoliberal Conservation and Restrictions on Resource Use

As discussed in the previous chapters, the principal features of the current regime of coastal resource management can be summarised as follows: the enclosure and delimitation of formerly open-access marine resources and the establishment of exclusive rights of access to the resources for certain groups of people in the municipality, fishing cooperative, or small business sector; the zoning and classification of municipal waters according to the market values of each resource; the delineation of substantial areas for the MPAs, in which small-scale fishing was prohibited while ecotourism was encouraged; and finally, the inculcation of the ideas of "obligation" and "responsibility," which particularly emphasises concepts such as "self-empowerment," "accountability," and "a sense of audit," concepts that fit well into the green neoliberal ideology, which lies behind the current regime of coastal resource management.

The current environmental governance summarised above puts substantial restrictions on Lito's fishing activities. The Fisheries Code reserves the right to utilise the resources within municipal waters exclusively to the fishermen residing in the same municipality. Owing to this, conflicts and disputes frequently arise when fishermen trespass into the municipal waters of other towns. *Likom* fishing, which Lito operated as a skipper, was one of the methods most affected by this change. The *likom* fishing groups were accustomed to operating in fishing grounds located in neighbouring towns, where the competition among the commercial fishers was less fierce than that in the municipal waters of Narra. However, under the new code, the *likom* fishers frequently began to be apprehended by the local enforcement agencies in the neighbouring municipalities. According to Lito, the fish warden of Aborlan, a town adjacent to Narra, was especially strict about the "illegal entry" of fishing vessels from neighbouring towns, and this warden apprehended him ten different times while he was fishing in the municipal waters of Aborlan. When apprehended, he was usually fined 5,000–10,000 pesos.

Furthermore, even within the municipal waters of Narra, the activities of Lito and other fishermen have been greatly restricted by the establishment of the MPA. Raza Island, for example, located near the shore of Panacan, used to offer a rich fishing ground for the fishermen of Panacan owing to the rich mangrove and coral reefs surrounding the island. By the end of the 1990s, however, an environmental NGO began to lobby for an ordinance declaring the island as an MPA through the municipal government of Narra. The NGO's aim was to protect the habitat of a rare and endangered species of bird called *katala*, or the Philippine cockatoo (*C. haematurophygia*), which is endemic to only some places in southern Palawan. The NGO also sought to conserve the coral reefs surrounding the island so as to promote scuba-diving tourism and increase revenues for not only the NGO but also the local government of Narra. In this way, Raza Island was declared an MPA in 2001 and, since then, any fishing activities, and even passing through the area, have been prohibited. The available area for the operation of Lito's *likom* fishing inside the municipal waters has been increasingly limited by this development.

In 2006, a crucial incident occurred that resulted in Lito having to stop his operation as a skipper.[5] Normally, the *likom* fishing groups in Panacan maintain several seasonal camps for their operations during certain months of the year. Particularly during the season of the northeast monsoon winds from October until March, some *likom* fishing outfits from Panacan transfer to the fishing grounds of Honda Bay and Ulogan Bay, which are at the northeastern side of Palawan Island facing the South China Sea. These bays are protected by the strong northeastern monsoon winds and abound in marine resources. As was usual in his *likom* fishing, Lito carried out his operation in Ulogan Bay in January 2006. On the night of January 31, 2006, he and his fishing group were apprehended by an enforcement team composed of the Philippine National Police, the Coast Guard, and a local environmental NGO. Because the waters of those bays fell within the jurisdiction of Puerto Princesa City, the capital of Palawan Province, the fishermen from Panacan were prohibited from operating in the area. As a result, Lito's fishing gear was confiscated, he was fined, and he had to face a criminal lawsuit in the provincial court. He was forced to stay in the provincial capital to go through the legal proceedings. The owner of this *likom* fishing operation had to spend more than 70,000 pesos for legal expenses and the retrieval of his confiscated gear. Even after he was able to return to Panacan, Lito was prohibited from operating the fishing group while his lawsuit was pending. Lito spoke about the incident, explaining, "I have been apprehended by the local Bantay Dagat in Narra and neighbouring towns many times. These people, some of whom I know personally, just ask me to pay an administrative fine of 5,000 pesos, then allow me to go fishing the next day. But if you are caught by an NGO, it's a different story altogether. The people of the NGO based in the capital are really strict!"

Generally, and traditionally, the small- and medium-scale fishermen of the Philippines, such as the *likom* operated by Lito, are accustomed to a rather mobile way of life, and seasonally migrate between several settlements depending on ecological factors such as monsoon winds, the flow of the currents, and the migratory routes of the fish (Seki 2000). However, the current trend of enclosure of local resources has greatly constrained the conventional ways of resource use by the fishermen, as demonstrated in Lito's story.

Living on Mining and Ecotourism

Although Lito's court case was eventually dismissed, owing to the financial damages he incurred from the confinement and fines, he opted to stop operating the *likom*. While subsisting with temporary labour for other fishing groups in Panacan, he was invited by his village mate to work with Roland Rodriguez, a businessman based in Puerto Princesa City who has stakes in the mining and tourism industries in Narra. Several mines that produce copper, nickel, and chromium are operating in Narra. Roland, a mining engineer, has been working in several mining companies operating within the municipality of Narra since the 1980s. Narra Nickel Mining and Development Corporation, where Roland was the chief operating officer, was looking for a licensed captain of fishing boats who could take charge of bringing workers from the pier to the ship when loading minerals on board. There is a stockyard of minerals in Barangay San Isidro, a *barangay* adjacent to Panacan, and loading is done once every month. Lito, hired by Roland as captain, operated the boat carrying the mine workers from the pier to the ship that carries the minerals to its destination, such as China or Japan. In an ordinary month, when there was a loading job from the mine, Lito could have 15 days of travel and earn 700 pesos per day. He was therefore able to earn 12,000–20,000 pesos per month.

However, the climate of public opinion in Palawan has increasingly become unfavourable to mining operations in the province. Some churches of various denominations, environmental NGOs, and the academic community were particularly concerned that the areas covered by the mining operations are forested, almost all of which are part of ancestral domain claims and community-based forest management agreements, and some are either declared or proposed watershed areas. Under these circumstances of a general anti-mining trend, the monitoring and regulation of mining activities by the local government tightened, and some mining pits were eventually closed for noncompliance violations. Furthermore, in November 2008, the provincial government of Palawan enacted a mining moratorium, which was consequently endorsed by the national government in January 2009.[6] Lito, who had been deprived of another source of income by the anti-mining trend in Palawan, says that "mining operation should be allowed as long as it observes the laws and appropriate procedures". His village mate, who invited Lito to work with Roland, is a more adamant defender of mining. He explained that the local economy benefits from the mining operation, citing, for example, the operation of Narra Nickel Mining and Development Corporation, which employed 500 local people: "Except for the specialists such as mining engineers and chemical engineers, the employees were all from Narra. The company paid them 3 million pesos as salary for 15 days. This means that 6 million pesos circulated in a month within the municipality of Narra. It was a huge blow to the local economy of Narra to have lost such an opportunity". He further criticised the environmental NGOs, which hold strong anti-mining stances, claiming that "those eco-NGOs are shouting for anti-mining in order to get money from the overseas funding agencies. They cannot receive funding if they are not anti-mining. So they shout for anti-mining and anti-development yet they themselves are beneficiaries of mining and development".

After the mining operation ceased, Lito's family was barely supported by remittances from his eldest daughter who worked in Kuwait as a cashier in a grocery shop. She earned 120 dinar (18,000 pesos) every month and sent some portion of it to her family in Panacan. However, the daughter became pregnant, and because the Kuwaiti government does not admit pregnant foreign workers, she was sent back to the Philippines. Meanwhile, Lito's eldest son worked in the stockyard of the Narra Nickel Mining and Development Corporation and earned a daily wage of 263 pesos but he lost his job when the governor issued a moratorium on mining operations in 2008. Faced with this financial predicament, Lito's family was presented another opportunity by the newly growing ecotourism industry.

Lito's former boss Roland has been engaged in the ecotourism industry aside from the mining industry in southern Palawan. To this day, southern Palawan, including Narra, has been relatively left out in terms of tourism compared with its northern counterpart where prominent tourist spots such as the "underground river" UNESCO World Heritage Site and El Nido are located. However, under the provincial government, the Palawan tourism council is now starting to promote the tourism industry in the south.

Roland owns an uninhabited four-hectare island called Arena Island, which is located 45 minutes from the pier of Panacan by fishing boat. Arena Island used to be inhabited by the indigenous people of Tagbanuwa, but during the 1980s, Roland applied with the Department of Environmental and Natural Resources for ownership of the island. Roland and his staff promote this island, which is also an MPA, as an ecotourism site through a conservation project for *pawikan*, a sea turtle native to the Philippines, which is designated as one of the world's most endangered species. It is said that the island is the only breeding area for *pawikan* in Palawan, where tourists can observe numerous eggs inside a cage located on the shore during incubation periods. Furthermore, to entice more foreign and "green" tourists, this island resort promotes a "*pawikan* adoption program me" in which tourists can adopt a *pawikan* for 1,000 pesos per head to sponsor related costs in keeping the baby turtles safe and healthy before they go back to sea. The hatchlings are tagged and registered to trace their return to the island to lay more eggs, on which occasion, the foreign "foster parents" are informed of the return of their adopted turtles (Pictures 6.1–6.3).

Picture 6.1 Conservation of eggs of sea turtle in Arena Island

Picture 6.2 Baby turtles bred in Arena Island

Arena Island strategically tries to entice tourists to visit through partnerships with other beach resorts and potential tourist sites in the vicinity. One of their partners is Cristal Paradise Resort, which is located near the town centre of Narra and owned by a Filipino-American medical doctor who currently resides in California. This beach resort, equipped with 12 lodging rooms and six villa-type cottages, opened in 2003 and accommodates mostly foreign tourists from the United States, Europe, and recently, Korea. Although the resort accepts an average number of 150–200 guests in ordinary months, the number of monthly guests substantially increases to as many as 300 during the peak season, such as Christmas and summer vacations. Another partner of Arena Island is Raza Island, which, as mentioned above, has been an MPA since 2001. A local NGO named the KATALA Foundation, which is funded by

Picture 6.3 Grown-up Pawikan and Lito's eldest son

European environmental NGOs and zoological societies in Germany, France, and the UK, has been vehemently promoting ecotourism around Raza Island through *katala* bird watching and conservation as well as scuba diving around the coral reef.

Recently, through this partnership with beach resorts and MPAs, the number of tourists being accommodated on Arena Island has substantially increased. Although fluctuations are seen according to the season, the island accepts 50–150 people per month, who are, aside from the local Filipino tourists, from various parts of the world such as Korea, Taiwan, and Singapore. During the past few years, Lito has been entrusted to operate a boat for transporting tourists plying between the ecotourism sites of Cristal Paradise Resort, Raza Island, and Arena Island. From the labour of frequent trips transferring the tourists, Lito earns a fixed monthly salary of 8,000 pesos, plus tips from the foreign tourists.

Today, Lito, still residing in Panacan, has seven children, three of whom are still minors in elementary and high school. Although Lito's monthly income from the ecotourism industry barely covers his children's tuition fees and his family's subsistence, he still considers himself lucky to have access to a steady, if meagre, monthly income. While working in the ecotourism industry, Lito is always ready to return to mining and commercial fishing operations as soon as the circumstances become preferable.

Discussion

From the life history of Lito presented in this chapter, we are able to understand the penetration of the institution of coastal resource management, as well as how an individual copes, and negotiates, with such institutions in the everyday practices of livelihood. Furthermore, his life history suggests the relationships between people and the environment, and livelihood strategies utilizing the environment, that cannot be fully explained by the concept of eco-governmentality, as discussed in the Prologue. In this section, I elaborate further on the implications of Lito's life history.

It can be argued that neoliberal natural resource governance regimes are at the same time a process of "state-space expansion" (Scott 1998), under which the indigenous practices of resource users, which are based on knowledge embedded in the complexity of local ecology and the environment, are "standardized" and "simplified," that is, "decomplification" (West, Igoe, & Brockington 2006), through decentralised co-management that mobilises an empowered civil society, community, and citizens, that is, "governing from distance" (Rose 1996b, 1999). As shown in the case of coastal resource management in Palawan, marine resources have not only been enclosed for the exclusive access of local residents, but also further divided into several zones according to a classification of the market values of the specific resource. Such enclosure and zoning of the formerly open-access waters signify the penetration of the administrative grid of the government according to which the "messy" activities of resource users became "legible" and "visible" to the state (Scott 1998). Furthermore, such an administrative grid, which determines a proper space for a proper activity, produces subjectivities with a proper sense of obligation and responsibility as rational managers of nature. Therefore, it can be said that resource management regimes, as the modern apparatuses of power and knowledge, exercise eco-governmentality under which the people go through a process of discipline and normalization to become rational, or more specifically, eco-rational subjects (Goldman 2004, 2005; Agrawal 2005b; Li 2007a).

However, the life history examined in this chapter suggests a subjectivity that cannot be easily reduced to fit the discourse of eco-governmentality and eco-rational subjects. This is because the transition of the livelihood of Lito, although certainly affected to a great degree by neoliberal environmental government, cannot simply be said as conforming to, or resisting, such governmentality and rationality. Time has passed since "the great fish race," (Butcher 2004) when the unhampered mobility of fishers, such as those of *muro-ami* fishing that Lito engaged in during his childhood, was a normal way of life in the waters of the Philippines and Southeast Asia. Now, particularly in Palawan, where the politics of environmental conservation are predominant and intense, the fishers increasingly fall under the surveillance and regulation of the central government, as well as the public opinion endorsed by the ideology of neoliberal environmental governance. The life history of Lito indicates that although he had sometimes been marginalised and dislocated as a result of neoliberal environmental governance, at other times, he had directly gone against such governance by working, for example, in mining operations, and still at other times, he had utilised and mobilised such environmental governmentality to his own advantage, for example, by earning a living from ecotourism.

As shown by Lito's life history, it is true that his access to resources has been greatly restricted since the late 1990s, when the conservation trend became predominant, as seen in the case when he was apprehended and his fishing gear was confiscated, and in the temporary termination of mining activities. The resultant situation, however, is neither a bare marginalization nor an exclusion from the community. In the same way, the situation does not automatically motivate him to resist the ideology and institution of neoliberal conservation. Rather, he simply exploited another opportunity, such as ecotourism, that opened up under the prevailing trend of eco-governmentality through utilizing his networks with his village mates. It is also true that Lito, as a boat man involved in the booming ecotourism industry, is living under the influence of the eco-governmentality ideology. Having examined his life history, however, it is not appropriate to consider the case as a process of subjectification or an indication of a "birth of an eco-rational subject". Rather, from his days as a *muro-ami* diver to his current status as an ecotourism boat man, what can be gleaned from his life story is the flexible mobilization and manipulation of dyadic social relationships, either kinship or non-kinship, for him to keep his head above water.

As another point reflected in Lito's life history, the livelihood strategies of Lito have been made possible through the flexible activation of social relationships, which should be contextualised into a broader feature of maritime Southeast Asian society. Having conducted research in the fishing community in Langkawi, Malaysia, where community histories reveal extensive demographic mobility, Carsten, based on her finding that the people reckon their relations "horizontally" in terms of siblingship rather than "vertically" in terms of descent, argued that "kinship in Langkawi is focused on the future rather than the past" (Carsten 1995: 319). Explicating her argument further, she suggests that some villagers in Langkawi had great difficulty remembering where their parents, let alone their grandparents, were born. Furthermore, very few people knew or cared much about the place of origin of their neighbours or fellow villagers. Discussing the importance of such "forgetting" as a collective act in the creation of a shared identity, Carsten summarises her point as follows.

> Kinship in Langkawi is an active, ongoing *creation* of relatedness between those who were previously unrelated or distantly connected, a process which is linked to the mobility of the local population. It is through the processes of kinship—hospitality, fostering, marriage, and having children—that newcomers to the island are transformed into kin. In these processes what is important is producing kinship in the future. To a considerable extent, the details of past diversity are gradually obliterated. In this sense, forgetting this past is part of an active process of creating a new and shared identity (Carsten 1995: 324, emphasis in original).

What is significant in Carsten's discussion is that it links such forgetting, or "genealogical amnesia," and population mobility to the relatively fluid concept of identity discussed as characterizing the Austronesian world, and to a predominant feature of Southeast Asian social and political organization. Taking another example from the Austronesian world, a study on the Vezo fishermen in Madagascar revealed a similar characteristic of fluid identity (Astuti 1995). Astuti noted that the Vezo identity is not determined by birth, descent, or an essence inherited from the past, but rather, is created contextually in the present through what people do and the place they live, or in a more concrete term, those who "struggle with the sea and live on the coast" are considered and accepted as Vezo (Astuti 1995). Astuti quotes a narrative by Vezo himself, "People are not Vezo because of their stock, but because they go out to sea, they go fishing, they live near the sea" (Astuti 1995: 3).

Returning to our case of Lito, it can be considered that his everyday livelihood practices since he settled in Panacan have also been realised through a "creation of relatedness" and "forgetting the details of past diversity" in a coastal community experiencing extensive demographic mobility, which is a characteristic of frontier societies such as Palawan. It is such continuous creation of relationships that made Lito's everyday negotiations with environmentality possible. Under the neoliberal resource management regime, social relationships and mutuality, which used to support the traditional livelihood of the people, have been marginalized and fragmented. Interestingly, however, neoliberal institution of resource management also induced people's practices of "an active, ongoing creation of relatedness" (Carsten 1995: 324). Such relatedness lies at the basis of emergent community, which we discussed in the previous chapter, which has a further possibility to expand into the vernacular public sphere for the people faced with the uncertainty of the maritime society.

Notes

1. This chapter is reprinted in a revised form from *Palawan and Its Global Connections,* Eder, James and Oscar Evangelista eds., (2014) pp. 161–194, Ateneo de Manila University Press, by permission of the Ateneo de Manila University. All personal names in this chapter are pseudonyms. The author first became acquainted with Lito in 1999. Since then, casual chats and unstructured interviews with him continued every time the author visited the Barangay Panacan. The conversations and interviews were conducted in Filipino and Cebuano. In 1999, the author also visited his hometown of Oslob, Cebu, for a week and had the opportunity to talk with his parents, brothers, and sisters, and other countrymen who used to work in the *Muro-ami* fishing industry.

2. The description of the Abines family and its *muro-ami* business owes much to the works of Butcher (2004), Olofson, Cañizares, and de Jose (2000), Olofson and Tiukinhoy (1992), and Sidel (1999), as well as my interviews with older fishermen in Oslob.

3. This figure more or less coincides with the number of vessels stated in another study conducted at the end of the 1980s, which says "(t)here are figures of 'over thirty' for the total and, for the largest operator, eighteen to twenty-four boats. Each boat employs a crew of about 350 fishermen" (Olofson & Tiukinhoy 1992: 36).

4. Young swimmers rather frequently escaped from *muro-ami* operations because of the inhuman labour conditions experienced during the expeditions while the vessels were docked in settlements in Palawan during the heyday of *muro-ami*. See, for example, Olofson, Cañizares, and de Jose (2000).
5. This case overlaps with Case 3.2 in Chapter 3.
6. See Austin et al. (2009) for details regarding the involvement of academes in this process.

Prologue to Part III

Mobility and Connectedness in Transnational Social Field

So far, this book has focused on urban and rural settings in the Philippines, but in the chapters of Part III, I place the Philippines in the "transnational social field". Owing to the remarkable increase in overseas migration since the mid-20th century, the "transnational social field" of the Philippines has been experiencing continuous expansion. The following chapters examine how the penetration of neoliberalism has prompted the transformation of "the social" in transnational settings as well as what kinds of solidarity and mutuality have emerged.

Overview of Migration from the Philippines

The Philippines, as one of the world's leading "migrant-exporting countries", has been attracting a wide range of interest in migration studies. According to the latest government statistics, as of December 2013, the number of overseas Filipinos was estimated to be about 10.24 million, which is roughly 10% of the population (CFO 2016). About 4.87 million of these Filipino expats are permanent residents, about 4.21 million are temporary residents, and about 1.61 million are irregular or illegal residents. The majority of the permanent residents are concentrated in North America, with about 3.14 million residing in the United States and 630,000 in Canada. Meanwhile, temporary residents under short-term employment contracts live in almost all parts of the world, with East Asia (including Southeast Asia), the Middle East and Gulf States, and Europe being the most popular destinations. In East Asia, about 790,000 have gone to Malaysia, and about 200,000 to Singapore and Hong Kong. Among the Gulf countries, Saudi Arabia and the United Arab Emirates stand out, with about 1 million people staying in the former and 820,000 in the latter. In Europe, about 270,000 are in Italy and 220,000 in the United Kingdom. In addition, about 400,000 Filipinos (many of them permanent residents) live in Australia, a major immigrant-receiving nation. Since the 1980s, Japan has been accepting young Filipino women who have obtained "entertainment visas" to work as entertainers in bars and other places. About 160,000 of these women have since married Japanese men and now have permanent residence in Japan.

The Philippines and the United States, where most of the permanent Filipino immigrants reside, have had deep historical ties since the Philippines was

DOI: 10.4324/9781003224273-9

colonised by the United States at the end of the 19th century. The flow of immigrants from the Philippines to the United States started at the beginning of the 20th century, when the population of Filipino immigrants and permanent residents started increasing, especially after 1965, when immigrants were legally allowed to bring in their families. In Canada, many Filipinos take advantage of the Live-in Caregiver Program, which grants permanent residency to foreigners who have worked for 2 years in live-in domestic or nursing care positions.

In contrast, temporary stays abroad with short-term employment contracts originated from the overseas employment policy launched in the mid-1970s. In the beginning, the main group of contract workers abroad were male workers engaged in engineering and construction work, for which demand increased in Middle Eastern countries against the backdrop of the oil boom. However, since the mid-1980s, the ratio of men to women in new overseas employment has reversed, and in recent years, women have accounted for 70–80% of the total. A phenomenon known as the "feminization of overseas work" or the "feminization of migration" is becoming increasingly prominent. This "feminization of overseas employment" is based on the structural background of today's globalisation, namely, the emergence of an international division of labour in reproductive labour. Since the 1980s, economic growth in newly industrialising economies such as Taiwan, Hong Kong, and Singapore has led to an increase in women's participation in society, creating a demand for female workers in the reproductive sectors of middle-class households in these countries. Such demand for reproductive labour in emerging countries was met by migrant female workers from the Philippines and other developing countries in Asia. Furthermore, since the 2000s, there has been a shortage of nurses and caregivers in developed countries such as Japan, Europe, and the United States as a result of the declining birthrate and aging population, a reduction in state welfare policies, and the privatisation of health care.

Thus, the phenomenon of the "feminization of overseas employment" suggests the international division of labour and the creation of a new hierarchical relationship among global women in which migrant female workers from developing countries, who can be employed at comparatively low wages, support the reproductive labour of middle-class women who have become productive labour in emerging Asian countries and developed countries in the West. The situation is further complicated by the fact that in the Philippines, it is the women from the further economically marginalised rural areas who are taking care of the reproductive labour of the families left without wives and mothers because of outmigration abroad. These "global care chains" (Hochschild 2000) of reproductive labour, which are stretched across national borders and between different socioeconomic strata, are the networks that support the "global supply chain", the international division of labour. The "global care chains" can be considered the "invisible" networks that support the more visible networks of the "global supply chain", and a characteristic feature of today's globalisation. These structural factors underlying today's globalisation are behind the migration of people from the Philippines to East Asia, the Gulf countries, and Europe (especially the United Kingdom and Italy) for work purposes.

Although international migration from the Philippines is broadly characterised as described above, much of the discussion in Part III, except Chapter 6, deals with the migration of middle-class people from the Philippines to the United States. In the following, I focus on the context of the Philippines as a sending country and the United States as a receiving country and examine how the transnational social field is restructured by neoliberalism.

The Postindustrial Era in the United States and Filipino Migrants

Much of the ethnography of the following chapters is related to the transnational social field stretching across the Philippines and the United States. Hence, as a background, I would like to examine the postindustrial labour market in the United States and how it has affected the situation of Filipino immigrants there. Particularly, as a broader context of each chapter, we need to focus on the influx of the so-called "new Asian immigrants" (Ong, Bonacich, & Cheng 1994) who came to the United States after the 1965 Immigration Act became law. Among these new Asian immigrants, a substantial number were from urban, educated, middle-class backgrounds, and they came to the United States as professionals, managers, and entrepreneurs (Ong, Bonacich, & Cheng 1994:4). The Immigrant Act of 1965 removed the national origin quotas that used to act as a racial barrier and constrain immigration from the Philippines and other parts of Asia. It also enabled family reunification, in which the parents and extended family of US citizens as well as permanent residents were given visa privileges. Furthermore, it had an occupational quota preferably allocated for skilled professionals and highly educated people such as physicians, nurses, and engineers. After the enactment of the 1965 Immigrant Act of 1965, the composition of immigrants to the United States drastically shifted from Europeans to Asians. About 4 million Asians immigrated to the United States between 1971 and 1989 (Ong & Liu 1994). The majority were Filipinos, but there were also Chinese (including those from Taiwan and Hong Kong), Indians, Koreans, and Vietnamese.

According to Ong, Bonacich, and Cheng (1994), such large-scale immigration from the Philippines and other Asian countries after 1965 did not merely coincide with the postindustrial economic restructuring of the United States; rather, the two phenomena were constitutive to each other. Postindustrial restructuring proceeded simultaneously with the erosion of the welfare state regime in the United States, in which government expenditures for social services, particularly those for the education or training of highly skilled professionals, had been drastically curtailed, while at the same time, the demand in the labour market shifted from that for unskilled manufacturing labour to professionals in the service sector. The professions most severely affected by such a transition of the welfare state regime in the United States were physicians and nurses. This situation resulted in a severe shortage, particularly of nurses, in the United States, and consequently, an increased demand for foreign-trained nurses. Therefore, the 1965 amendment to the Immigration Act was not only a response to these changes in the domestic labour market in the United States, but it also made the postindustrial trend in the United States more pronounced because of the large number of foreign health-service workers who immigrated into the country from that time (Ong, Bonacich, & Cheng 1994).

Another reason for the shortage of nurses in the United States was the deterioration of working conditions, particularly decreasing wages, owing to the cutting of public expenditures for medical services and the privatisation of health insurance (Ong & Azores 1994). Under this situation, the demand for foreign-trained nurses increased, particularly for those from the Philippines and India, who were considered highly adaptable to difficult working conditions such as low wages and long working hours (Ong, Bonacich, & Cheng 1994; George 2005). Reflecting such trends, Filipinos accounted for 27.6% of the 28,832 foreign nurses working in the United States at the end of the 1970s (Ishi 1987: 288).

A more recent factor that should be considered as having influenced the structure of the labour market for Filipino immigrants in the United States is the predominance of the neoliberal ideology. By the 1990s in the United States, "neoliberal multiculturalism", which celebrates cultural diversity among immigrants to attract international investors, global talent, the "creative classes", and high-tech industries, became one of the ways cities could rebrand and gentrify themselves (Glick Schiller 2011). This ideology insists that the market should be the supreme regulator of immigration policies that determine which immigrants to welcome. This ideology has become predominant in the context of the post-welfare state transition summarised above, under which public social funding for the support of marginalised immigrants is increasingly curtailed while visas are preferentially granted to primarily middle-class immigrants who are capable of optimising their skills, knowledge, and capital and are considered self-reliant and "cost-effective".

Against this backdrop, care work, including nursing and personal care in hospitals, nursing homes, and households, has continued to absorb many Filipino immigrants as a niche in the immigrant job market (Parreñas 2001, 2008; Boris & Parreñas 2010). The context of the host country described so far may suggest that for Filipino immigrants, the United States immigrant labour market in the postindustrial era is increasingly characterised by tight competition. Under the immigrant labour market regime in the United States, it is understood that Filipino immigrants are increasingly persuaded to be enterprising individuals who engage in the everyday practice of enhancing their "marketability" and "employability" in the competitive labour market of the postindustrial United States.

The Philippines as a "Brokering State"

Understandably, the emigration and labour-exporting policies of the Philippines have inevitably been influenced by the postindustrial structural transition of the major countries of destination, such as the United States, as mentioned above. It is argued that the recent neoliberal government strategy of labour exportation has transformed the Philippines into a "labour-brokering state" (Ong 2006; Guevarra 2010; Rodriguez 2010). Guevarra (2010) noted that "the state and employment agencies exercise a kind of disciplinary power toward migrant Filipinos that aims to govern their social conduct through the notion of 'empowerment' and promotion of an ethic of responsibility to their nation, families, and the image of the Great Filipino Workers" (Guevarra 2010: 5). Such labour-brokering processes reflect "a neoliberal mode of governing from a distance, where the goal is to regulate workers' conduct and produce disciplined labour commodities that are useful to transnational capital, the Philippine state, and workers' individual families" (Guevarra 2010: 5).

Such labour-brokering polices pursue the "professionalization" of workers, under which various training programs are offered by government agencies, private recruiters, and non-government organisations (NGOs) to produce highly skilled and competitive workers for overseas markets. Through this policy of "professionalization", migrant workers are formed not only into "supermaids" who possess advanced skills in English competency, basic nursing, and medical practices, but also nurses who have developed the inner abilities of "diligence", "hospitality", "docility", and "tender loving care" (Guevarra 2010: 132–136). This advanced skill set has become a requirement in the competitive working conditions of "emotional labor" (Hochschild 1983) under the post-welfare state regime of the United States and other Western countries. Through this process, migrants are commodified into an ideal labour good with "added export value" that gives them a global comparative advantage (Guevarra 2010: 125). Under such a transformation of the Philippine state, the people are increasingly governed to be entrepreneurs who are "flexibly altering their bundles of skills and managing their careers, but they also become the bearers of risk, thus shifting the burden of risk from the state to the individual" (Dunn 2004: 22). These aspects—the postindustrial labour market and the "brokering state"—form the structural backgrounds against which the chapters of Part III can be properly contextualised.

The argument so far suggests that a transnational social field stretching across the sending and host countries cannot be considered a homogeneous social field that accommodates the smooth and unidirectional assimilation of immigrants into the host society; on the contrary, it is a highly differentiated field constituted by asymmetrical power relations among the people. According to Levitt and Glick Schiller (2004), the contemporary transnational social field can be defined as "a set of multiple interlocking networks of social relationships through which ideas, practices, and resources are *unequally* [italics added] exchanged, organized, and transformed" (Levitt & Glick Schiller 2004: 1009) in the process of the incessant circulation of goods, cash, information, and people across the borders of nation-states. Furthermore, such a field is constituted by social relationships structured by power and "created by the participants who are joined in struggle for social position" (Levitt & Glick Schiller 2004: 1008). It can be considered that the transnational social field today is strongly restructured by neoliberal ideas, values, and institutions. Under such a trend, the protection and welfare of migrants are not the responsibility of the governments of the host or sending countries, but rather, are expected to be achieved through the self-help and self-reliance of the "empowered" migrants. The chapters of Part III discuss, based on concrete ethnographic cases, how the transnational social field is experiencing neoliberal restructuring, and, in the process, what kind of an alternative public sphere for the mutuality, solidarity, and political actions of the people is emerging.

7 A Woman and the Community of Empathy
Life History of a Widow of an Overseas Migrant Worker

The transnational social field is constituted not only by those who migrate abroad, but also by those who remain, or who are left behind in their own countries but remain closely connected to those living abroad. In the Prologue of Part III, I pointed out the "feminization of overseas migration", but the uncertainty and vulnerability brought about by overseas employment is not experienced only by women who actually migrate abroad. Rather, the difficulties experienced by women left behind in the Philippines by their husbands' overseas employment as wives and mothers have been widely pointed out in recent years as a social cost of overseas migration. The "broker state regime" and the professionalisation of female labour, also discussed in the Prologue, revealed a situation where the risks and costs of overseas employment have to be borne by the women workers themselves. However, the social costs of the overseas employment of the husbands fell on the remaining wives and their families as much as or more than that on the husband. In this chapter, I present the life history of a woman left behind in order to consider how uncertainty and vulnerability were experienced by her. From this, we can understand the difficulties and marginalisation that wives, mothers, and families experience as a result of their husband's/father's overseas employment; at the same time, we can clearly see the agency of the women who deal with such uncertainty and vulnerability while utilising networks with various non-state actors. Through such practice of constructing network and relatedness, we can see the emergence of the community of affect which shares compassion, sorrow, pity, and anger. The vernacular public sphere that the current study is searching for would be created by those women living in the community of empathy.

Life in an Urban Poor Community and a Husband's Migration Overseas

Gracia Corpus, born in 1947, is a woman living in Barangay Malanday, Marikina City, in Metro Manila.[1] As mentioned in the chapters of Part I, until the early 1990s, many residents in Marikina made a living by subcontracting and sub-subcontracting the manufacture of shoes as a local industry; however, the shoe industry in Marikina has become a declining industry as a result of cheap shoe imports from China. Gracia's childhood was the heyday of the shoe industry in

DOI: 10.4324/9781003224273-10

Marikina. Her father (1911–2004) started working in the shoe industry after graduating from elementary school, and during Gracia's childhood, he was engaged in a contract cottage industry with six employees, producing about 300 pairs of shoes a week. The existence of a small but continuous cash income from the shoemaking business allowed Gracia to finish high school and go on to technical school, where she studied secretarial courses.

In 1970, Gracia met and married Romeo, a high school dropout from the province of Nueva Ecija in Central Luzon who was working in a shoe factory in Marikina. However, the couple's income as workers in a small cottage industry was insignificant and unstable. Romeo earned his daily cash income by performing odd jobs such as street sweeper and tricycle driver. His life of poverty continued as he shuttled back and forth between work in the rural areas of his hometown of Nueva Ecija and precarious employment in the urban informal sector. At the time, they were short of three meals a day, and the family of four, including their two children, would sometimes share a single fried egg.

The turning point in their lives came in 1985. At that time, Gracia and her husband were making a living by running the three tricycles that they had purchased with a loan from the *paluwagan* (a sort of mutual loan association among neighbours). Romeo then heard from a friend about a job opportunity for construction workers in Saudi Arabia, so he sold one of the tricycles he owned to pay for a placement with an overseas employment agency. Consequently, in 1985, Romeo went to Saudi Arabia to work. Romeo's work in Saudi Arabia consisted of manual labour at construction sites. For the first year or two, he sent regular remittances. In 1987, he returned to the Philippines for his first vacation and spent two months with Gracia and the children, but this vacation was the last time Romeo and Gracia would ever be together.

After Romeo returned to Saudi Arabia from his vacation in 1988, he stopped sending money to Gracia and she was unable to contact him. Romeo's brother, who was also a migrant worker in Saudi Arabia, confided in Gracia that Romeo was having an affair with another Filipino woman who was also a migrant worker in Saudi Arabia. With remittances halted and a shortage of funds, Gracia was forced to sell her two tricycles. After that, Gracia and her four children were in dire straits. During this time of hardship, Gracia received both material and spiritual support from her neighbours. For example, from 1988 onward, Gracia was able to run a *sari-sari* store (a small grocery store in front of her house) with a loan from the *paluwagan*. Also, from 1992 to 1994, a neighbour offered her a job as a contract shoemaker. However, emotional support has been as great of a help, if not greater, to Gracia than the material support she received. This moral support came from her neighbours in the barangay and NGOs (see below) organised by families of overseas migrants who shared the hardships brought about by overseas migration. The neighbours and NGO staff shared with Gracia feelings of anger about her husband and his lover. Gracia recalls, "they were able to feel exactly what I was feeling (*nararamdaman nila ang nararamdam ko*), because they were a family of migrants like me. Without the support of these neighbors and family members, I would have ended up in a mental hospital".

In 1992, Romeo returned from Saudi Arabia with his lover, and they moved to a newly built house. He never returned to Gracia. The children, who had not yet reached adulthood, missed their father, sometimes blamed their mother, Gracia, for the separation (see the narrative of Marco, the eldest son, below), and sometimes went to live with their father for a short time. In this way, the relationship between Gracia and her children became strained.

It was during this difficult period for Gracia, in 2005, when tragedy struck. Romeo and his lover had returned to their hometown in Nueva Ecija, where they had built a new house together. Between Romeo and his brothers, a conflict had arisen over the inheritance of the land left to them by their parents. One day, Romeo's younger brother became angry with Romeo's lover for interfering in the inheritance discussion and fired a gun at her. The bullet hit Romeo, who had taken a stand to protect his lover, and he was killed.

From then until 2017, Gracia's life and that of her family has not only failed to improve, but they have also experienced from a variety of additional hardships. Gracia currently lives with her youngest daughter, who was born in 1985 and is still single. Gracia has no fixed income and relies on the small income of her daughter, who occasionally works as a domestic helper for the neighbours to make ends meet.

In addition, her eldest daughter, Nelly (born in 1972), her husband, and their children also live with Gracia under the same roof, although they have separate finances. This situation gives us a sense of the everyday reproduction of the "intergenerational cycle of poverty". Nelly's husband, Boboy, is a street vendor who sells fruit and *binatog* (a local snack made from boiled corn topped with grated fresh coconut) on the back of his bicycle. With a meagre income of about 300 pesos a day, it is all he can do to feed his family. If it rains or his bicycle breaks down, he has no choice but to stop peddling. Boboy somehow strategises his livelihood by changing the items he sells according to the seasons, but he has gradually lost interest in his work. Nelly and Boboy have two sons, the first born in 1993 and the second in 1999. Both of them managed to graduate from elementary school, but after entering high school, they tended to miss class. Gracia often scolded her grandchildren for not going to school, but Nelly and Boboy did not particularly encourage their children to attend. In the midst of all this, their sons gradually lost interest in their studies, and eventually dropped out. Shortly thereafter, the elder brother moved in with a neighbourhood girl and became a father in his teens. As of 2017, he had two children and was supporting his family through casual construction work.

With irregular income and unstable work, Boboy lost his desire to peddle street food and gradually became involved in drugs. In Malanday, where there are many poor people, it is easy to get drugs. Boboy became not only a drug user but also a drug dealer. People around Boboy, including Gracia, wondered why he had suddenly become so profitable, and assumed that he was probably getting money from drug sales. However, Boboy did not use his newfound income to support his family. Rather, the rumour that had been spreading among the neighbours was that Boboy was giving the money he earned from drug sales to a neighbourhood woman with whom he was having an affair. Nelly and Boboy began to fight frequently and eventually separated. Around this time, Nelly became increasingly desperate and began to care less and less about her own life. She stopped eating meals and sated her hunger with junk food that she bought for a few pesos at a *sari-sari* store. She began staying up late playing games at the neighbourhood computer shop, and as a result, she never got enough sleep. Around the beginning of 2016, she started to feel sick and often spent the day just lying on the floor. She began to cough violently and had a distended lower abdomen. By March, the swelling had spread from her lower abdomen to both legs, and her calves were also swollen and enlarged. Gracia and other neighbours convinced her to go to the hospital for an examination and took her to one of the public hospitals in Quezon City. The public hospital was very crowded with people who could not afford the more expensive private hospitals, so Nelly and her family had to wait for a long time in the scorching sun, after which, they were told that the hospital was closed and they had to go home. After this, Nelly began to refuse adamantly to go to the hospital for tests and treatment, and began to say things like "I want to die" and "Please let me die". Despite the desperate efforts of Gracia and her neighbours to provide care, Nelly passed away at the end of April 2016, at the age of 44 years.

The Filipino overseas migrant workers are hailed as "heroes of the day (*bagong bayani*)" because of the positive impact that their remittances and investments in the country have on the Philippine economy, and they enjoy various privileges such as tax exemptions. However, Gracia's life history demonstrates how the expected contributions from overseas migrants to families and the nation often create new risks, making the lives of the families left at home more vulnerable and uncertain. Gracia says, "The real heroes are not the people who go abroad to work, but us, the people left at home". Indeed, the life history recounted by Gracia reveals the hardships that are faced, and endured, by a wife/mother while protecting her family left at home. Interestingly, however, Gracia's eldest son, Marco (born in 1970), describes a different image of motherhood. In particular, Marco tells another version of his father's trip to Saudi Arabia and his subsequent separation from his wife that differs from the story that Gracia told. The following is an examination of Marco's recollections of his father.

Another Version Told by Marco, the Eldest Son

According to Marco, his father, Romeo, was very industrious. Even before he went to Saudi Arabia, he earned money by driving one of the three tricycles he owned. At dawn, he woke up before anyone else in the family to drive a tricycle. Around 8:00 a.m., he would come home and prepare breakfast for the family. After eating breakfast, he swept the front of the house with a broom and went back to driving the tricycle. "The house was always cleaned by my father, not a speck of dust. The refrigerator was always stocked with soft drinks". When Marco had a fever, Romeo would immediately get him some medicine. When Marco had a cough and was having trouble breathing, "he would take me to

Luneta Park (a park in downtown Manila, also known as Rizal Park) early in the morning and bathe me in the morning dew (*hamog*). Then, strangely enough, my breathing became easier", Marco said, recalling childhood memories of his father.

When Marco was 15 years old, his father left for Saudi Arabia. According to Marco, during his father's absence, "I was the one who took care of my sister, who was still a baby. I always held her, nursed her, gave her milk, and gave her medicine when she caught a cold. I was also the one who cleaned the house. My mother and eldest daughter never cleaned the house, so naturally, I did it myself. I was always watching my father do the house chores, so I guess it just came naturally to me". In 1987, Romeo returned to the Philippines for a while and asked Gracia if he could buy a jeepney in addition to his tricycles to make a living so that he would not have to go back to Saudi Arabia. However, Gracia did not want to do that. She wanted Romeo to go back to Saudi Arabia. Marco remembers that his parents often argued over this issue. Sometimes Romeo would raise his hand to Gracia. The fighting between Romeo and Gracia was not only about him going back to Saudi Arabia. Romeo did not like the fact that Gracia was often away from home, gambling and gossiping with the neighbours. Marco says they fought so often that he began to think that their relationship would not last much longer. According to Marco, his mother became very aggressive when she felt attacked and her personality was such that she would never back down. Marco says, "It was because of this that my mother became very aggressive. My father's mind gradually drifted away from her because of her personality". He continues, "I can't say that it was all my father's fault that he ended up with another woman in Saudi Arabia".

Romeo returned from Saudi Arabia for the second time in 1987, started living with another woman, and never returned home. Marco says, "Nevertheless, when it came to us, the children, my father was never lacking in fatherly love. My brothers, sisters, and I supported our father as much as we could as children. He was a very kind father. (...) But our mother often blamed him for our failure to finish their schooling, saying that it was because they lacked support from their father". According to Marco, although his father was not entirely responsible, his disappearance certainly affected the family's problems in many ways. Marco's younger sister, Nelly, spent her days wandering around and neglecting her children, who had stopped going to school, without trying to get any kind of work to supplement her husband's meagre income from peddling.[2] Marco thinks that his father is probably the reason why his younger brother (born in 1976) keeps getting married and divorced, and why his youngest sister can never get married. Finally, he says "Some families stay together even though the parents have been separated for years because of migration. But there are also families like ours in which one of the parents goes abroad to work and make some money, but ends up destroying the family".

Thus, Gracia and her son Marco have different versions of the same story that explains why Romeo had to leave to work in Saudi Arabia. It is pointless to ask which narrative reflects reality. Rather, the purpose of relaying these stories is to suggest the importance of understanding how the difficulties of a family in a transnational social field are subjectively experienced and how they are interpreted differently depending on the position within the family.

In the meantime, despite her own material and emotional hardships since she lost contact with Romeo and stopped receiving his remittances while he was working in Saudi Arabia, Gracia has been providing various kinds of support to overseas migrant workers and their families left at home in her neighbourhood of Barangay Malanday. In the following, I examine such activities of Gracia through two cases.

Death of an Overseas Migrant Woman and Compensation to the Bereaved Family

On August 1, 1996, Sara Balabagan, a domestic worker who was sentenced to death for murdering her employer in the United Arab Emirates and later released after having been judged to have acted in self-defence, safely returned to the Philippines. Upon her arrival, she received a warm welcome from the Filipino people and the media as the "hero of the day" (*bagong bayani*). However, few people knew about Ellen Macabayan, who silently returned home in a coffin, on the same airplane as Sara, without attracting any attention.

Ellen, who had been employed as a domestic worker in Jordan, died of unknown causes and was quietly returned home in a coffin on August 1, 1996. Before she had gone abroad, Ellen and her mother, who lived in Marikina, earned a meagre income as a laundrywoman. However, she needed money to pay for her mother's breast cancer treatment, so she went to Jordan to work. Gracia, who had known Ellen as a neighbour, attended her wake and wondered why she had so many scars and bruises on her body. When Gracia spoke with her mother, she discovered that shortly before her death, her mother had received a letter from Ellen in Jordan complaining about the abuse she was being subjected to by her Jordanian employer. Her letter stated that she had been violently assaulted by her angered employer for simply locking herself in her room.

Concerned about the cause of Ellen's death, Gracia contacted KAKAMMPI (*Kapisanang ng mga Kamag-anak ng Migranteng Manggagawang Pilipino, Inc.*), an NGO that assists the families of Filipino overseas workers. Gracia, as the wife of an overseas migrant worker, had already been in close contact with this NGO for years. KAKAMMPI, which was organised in 1983, has a network with communities in several areas of Metro Manila and provides various kinds of support. Specifically, KAKAMMPI provides emergency assistance to workers caught up in conflicts and incidents overseas, as well as educational activities and livelihood projects for families who remain in the country. Gracia, together with KAKAMMPI staff, reached out to the local congressman from their district to publicise Ellen's case and arrange for an autopsy. The results of the autopsy found no evidence of suicide by jumping, which had been claimed by the Jordanian employer as the cause of Ellen's death. In response, both the lower house (the Congress) and the upper house (the Senate) of the Philippine government decided to hold a hearing, summoning the Jordanian ambassador and others. Ellen's family members (mother, husband, and then 6-year-old child) were eventually able to obtain compensation from the Jordanian government and her employer. In addition, Gracia and others provided information to Ellen's family about the rights of the families of overseas Filipino workers to obtain compensation from the government and the necessary procedures, which made it possible for them to obtain compensation from the government and scholarships for their children.

Rescuing Workers Caught in the Lebanon War of 2006

Sylvia, who was born in 1971, was one of Gracia's neighbours in Malanday. She went to Lebanon in May 2005 to work as a domestic worker. While she was there, she was treated unfairly, by not only her Lebanese employer but also her dispatch agency in the Philippines. For example, according to her contract, she was supposed to have 1 day off per week, but in actuality, she was allowed to go out only when she went to the bank to send money to her family in the Philippines, so her communication with the outside world was quite restricted. In addition, she sometimes did not receive her wages.

On July 4, 2006, Sylvia learned about the bombing of Beirut's airport by the Israeli army when she saw a news report on TV. She asked her Lebanese employer what was going on, but he did not tell her anything; from July 12 to 14, the fighting intensified. On her way to the bank, she was surprised to see many soldiers and tanks and realised the gravity of the situation for the first time. Her employer's wife and children were then evacuated to London, but Sylvia was not allowed to return to the Philippines. Her passport was in the hands of her employer, and there was nothing she could do about it. During this Lebanon War of 2006, many Lebanese employers often entrusted the maintenance of their homes to Filipino house cleaners while they evacuated overseas.

Sylvia usually kept a cell phone concealed on her person, despite her employer forbidding her from doing so. She used it to frequently exchange e-mails with her family in the Philippines as well as Gracia, her neighbour in Malanday. Gracia also communicated with her on a daily basis, for instance, sending her a message on Mother's Day. In the chaos of the Israeli attack on Beirut, Sylvia was left at her employer's house and sent a message to Gracia from her cell phone, asking for advice on what to do. Gracia then consulted with the KAKAMMPI staff mentioned in the previous section, and gave the Philippine Embassy and the Catholic Church in Lebanon the name and phone number of Silvia's employer, requesting them to take immediate action. The Philippine Embassy then called her Lebanese employer to request that Silvia be allowed to return home, but the employer did not comply with the embassy's request. Gracia and the KAKAMMPI staff gave Silvia the phone number for the Philippine Embassy and instructed her to ask for help directly. Silvia called the Philippine Embassy while her employer was away and was later taken into custody by the embassy staff. Her Lebanese employer strongly objected to such a step, but finally gave up after some persuasion by the embassy staff. The employer then evacuated to London.

After spending half an hour filling out paperwork at the embassy, Sylvia was forced to wait for four days with other Filipino workers at a nearby Catholic church, but was not even given water. After that, everyone was put in the back of a truck for the 8-hour drive to Syria and then flown via Bahrain to Manila, where they returned safely on August 9, 2006. Looking back on the events in Lebanon, Silvia says, "Without Gracia and KAKAMMPI's help, I would not have had the courage (*lakas loob*) to call the embassy under the watchful eyes of my employer". With the help of Gracia and KAKAMMPI, she is now preparing to file a lawsuit against the dispatch agency in the Philippines, which has violated several contracts.

Discussion

The life history of Gracia presented in this chapter clarifies the situation of contract migrant workers and their families remaining in the Philippines. The labour export policy of the Philippines was initiated in the mid-1970s against the backdrop of a growing demand for construction labour in the Middle East due to the oil boom. Romeo went to Saudi Arabia as part of such an outgoing labour flow. Gracia's life history clearly demonstrates the difficulties experienced by wives/mothers and families left behind. However, unlike Gracia's story, which emphasised the "enduring wife/mother", her son Marco's narrative showed the subtle conflict between the husband and the wife over migration and overseas work. It also revealed the conflicting aspects of Romeo's gentle character and diligent work ethic and Gracia's lack of understanding about Romeo, as well as Romeo's desire to spend more time with his family at home and Gracia's demand for more income from working abroad. Further, the sad death of Gracia's eldest daughter, Nelly, in 2016, can be seen as a long-term consequence of the risk derived from the absence of her father. Such risks are entangled with various factors surrounding the poor, such as unstable informal sector jobs, easy access to drugs, inadequate health care, and a poor public education system, all of these accelerated the desperation of Nelly and ultimately resulted in her unexpected death.

The chapter also dealt with the cases of women, Ellen and Sylvia, who went to the Middle East to work as domestic workers. These cases can be considered to represent the situation of women who are incorporated into the global care chain, the formation of which results from the current phenomena of the "feminization of migration" and the globalisation of reproductive labour, as discussed in the Prologue.

The retreat of the state and the spread of neoliberalism in the transnational social field, as discussed in the prologue, pose various risks, particularly to women who work abroad, as well as to those who remain in the country; such risks include the breakdown of the family, exploitation by agents and employers, war and conflicts, and so on. However, such risks are often hidden in the domestic space, where domestic and care workers make a living, which makes it difficult for state support to reach them. Therefore, in a situation where the state cannot fully bear the costs of overseas employment, workers and women are called upon to deal with everyday uncertainty and vulnerability through self-help and self-responsibility. At the same time, however, women, as the nexus of neighbourhood groups and grassroots community organisations, are the agencies that actively build and mobilise networks with NGOs, the media, and government agencies.

In particular, I would like to emphasise Gracia's words, "They were able to feel exactly what I was feeling (*naramdaman nila ang nararamdam ko*) because they are also families of migrants like myself". Her words suggest that Gracia's actions are enabled by her ability to empathise with others. I refer to this mutuality realised by empathy as *community of empathy*. What really helped Gracia in her time of difficulty was not the government or civil society organisations, but rather, a community of people who shared sorrow, anger, and despair with her. It is worth examining the significance of this *community of empathy* not only as the intimate sphere of a closed community but also as an alternative public sphere that can give voice to marginalised people and even encourage them to forge solidarity for political action. Recently, the concept of civil society, based on the Western notion of free and autonomous individuals, has been criticised based on various cases of political and social movements observed in non-Western contexts. For example, based on the reality of slum colonies in Kolkata, India, Chatterjee defines civil society as "the closed association of modern elite groups, sequestered from the wider popular life of the communities, walled up within enclaves of civil freedom and rational law" (Chatterjee 2004: 4). Rather than civil society, which often works as a power to oppress the demands of the people, according to Chatterjee, popular politics is realised through a "political society" made up of subaltern groups whose demands and struggles for living and work often "transgress the strict lines of legality" (Chatterjee 2004: 40).

Similarly, the life history presented in this chapter indicated that it was not the civil society, which is an association of middle-class professionals "walled up within the enclaves of civil freedom and rational law", that gave courage and strength to the women when she was at loss with small children because her husband had stopped sending remittances, when she was struggling to cope with the loss of her daughter in an inexplicable situation abroad, or when she was fleeing from an armed conflict abroad. Rather, it was a *community of empathy* made up of people who shared the experience of working abroad, or of being left behind, and emotions of misery and pity. While the KAKAMMPI, the NGO that Gracia relied on, can be considered as part of civil society, it is composed of former migrant workers and the families of workers who are currently abroad. Therefore, KAKAMMPI, while maintaining broad networks with other NGOs, governments, and international organisations, is a part of this *community of empathy*.

Regarding the importance of empathy for solidarity and political actions, Curato, based on research in the post-disaster community in Leyte, discussed the potential of the emerging public sphere made possible by the "affective agency" of disaster victims, who are capable of carrying out political action by sharing emotions such as sorrow, misery, and pity (Curato 2019). Through focusing on "affective agency", Curato criticises the privileging of the discursive public sphere, which focuses exclusively on the capacity of citizens for speech and verbalised actions. Similarly, the life histories given in this chapter require a shift of focus into the alternative public sphere, where solidarity and political actions are made possible by the speechless and nonverbal capacity of the people mobilised by empathy and affect. The individual actors presented in this chapter are not free and autonomous citizens with clear plans and strategies to solve problems; however, their political actions are enabled by "affective agency", the capacity of which to act is derived not only from the ability to affect others but also to be affected by others through empathy (Clough 2007)[3]. It should be emphasised that it is not the intention of this chapter to romanticise the intimate sphere of tightly-knit, cohesive communities. Rather, what we can observe from the life histories given above is that the neoliberal restructuring of the transnational social field can create a space for an alternative public sphere for solidarity and political action by the people who belong to the *community of empathy*.

Notes

1. For more information on the Barangay Malanday of Marikina City, see Chapter 1. I have been acquainted with Gracia since 1991. Especially since the mid-2000s, when I started my field research on social policy in urban slums in Malanday, she has been my close collaborator who has provided me with various supports during my research. The life history presented in this chapter is a compilation of the episodes she has shared with me over the years. All personal names in this chapter are pseudonyms.
2. The interview with Marco was conducted while Nelly was still alive.
3. My discussion here can be further developed by referring to the recent discussion of the "affective turn" (Clough & Halley 2007). This, however, remains as a future task.

8 Migration as Practice of Differentiation

Focusing on the Identity of the Middle-Class Professionals

This chapter will shift the focus from the individual level to the level of social class in discussing the neoliberal restructuring of the transnational social field.[1] Particularly based on the case of the migration of middle-class professionals, it will discuss the divide and differentiation between the social classes would become more prominent in the process of such restructuring. In the following, I will briefly explain the significance of focusing on this specific social class.

Particularly, since the late 1980s, the emergent middle classes of Asian countries have been seen as pivotal in the democratization process and as significant in pushing for economic liberalization and maintaining a vigorous civil society (Robison & Goodman 1996). In the Philippine setting, studies suggest that the middle class, together with the business elite, is crucial for realizing the public sphere by integrating other social classes and marginalised peoples into mainstream civil society (Ferrer 1997; Silliman & Noble 1998; Hilhorst 2003). Notwithstanding the significant role of the middle class in political and economic development processes, a cultural analysis focusing on the identity of the middle class brings into sharp relief its ambivalent character. This ambivalence derives precisely from its position of being in the middle. While the middle class engages itself in social practices of distinction and differentiation by improving its economic status and attaining its desired lifestyle, its newly acquired wealth and status are always contested particularly by both the labouring and the upper classes.

A cultural analysis of the identity of the middle class and its relationship with other social classes takes "class" not as an objective category measurable by certain productive or economic relations, but as a cultural construct emerging through the contestation of identity and representation, and differentiation from other classes through the manipulation of various forms of symbolic capital. As such, people of the middle class are involved in the politics of representation, in which "they struggle to distinguish themselves from the working class, with reference to such qualities as sobriety, rigour and neatness; on the other [hand], they go out of their way to emulate the bourgeois, but in doing so are distinguished by the bourgeoisie as 'pretentious' and 'flashy'" (Pinches 1999, 34; cf. Bourdieu 1984, 246–247).

Especially in the Philippines, a cultural analysis of middle-class identity should be discussed in the context of the increasing fluidity of social classes brought

DOI: 10.4324/9781003224273-11

about by transnational migration. Although both permanent and temporary labour migrations widen the socioeconomic gap between social classes—particularly between the lower and middle classes—and reproduces the difference between them, this same process leads to the emergence of a new category of middle-class people called the "new rich". They are those who used to belong to the lower labour class but have attained a certain level of economic status and purchasing power after their successful overseas employment (Pinches 1996). In other words, the relations of the social classes in the Philippines today are becoming "hybrid" and "overlapping" (Aguilar 2003, 154) in the sense of fluid mobility between the social classes, and the blurring of their boundaries. Paradoxically, the increasingly blurred boundary between the middle and lower classes actually encourages the members of the middle class to construct a symbolic boundary between themselves and other social classes through the practice of distinction and differentiation. Such cultural analysis should give attention to the fact that the identity of social classes has never been static but has always been contested by other classes, consequently bringing about conflict and distinction between different social classes rather than integration in a homogeneous civil society (Schaffer 2005, 2008; Garrido 2008). This chapter argues that such practice of distinction and differentiation by the middle-class professionals would further accelerate in the process of neoliberal restructuring of the transnational social field.

The Philippine Middle Class and Migration

Philippine society has been commonly characterised as a two-class structure, composed mainly of a small number of landed oligarchs and numerous tenant farmers, or the so-called big and little people (Lynch 2004), respectively, a system that had remained basically unchanged since the nineteenth century. However, the Philippines has been undergoing a remarkable transformation of its class structure owing mainly to democratization, stabilization of the government, and the liberalization of trade and the economy particularly after the end of the dictatorial regime by Ferdinand Marcos. This transformation is seen in the emergence of a "new middle class", which is composed of the growing corps of professional managers, administrators, and technical experts (Pinches 1996: 106). This chapter focuses on the middle class that has grown in political and economic presence during the democratization process, which started under the presidency of Corazon Aquino in the late 1980s. It includes particularly middle-class professionals who have attained a level of education equivalent to or higher than a college degree and are licensed professionals such as doctors, nurses, engineers, lawyers, certified public accountants (CPAs), architects, as well as businessmen and corporate managers employed particularly in multinational corporations.

The Filipino diaspora, composed of Overseas Contract Workers (OCWs) working mainly in the Middle East and East Asia and immigrants in Europe, the United States, and Canada, has reached about 9.45 million people as of December 2010 (Commission on Filipino Overseas, n.d.), which represent

10 percent of the Philippines's estimated population of 92.34 million as of May 2010 (Philippine National Statistics Office 2012). A conspicuous feature of today's emigration from the Philippines is a drastic increase in the number of nurses migrating to North America, Europe, and the Middle East, following the rise in demand for health-related workers in those parts of the world. Although the exodus of Filipino health professionals, such as doctors and nurses, particularly to the United States, has been a phenomenon since the mid-1960s (cf. Choy 2003), the current migration presents an interesting trend in that middle-class professionals such as engineers, CPAs, architects, teachers, corporate managers, and doctors are shifting careers and trying to secure nursing licenses for the expediency of working and migrating abroad. Thus, for these Filipino middle-class professionals, a nursing license is akin to a "second passport" to help facilitate their immigration.

Statistics released by the Philippine Overseas Employment Authority (2008) indicate more or less 5,000 to 10,000 nursing professionals who left the country annually to work abroad during the period from 1994 to 2006. The total number of Filipino nurses working abroad during those twelve years was over 102,000. Their destinations covered the Middle East, East Asia (such as Singapore), and the United States and Europe (particularly the United Kingdom). The main destination in the Middle East is Saudi Arabia, which accepts about 5,000 Filipino nurses every year (Philippine Overseas Employment Association 2008). While the United States accepted 2,833 nurses in 1994 and 3,690 nurses in 1995, the number decreased drastically to only 5 in 1998. But the number increased again to 3,853 in 2005. In the same way, the United Kingdom has been receiving none or only a few nurses during the 1990s, but it employed 5,383 nurses in 2001. Thus, it can be inferred that the employment of nurses abroad fluctuates markedly in accordance with the demand for health professionals or the immigration policy in host countries.

It is worth emphasizing that middle-class professionals who have retrained to secure nursing licenses already possess non-nursing college degrees and oftentimes have government licenses to practice their own professions. To meet this need for retooling, many nursing schools have started to offer a special curriculum aimed specifically at middle-class professionals, enabling the completion of the course in a period shorter than that of the normal nursing curriculum. Table 8.1 indicates the number of enrolees in major nursing schools and colleges in Metro Manila that offer this special curriculum for so-called "second coursers".

Unmistakably the number of enrolees in those schools has increased drastically in the few years of early 2000s. Furthermore, interviews with university registrar's offices confirmed that enrolees in the second-coursers curriculum were already college-degree holders and many of them had been working as middle-class professionals such as doctors, engineers, certified public accountants, architects, corporate managers, and self-employed businessmen. This chapter focuses on this type of middle-class professionals as an exemplary case of middle-class adaptation strategy to transnational social fields and their identity emerging from such practice.[2]

Table 8.1 Transition in the Number of Enrolees in Major Metro Manila Nursing Schools Offering a Curriculum for "Second Courser", during the early 2000s

	School A (Manila)	School B (Manila)	School C (Manila)	School D (Valenzuela)	School E (Caloocan)	School F (Quezon City)
AY2000	103	—	138	n.a.	41	170
AY2001	258	—	201	1,766	72	603
AY2002	886	—	970	1,728	153	1,225
AY2003	2,133	427*	1,214	2,135	426	2,316
AY2004	3,447	744	1,465	2,978	577	3,753
AY2005	4,728	895	1,612	3,128	772	4,446

Source: Interview with the University Registrar's Office of the respective schools.

* Initial batch.

The Middle-Class Identity and Its Ambivalence

The narratives of middle-class professionals regarding their motivation and plans for migration highlight middle-class identity and its ambivalence. This identity is constructed through practices of boundary making between members of the middle class and other social classes, namely the upper elite class and the labouring class. Such practices are observed in their narratives of distinction and differentiation from other social classes and, furthermore, from their country itself. Also shown in the narratives presented below (Cases 8.1–8.9) is ambivalence characterizing their identity. The middle class harbours a double-sided sentiment: while desiring to immigrate to a developed country to attain more wealth and a better lifestyle than in the Philippines, at the same time members of the middle class are hesitant to leave the country.

Case 8.1: "This country is going nowhere" (Walang patutunguhan ang bansang ito) (Interview on September 2, 2005)

Born in 1970, Alma Cruz is a doctor of medicine. She passed the medical board examinations in 1995, and is currently working as a dermatologist in several clinics in Metro Manila. In 2002, she enrolled in a nursing school for a two-and-a-half-year course. The tuition fee for the nursing school, quite steep at P120,000 for the entire course, was shouldered by her husband, a well-known veterinarian in the Veterinary Inspection Section of the City Hall of Manila. Since then, Alma has been steadily preparing for her immigration to the US. After graduating from nursing school, Alma took and passed the nursing board examinations in June 2004. In November of the same year, she passed the examination given by the Commission on Graduates of Foreign Nursing School (CGFNS), which is necessary for working in medical institutions in the United States. She applied for a working visa to the United States in March 2005, and at the time of the interview had been waiting for the visa, hoping to receive it by the end of 2006.

Regarding the motivation behind her endeavour to be a nurse and to migrate to the United States, she says, "It is for my child". She has a daughter who is four years old, and she says,

> I want her to have an option as to where she would like to stay, to experience the best of both countries. There is a difference between the social welfare and system of benefits that you can avail of in the Philippines and the United States. I want my daughter to be able to avail of the best benefits from both countries.

Furthermore, Alma emphasises that her reason for migration is not a financial one. Her income combined with that of her husband, who is well known in his field, is sufficient for a comfortable life in Metro Manila. Rather, Alma explains that the true motivation lies in her anxiety about living in the Philippines, where the political situation seems to be quite unstable and lacking direction. She expresses her feeling by saying that "Nothing can be changed by People Power. Nothing can be gained by People Power (*Wala namang nakukuha sa People Power*)".

In the Philippines, the memory of the "People Power Revolution" in 1986, which toppled the Marcos dictatorship, has been called upon repeatedly in times of political turmoil, which have been caused primarily by the perceived corruption of politicians in government positions. To many Filipinos, it seems to have provided a framework where street demonstrations and civic movements are regarded as the most effective means of fighting against a corrupt incumbent government. Particularly in January 2001, then-President Joseph Estrada, who had been accused of graft, was ousted from the presidency by tens of thousands of people who protested in the streets of Metro Manila, an event that came to be called "People Power 2". Nevertheless, the political unrest remained unabated and street protests in varying scales continued despite the extraconstitutional ascent of Gloria Arroyo, then vice president, to the presidency. Alma indicates her disappointment with the political instability brought about by "People Power", saying, "This country is going nowhere" (*Walang patutunguhan ang bansang ito*).

Such anxiety and disappointment coexist with a somewhat critical gaze towards the masses, the lower class known colloquially as the *masa*, who are often present at street demonstrations. Alma, for instance, says that "The masses are very spoiled. If you ask them, they respond that they are pitiful" (*Masyadong i-spoiled ang masa, if you ask the masa, sila ang kawawa*). At the time of the interview in September 2005, street protests clamouring for the resignation of President Arroyo, who had been accused of cheating in the 2004 presidential election that gave her a full presidential term, were frequently held in the streets of Metro Manila. The masses were the main component of the crowd protesting in the streets, and they sometimes clashed violently with the police. Alma's comment reproaches the masses whose street demonstrations are perceived to be disorderly, with the *masa* demanding violently for what they want. According to her, the masses are so spoiled that they think anything can be provided to them as their due right, as the price for their "miserable situation". Alma's comment expresses a strong rebuke for the self-pity of the poor.

Yet, while expressing her feeling of deep frustration with the political situation in the Philippines and her desire to immigrate to the United States, Alma explains that immigration for her is nothing but a "fallback option". In other words, it is a security or safety net for her and her family should the country's situation is getting worse. To migrate is neither an urgent need nor a dire necessity that for her would require an immediate decision; rather, it is one of the options she merely wants to secure. This is because, Alma concludes, "To leave your own country is not an easy thing to do.

There might be severe discrimination in the United States. My brain is enticed by the United States, but my heart remains here" (*Malapit ang utak sa States, pero ang puso nandito*).

Case 8.2: "It is of course hard to leave everything you have achieved in the Philippines" (Interview on February 24, 2005)

Born in 1969, Vilma de los Reyes graduated from the law school of the University of the Philippines. As a lawyer, she has been working as a senior manager in a multinational pharmaceutical company in Metro Manila for several years now. Despite having an economically remunerative job and a financially stable life, she is planning to immigrate to Canada with her husband and three children. They also intend to transfer to the United States after they secure Canadian citizenship.

She narrates her motivation for migration as different from that of OCWs:

> OCWs go abroad in order to acquire status symbols such as a sturdy house (*bahay na bato*), an owner jeep, and a *sari-sari* (variety) store in the Philippines. But we, the middle class, can only achieve our desired lifestyle and quality of life abroad. This is quite a sad situation that the middle-class people have in the Philippines. Such feeling can never be understood by the Japanese like you.
>
> ...
>
> The middle class people migrate abroad because we have capability, competence, and resources that can be utilized in foreign countries. Through migrating, we avoid competing with the lower class people who only have limited resources, and leave much local opportunities to them.

However, she adds, expressing her anxiety about migrating, "It is of course hard to leave everything you have achieved in the Philippines, and start from scratch".

Case 8.3: "I started to be quite anxious about a society" (Interview on August 17, 2005)

Born in 1969, John Devara is an electronics and communications engineer, and is currently working in a research institution in Metro Manila. Although he has harboured an intention to migrate since around 2001, he was hesitant to leave in the beginning because he was not sure if he could find a steady job abroad such as the one he now has in the Philippines. Yet, according to John, the positive aspect of migration has overwhelmed the negative aspect, given the fact that he has increasingly felt the corruption and instability of the government under the Estrada administration.

John's wife, May, majored in fine arts at the University of Santo Tomas and is now working as an interior designer. May narrates that her anxiety about staying in the Philippines began in 1998, when Estrada announced his candidacy for president. She explains her feeling,

> I started to be quite anxious about a society in which the politician who doesn't have capacity for governance can be elected as a leader through

mobilization of the masses; and in effect, the masses who have been mobilized in that way actually had the final say regarding which direction the country will be heading.

The statement above expresses the feeling of helplessness entertained by the middle class in view of their realization that the direction of the country will not be decided by them but by someone else, in particular the *masa*, who can bring bulk votes to politicians who, in the opinion of the middle class, are populists and quite often corrupt. This observation is also reflected in the following two cases.

Case 8.4: *"You have to secure the option to come back home anytime"* (*Interview on August 21, 2005*)

Peter Ocampo, like Alma in Case 8.1, is also a doctor of medicine. Peter, about 40 years old at the time of the interview, is an ophthalmologist who passed the medical board examinations in the early 1990s. While working as a doctor in several hospitals in Metro Manila, he enrolled in and completed his nursing education and then secured a nursing license. His wife, Maria, born in 1969, graduated from the University of the Philippines, College of Business Administration, and has worked as a senior manager in several multinational corporations.

Mr. and Mrs. Ocampo are hoping to migrate to the United States, and they explain their motive for migration by saying, "We want our kids to spend their lives in a First World country". Peter and Maria have two children, a 12-year-old boy and a 7-year-old girl, who are both studying in "exclusive schools" in Metro Manila.[3] Maria cannot help but feel anxious about the future of her children. According to her,

> In order to spend a comfortable life in the Philippines, you must at least find a job in a multinational corporation. You also need to study in the University of the Philippines, or Ateneo de Manila, or De la Salle University, and you have to graduate with outstanding grades.[4] Yet, today, even if you have graduated from those schools, you sometimes end up working in a call center.

Maria's anxiety regarding the future of their children is associated with the political situation in the Philippines. Maria narrates:

> When President Marcos was ousted in February 1986, I had high hopes that the new political system and nation building would begin in the Aquino administration. I was thinking that the Philippines will soon join the progressive countries. But the current situation is worse than the dictatorship of Marcos.

She started to think seriously about migrating, particularly after Estrada became president in 1998. Maria says, "Although the Arroyo administration is also criticised for corruption and injustices, Arroyo is the lesser evil". She adds, "Even if President Arroyo is ousted through impeachment or another People Power, there will be no one to replace her. The Philippines will not get anywhere" (*Walang patutunguhan ang Pilipinas*).

While expressing feelings of disappointment with the country, which they share with Alma in Case 8.1, and their desire to migrate to the Unites States, the Ocampos say that definitely "you have to secure the option to come back home anytime". Particularly for Peter who can practice ophthalmology in the Philippines anytime, it is crucially important to "have several options" for which purpose he points out, "Don't burn your bridges".

Case 8.5: "Nothing can be fundamentally changed by People Power" (Interview on August 20, 2005)

Born in 1963, Fe Padilla is a certified public accountant who has been working in one of the major Philippine banks and multinational companies. Among her prospective destinations for migration are Canada, the United States, and Australia. The reason behind her desire to migrate is to prepare a better environment for her 10-year-old daughter. It seems that Fe does not want her daughter to grow up in the Philippines where the political situation is so unstable. According to her,

> The Filipinos are never satisfied with the person whom they voted for. When the people are not satisfied with the leaders they elected, they simply want to kick them out by People Power. But nothing can be fundamentally changed by People Power, regardless of how many times people repeat it. Corruption will never be gone. GMA [President Gloria Macapagal-Arroyo] should resign, but even though Noli [Vice-President Noli de Castro] takes over, he will be ousted again by the people.

Aside from the feeling of helplessness, the narrative above indicates a cynical view by members of the middle class, who stand aloof from the political events happening in the Philippines. From the cases above, it can be understood that the desire of middle-class professionals for migration and a new lifestyle abroad coexists with a strong feeling of reproach for the lower class, that is, the "masa", or "the people", as well as for the corrupt political elites who are largely seen as belonging to the upper class of society. In other words, migration for the middle-class professionals is seen as a practice of distinction made through differentiating themselves from the other social classes in the country as well as from the country itself. Furthermore, the other feelings entertained by middle-class professionals are anxiety, disappointment, and distrust against the state and the system of government, which can also motivate migration. The following cases (Cases 8.6–8.9) indicate these feelings.

Ruth's family is Chinese-Filipino and runs a family business in the construction industry. She sometimes goes back to her parents' house to help them with their business, but "once I got married and went back home, I felt like I didn't belong there, I didn't feel comfortable". This also made her wish for a space just for her and her daughters, and she began to think about a new life in the US.

Ruth has relatives who have already immigrated to the United States. Two aunts on her father's side already immigrated to the US over 20 years ago and are currently running a nursing home in Pittsburgh. Ruth's older sister came to the United States with the help of her aunt, and while in the United States, she married a Filipino with US citizenship. Currently, she and her husband are running a nursing home in California. This sister strongly recommended Ruth to get a nursing license and paid all the tuition fees for nursing school.

She was also influenced by her husband's relatives. Many of her husband's maternal uncles and aunts were doctors, and one of them, who was an obstetrician and gynaecologist, recommended that she get her nursing license. Another aunt on her husband's side was an experienced nurse who had been working in Pennsylvania for about 20 years. When she temporarily returned to the Philippines in 2004, she offered Ruth, "I will find you a job when you come to the U.S. as a nurse".

Case 8.6: "I am becoming hesitant to pay taxes (Nakakahinayang magbayad ng tax)" (Interview on September 15, 2005)

Corazon Sison is a businesswoman. She was born in 1963 in Leyte Province and studied at the University of the Philippines in Tacloban, the capital of Leyte. After graduating in 1984, she went to Manila and met her husband, who was a graduate of the University of the Philippines, Diliman, majoring in architecture. They married in 1986. Corazon and her husband are now engaged in the manufacture and sale of acrylic plastic products such as key holders, trophies, and signboards, and are expanding their sales outlets in major commercial establishments such as SM Shoemart.

While engaged in running their business, Corazon began to study nursing in 2004. She plans to migrate to the United States after securing her nursing license. Her motivation for migration is similar to the other two cases presented earlier, "to give the children the choice of studying in the United States". Her children, four in all, the eldest of whom is 16 years old while the youngest is 4 years old, are all studying in prestigious private schools such as the Ateneo de Manila. Nevertheless, as a mother, her anxiety about the future of her children remains. According to Corazon, "There are good schools in the Philippines, but the problem is that there are no jobs available after graduation". Further, her anxiety apparently is not only about the lack of employment opportunities or financial issues. She adds, "I don't want my kids to grow up in the Philippines, because the government is so unstable". Corazon's criticism of the government is not merely an expression of fear of its instability but also of a deep distrust in the system. As a person who regularly engages in private business transactions, she is strongly dissatisfied with how the government manages the operation of businesses within its jurisdiction. Corazon points out that the government has no set of consistent and written rules and regulations regarding business operations, and often rules for transactions are merely dependent on instant negotiations with whoever is in charge, who makes on-the-spot decisions. She deplores such situation, saying, "There are so many gray zones here". She feels frustrated that in some situations she has had no choice but to go along with what she believes is a corrupt system. She deplores,

You don't know what the real rules are because they are not clearly written. Under such system, the unscrupulous person who is good at bending the law for his own interest always benefits the most. You cannot survive unless you ride the tide, even though you know well that the system is corrupt. Under this situation, whether you like it or not, you are swallowed up by the system [*Makakain ka ng sistema*].

Furthermore, such cynicism towards the system of government makes her hesitant to observe a basic obligation as a citizen and she says, "I am becoming hesitant to pay taxes" (*Nakakahinayang magbayad ng tax*).

Another motivation for Corazon to move abroad is to expand her current business without any hindrances from the untrustworthy system of the government. After her migration to the United States, she plans to maintain her retail stores in several locations in the Philippines and further expand her sales channels in the United States. She considers her nursing license as part of this transnational business strategy. A similar strategy can be read into the Case 8.7 below too.

Case 8.7: "I will never change the diaper of elderlies in the US" (Interview on September 19, 2005)

Vincent Salazar, a male born in 1964, graduated from the medical technologist course of a private university in Manila in 1984. After graduation, he worked for a major multinational pharmaceutical company for eight years. On the other hand, his wife, a clinical technologist, has been working for the same company as a manager in the human resources department for the past 19 years. Vincent is currently attending nursing school and is considering moving to the United States or Canada in order to expand his current medical transcription business globally.

Since around 2003 in Metro Manila, according to Vincent, there has been a sharp increase in the outsourcing of digital medical transcription from the hospitals and clinics of North America. Since then, Vincent has partnered with major university medical schools and nursing schools in Manila and Cebu City to provide curricula for digital medical transcription, and plans to open an independent school for the digital medical transcription in Quezon City by the end of 2005. After he moves to the United States or Canada, Vincent has plans to expand this digital medical transcription business transnationally. Vincent has several relatives on his wife's side who work as nurses in medical institutions in Canada and the United States and run nursing homes, and he is planning to migrate with his wife by relying on these relatives. Vincent further plans not only to participate in the management of these medical care facilities, but to operate the business of recruitment of nurses in the Philippines, and then send those Filipino nurses to the United States and Canada. After he settles in the United States or Canada, he will outsource the digital medical transcription from the medical facilities in the United States and Canada to his own office in the Philippines. This is the grand plan entertained by Vincent for his transnational healthcare business across the pacific and nursing license that he currently pursues is just a part of such plan. He says, "Even if I get certified as a nurse and immigrate to the U.S., I will never actually work as a nurse there. I will never change the diaper of elderlies in the US. The nursing license is just a passport". Succeeding two cases (Case 8.8 and 8.9) indicate the significance of a nursing license which would provide them with a sense of "insurance" and "security" for the middle class who are faced with the unpredictable system of the country.

Case 8.8: "Here, we are not ruled by the law, but by the people" (Interview on September 19, 2005)

Diana Yu, born in 1961, is a dentist who practices in her own clinic as well as in other clinics in Metro Manila. She studied her nursing course from 2004 to 2006, and is now preparing to migrate to the United States as a nurse. One of her motivations behind migration is the "corruption in the government", which she encounters in everyday transactions in government offices. For example, she narrates,

> Once, at the city hall, I applied for a business permit and was asked by an assessor to pay P5,000. But I was asked to pay only the minimum amount of P600 in the following year even though I submitted the same documents and no conditions of my business had been changed since the previous year. You don't know who is right and who is wrong, everyone has their own rule (*Hindi mo alam kung sino ang tama, kanya-kanya ang ruling*). When the city mayor is replaced and, accordingly, his underlings in the government office are also replaced, the rules change as well. Here, we are not ruled by the law, but by the people.

Further, the nursing license for Diana is an "insurance" against the deteriorating peace and order situation in the Philippines. As a Chinese Filipino, she is fearful of the increasing kidnap-for-ransom incidents victimising wealthy Chinese Filipinos in Metro Manila. Under such a situation, the nursing license and the option to migrate abroad provide her a "security" or "insurance" in case the peace and order situation of the country turns for the worse.

Case 8.9: "We have no choice but to be swallowed by the system (makakain ka ng sistema)" (interviewed on September 19, 2005)

Manuel Tan (male, born in 1965) is from Naga City, the capital of Camarines Sur Province in the southern part of Luzon, and has been working in Naga as an underwriter for one of the country's largest insurance companies since 1987 after graduating from a university in Legazpi City in 1985. On the other hand, his wife is a certified public accountant who also lives in Naga City. However, his wife does not like the relationship with the local officials of the Internal Revenue Office and tries not to work as an accountant. The reason is that "bribes are necessary to facilitate negotiations with local government officials. We have no choice but to be swallowed by the system even if we don't like it (*makakain ka ng sistema*)". Initially, his wife wanted to get a nursing license and move abroad, but he thought it would be difficult due to her age, so he and his wife discussed it and decided that only Manuel would enter nursing school.

Manuel graduated from nursing school in 2005, and is currently attending a preparatory school in Manila to prepare for the board exam. The couple hopes to move to the United States after Manuel gets his nursing license. The main motivation for moving to the United States is the security after retirement and old age. Manuel said, "In the Philippines, no matter how much you work, when you get old, you have nothing left. In the U.S., even if 30% of your salary would be withheld, after you retire at 60, you get benefits that you can't get in the Philippines", he continues, "in the Philippines, once you get a serious illness, your savings will be wiped out, but in the U.S., you don't have to worry about that because of the well-developed health insurance system". Finally Manuel said "it is quite worrisome that good doctors are leaving the Philippines altogether".

What kind of identities of the Filipino middle class living in the transnational social field can be read from the cases presented so far? What are the characteristics of the transnational social field highlighted by their practices of identity construction? I would like to discuss these points below.

Discussion

Some similarities indicative of middle-class identity can be gleaned from the cases presented above. The sentiment common to middle-class professionals who desire to leave the country is expressed, for example, in the despondent phrase, "This country is going nowhere" (*Walang patutunguhan ang bansang ito*). The implication of this phrase, mentioned by several informants, can be properly considered by locating it first in the specific circumstance prevailing at the time of the interviews. It is a criticism against the governance of then-incumbent President Arroyo as well as that of deposed President Estrada. Estrada, who used *Erap Para sa Mahirap* (Erap for the Poor) as a campaign slogan, overwhelmingly won the presidency in 1998 owing to the huge support garnered from the lower class (Picture 8.1). His administration, according to informants, had continued the populist policy of dole-out without any clear and long-range plan.

In 2001, Estrada was ousted by street demonstrations that involved numerous middle-class people, his then Vice-President Arroyo subsequently assuming the presidency. She went on sitting as president by winning the 2004 presidential elections. However, the Philippines has remained in a political stalemate and chaos caused by political scandals and the alleged fraud committed by Arroyo in the 2004 elections, prompting opposition politicians to demand her impeachment and instigating civil groups to plan and stage yet another "People Power" to kick her out of office (Picture 8.2). It is in this situation that middle-class professionals expressed disappointment and distrust towards the drifting state, as seen in the cases presented above. Most of the informants actually joined the two People Power events of 1986 and 2001 in order to express their political will. Their disappointment has been further deepened by the sense that unscrupulous politicians and the corrupt system of government have stolen the fruits attained by the two People Power events.

Similarly, the frequent mention of the phrase by many informants, "You are swallowed up by the system" (*Makakain ka ng sistema*), indicates a deep-seated distrust of the system of government as a compelling reason behind the

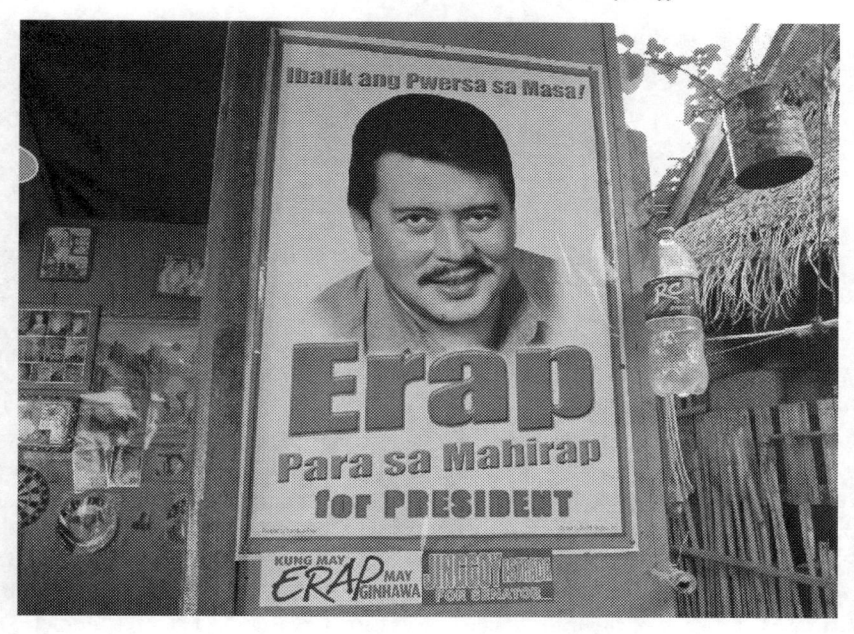

Picture 8.1 Poster of Joseph Estrada for the presidential election campaign. It says recover power to the poor

Picture 8.2 Crowd demanding the resignation of then-President Arroyo (February 2008)

middle-class professionals' desire to emigrate. Such distrust is connected to the dissatisfaction that the taxes they pay are not properly compensated for. As one informant reasons,

> We cannot decline to pay the taxes because it is withdrawn automatically from our salary. The masa are not paying the taxes. But the masses can have what they want realized through their votes in elections owing to their huge numbers. While we, who are paying taxes, cannot choose the leader of the country; the masses, who are not paying taxes, have the power to elect their chosen leader.

Thus, on the one hand, the middle-class professionals hold a deep-seated distrust towards upper-class political elites and the system of government implemented by those elites. On the other hand, their reproach for the lower-class poor, the masa, is just as entrenched. As shown in the informants' narratives, such rebuke is directed particularly towards the poor people's seemingly relentless demand for pity and compassion for their miserable situation from the populist-styled politicians. This critical gaze indicates that the middle-class professionals are trying to define who they are in contrast to the poor (Schaffer 2005: 20). Such narratives and gaze of the middle-class professionals can be considered a practice of boundary making, which lies at the basis of their identity. As Schaffer (2005: 21) points out in a similar situation in Metro Manila, such practice serves "to remind middle class … of who they are and how they are different from—and morally or politically superior to—the poor". The middle class's distrust and disdain towards both upper and lower classes have led to their disappointment and frustration with the country and its future direction. Under this situation, migration is an opportunity for the middle class to leave behind such disappointment and resignation, and to seek an alternative lifestyle abroad hoping for an improvement of one's career, a good quality of social security and welfare, and better education for their children.

Yet, while migration for middle-class professionals enables them to distinguish themselves from other social classes, the informants display *a conspicuous hesitance* to leave the country. Compared with the flexible and fluid mobility of "multiple-passport holders" and "astronaut" Chinese professionals discussed by Ong (1999), the Filipino middle-class professionals examined here stand out for their indecision, despite all compelling reasons, to leave the Philippines. As told by Alma of Case 8.1, for the many informants of this study, to immigrate to the United States and other foreign countries is a mere "fallback option" or "insurance" in case the political economic situation in the Philippines turns for the worse. While securing the option to leave the country, and at the same time desiring to leave, the middle-class professionals in this study opt to actually remain and stay where they are, thereby containing their disappointment and resignation. Such ambivalence is clearly expressed by Alma of Case 8.1, "My brain is enticed by the United States, but my heart remains here" (*Malapit ang utak sa States, pero ang puso nandito*), and also by Vilma of Case 8.2, "it is of course hard to leave everything you have achieved in the Philippines, and start from scratch".

Another informant, a doctor who specialised as an anesthesiologist and who is now a nurse in the United States, narrates,

> There are many doctors who turned to nursing like me but who are still hesitant to leave the country. This is because it is difficult for them to give up all the comforts they have in the Philippines. In the Philippines, you can depend on many persons to help you such as a *yaya* (dry-nurse), a helper, and extended family. Those doctors will finally leave the country only when the situation of the country worsens. If not, they will remain here.

In addition, the motivation for overseas migration was cited by many informants as "for the sake of the children", especially for the sake of their education. Many parents with such motivations express the desire to return to the Philippines once their children have finished school, found jobs, and are conveniently settled abroad. Overseas migration is a means of providing options for their children, and is not intended to sever the physical and emotional ties between themselves and the Philippines. In other words, the adaptation strategies of the middle-class professionals in the transnational social field are summed up in Peter's words in Case 8.4: "don't burn your bridges". Particularly, as seen especially in Cases 8.6 and 8.7, middle-class professionals who attempt to further expand their business by migrating abroad aim to secure multiple business options in the transnational space, including the Philippines. For them, ties to the Philippines have become an indispensable resource for them to maintain and expand their businesses. Just as migration abroad is a "backup option" for many informants, for middle-class professionals trying to do business abroad, ties to the Philippines are such a "backup" or a "bridge" that they have to maintain.

This strategy of middle-class professionals to leave multiple options open without "burning their bridges" can be attributed precisely to their position of being in the middle. As Bourdieu pointed out "the anxious pretension" of the promoted petite bourgeoisie in France (Bourdieu 1984), today's Filipino middle class professionals are incessantly urged on promoting themselves in the face of uncertainty about when they will fall. It is precisely this "fear of falling" (Ehrenreich 1990) that is implicit in their anxious practices of differentiation and distinction. This "fear of falling" is also related to the increased fluidity of social class relations brought about by the recent transnational migration from the Philippines. Such fluid mobility between the social classes would result in the blurring of their boundaries. The increasingly blurred boundary between the middle and lower classes further encourages the members of the middle class to construct a symbolic boundary between themselves and other social classes through the practice of distinction and differentiation in order to maintain their "middle" position.

For example, in Vilma's narrative of Case 8.2, where she sees migration for the temporary contract labour as an act of acquiring goods that provide short-term security, such as a "concrete house" a "private jeep", and a "small grocery store", and counter-poses her own migration as something different, we can see an aspect of symbolic boundary construction between hierarchies of social classes. While attempting to differentiate and make distinction through migration, however, the "fear of falling" that they entertain owing to their position as being in the middle is reflected in their practices of securing the multiple "backup options" in the transnational social field.

The identity and subjectivity forged under contemporary neoliberal governmentality are characterised by instability, fragmentation, individualization, and social fluidity (Harvey 2005; Crompton 2008). Under such conditions, class identities, or consciousness, emerge not from a sense of collective belonging but from a process of differentiation from others (Crompton 2008: 92). The transnational migration of Filipino middle-class professionals examined in this chapter suggested the "individualized identities, generated by a continuous process of comparison 'up' and 'down'" (Crompton 2008: 92). The cases in this chapter reveal that the middle-class professionals' migration is motivated by a highly individualistic upward mobility and orientation for security. Their migration as an attempt to enhance their marketability and employability in the highly competitive transnational market accelerates the further polarization, fragmentation, and individualization, rather than the mutuality, cohesion, and solidarity in the transnational social field. The question that should be asked now is where we can find the alternative public sphere for the possible mutuality, connectedness, and solidarity spreading beyond the difference of social classes? Before this question will be dealt with in Chapter 10, the next chapter will discuss what had happened to the children who were brought to the United States together with the parents such as those presented in this chapter.

Notes

1. A part of this chapter is reprinted in a revised form from *Philippine Studies* Vol.60.2 (2012): 187–222, by permission of the Ateneo de Manila University.
2. The data is based on interviews conducted in Metro Manila in August and September 2005. The informants were selected mainly from the enrolees of two schools, one a nursing college in Quezon City and the other a review school in Manila for nursing board examinations. The basic questionnaire sheets were distributed in two classes (107 attendants in total) of the school in Quezon City, and also in one class (156 attendants in total) of the review school in Manila, where basic information such as personal profile and intention for overseas migration were provided. 45 informants were further selected according to their type of occupations, age, and sex and so on, for the purpose of the interview. The names of all informants in this text are pseudonyms. Thus, the "ethnographic present" of this chapter is the mid-2000s. Today, more than a decade later, we can assume that there have been some changes in the trends of overseas migration of middle-class professionals. However, I believe that the basic argument of this chapter regarding their identity reflected in their practices of migration is still valid today. As for the migration of Filipino nurses in recent times and overseas employment in the hotel and resort management (HRM) sector as a more current trend of the middle-class migration, see Ortiga (2018).

3. An exclusive school in the Philippines has the literal meaning of exclusivity in terms of gender, that is, "exclusive for boys" or "exclusive for girls", but it is a common conception among Filipinos that such exclusivity also, in a financial sense, pertains to the upper and middle classes of the enrolees whose families are able and willing to pay more for a perceived better education.
4. The three schools mentioned here are considered the three most prestigious universities in the Philippines which have produced elites in various areas such as in politics, business and economics, bureaucracy, and academic fields.

9 "The Family" in Contestation
Identity Construction of 1.5-Generation Filipino Children in the United States

As discussed in the previous chapter, most middle-class professionals mentioned that their migration abroad was motivated "for the sake of their children". The reasons behind vary: permanent political instability, poor security, deteriorating quality of education in public schools, lack of good jobs even after graduation from one of the most prestigious universities in the country, and so on. They want to leave the Philippines and go abroad to give their children a better education and a better job. Such a desire was the basis of their practice of distinction and differentiation. However, the situation of children who are brought abroad at an early age due to such desires of their parents does not always turn out the way the parents wanted. Rather, the experience of being abruptly separated from their peaceful childhood environment, without any consideration of their own feelings, causes various inner conflicts in the children.

This chapter will examine the identities of such border-crossing children.[1] In particular, I would like to discuss the meaning of the "family" represented by those children as something lying at the core of their identity as "Filipino" even being faced with marginalisation and exclusion in the host country, and even having conflicts and disputes with their parents. In the first section, I will briefly discuss the significance of examining children's migration and their representations of the "family", and then explain the feature of the children covered in this chapter. The second section examines the experiences of grief, anger, and acceptance felt by children who are suddenly separated from their childhood environment. While children come to accept and understand their parents' decision to migrate over time, they also continue to have various conflicts with, and grudge toward, their parents in their daily lives in the host country, as will be discussed in the third section. This chapter argues that, in the midst of the marginalisation and exclusion they experience in their new environment, "family" is mentioned as a place to base their own identity. In other words, while the real family contains various conflicts and frictions, it will become clear that its representation is mobilised as a symbolic resource to counter the marginalisation and exclusion experienced in the transnational social field.

DOI: 10.4324/9781003224273-12

Migration of Children and Representation of the "Family"

As one of the major destinations of migration from the Philippines, the Filipino communities in the United States have so far attracted extensive interests of migration studies (Choy 2003; Espiritu 2003; Guevarra 2010; Rodriguez 2010). Among them, recent literature focuses on the sometimes neglected but important actor of migration, that is, the children of immigrants (Espiritu & Wolf 2001; Portes & Rumbaut 2001; Wolf 1997, 2002). These studies on children of immigrants thus far, however, have been mainly focused on either the "children left behind", who were separated from their migrant parents, or the second-generation children who were born and raised in the host country. Set in this context, this chapter focuses on the 1.5-generation youth who were brought to the host country by their parents during their childhood, and often continue to shuttle between the host and origin countries even after their migration. In this way, they are made to go through their socialisation and identification both in the host and the origin countries. Hence, the more complex process of identity construction within the contemporary transnational social field can be readily understood by focusing on the 1.5 generation.

Although there is still no clear definition of 1.5-generation immigrants shared among the scholars, Danico, who has studied the 1.5 generation of Koreans in the United States, describes them as "those who are bicultural and bilingual and who immigrated to the United States during their formative years. They are socialized in both Korean and American cultures and consequently express both sets of cultural values and beliefs" (Danico 2004: 2). Thus, a distinctive feature of the experience of the 1.5-generation children is that they have had to go through dual socialisation and identity formation both in their home country and in the host country. Attention to their experiences will highlight the ambivalence and difficulty of having ties to both the country of origin and host, but not being able to achieve full belonging in both. Such children's subjective experiences of border crossing will reveal the subject formation and identity construction while carefully paying attention to the subtle differences and nuances derived from the power relationship inherent in the contemporary transnational social field.

As has been mentioned in the prologue to Part III, the transnational social field, according to Levitt and Glick Schiller (2004: 1009), can be defined as "a set of multiple interlocking networks of social relationships through which ideas, practices, and resources are *unequally* [italics added] exchanged, organized, and transformed" in the process of incessant circulation of goods, cash, information, and people across the borders of nation-states. Further, such a field is constituted by social relationships structured by power and "created by the participants who are joined in struggle for social position" (Levitt & Glick Schiller 2004: 1008). Thus, a transnational social field cannot be considered as a homogeneous social field that accommodates the smooth and unidirectional assimilation of immigrants into the host society; on the contrary, it is a highly differentiated field constituted by asymmetrical power relations among the people. Hence, an ethnographic approach to the specific ways in which the transnational social field is structured by power, and how the identity and subjectivity are formed within such field, is indispensable to scrutinising the contemporary aspects of globalisation.

In order to examine the identities of migrant children as they are constructed in the transnational social field explained above, this chapter focuses on the representation of the "family" among them. The importance of the idea of family among the Filipino immigrants has been already pointed out in previous studies. Wolf (2002: 261), for example, studied on the Filipino second-generation youth in California, and found that "when asked what it means to them to be Filipino, [...] the most common response was a strong, spontaneous, and emotional statement about family as the centre of what it means to be Filipino". An interesting point in her argument, however, is that "although families create the ties that bind and bond, they can also be sites of intense conflict and contradiction, especially among immigrants" (Wolf 2002: 285). The second-generation Filipino children, according to the study, face intense pressure from their parents, who have mostly immigrated to the United States as middle-class professionals, to maintain good academic scores and attain upper-middle class status jobs after their graduation. Wolf's study concludes that such pressure from the parents quite often results in serious psychological depression in the children, which sometimes leads further to suicidal thoughts or attempts among the second-generation youth.

While appreciating the insight made by Wolf, this chapter maintains that the study of the identity of immigrants' children should be more sensitive to the nuanced differentiation recognised by the immigrants themselves. Particularly, as will be mentioned later, the second-generation Filipino immigrants and the 1.5-generation explicitly differentiate themselves by calling each other "Fil-Am" for the second generation and "Fil-born" for the 1.5 generation. Hence, it is important to focus on the identity of the 1.5-generation children, which emerges contradistinctively with that of the second generation. A "sense of family" as the centre of what it means to be Filipino, for example, is recognised quite differently by the 1.5 generation from the second generation. As indicated in the narratives in this study, it should rather be considered a contested notion that is mobilised into the representation of the 1.5 generation's identity. In this chapter, I will use the term "family" in parentheses to refer to the family as a representation presented to others that does not necessarily reflect the reality of the family. For children in this chapter, "family" does not necessarily mean the nuclear family nor blood relations, but rather a group of close relatives such as grandparents, grandfathers, mothers, cousins, and sometimes non-relative nannies and neighbours who have raised, and cared for, them for many years in the Philippines and also in the United States. It is argued that the focus on the identity of the 1.5-generation children brings into sharp relief the difference and power relation among the immigrants in the United States, an aspect of which is indispensable to understanding the contemporary dynamism of the transnational social field.

Profiles of the 1.5-Generation Migrants

Here, I would like to briefly touch on the feature of the 1.5-generation migrants that will be examined below, especially the social class background of their parents. Many of the parents of the children interviewed immigrated to the United States in the late 1990s to mid-2000s. Many of them worked in the Philippines as government employees, engineers, clerks, self-employed businesses, teachers, and other middle-class jobs. As mentioned in the previous chapter, this period saw the emergence of a serious political and economic crisis and social unrest in the Philippines under the administrations of former Presidents Estrada (1998–2001) and Arroyo (2001–2010). Against the backdrop of domestic chaos and the resulting increased distrust of government and society, and in response to the surging demand for nurses and caregivers in the United States and other Western countries during this period, many middle-class Filipinos migrated to these Western countries. The 1.5 generation of immigrants covered in this chapter are children who were brought to the United States by such middle-class parents. Therefore, while the following data are not about the actual children of the middle-class parents examined in Chapter 8, it is safe to assume that the parents of the children dealt with in this chapter share their socioeconomic background and motivation of migration with the middle-class professionals discussed in the previous chapter.

Interviews with the 1.5-generation children were conducted in some colleges and universities located near Daly City in the northern San Mateo County, adjacent to the City of San Francisco, California. The ethnic composition of Daly City is characterised by the large number of Asian immigrants: of the 101,123 residents as of 2010, 23.6% were white, 3.6% were black, and 23.7% were Hispanic. Of the total population, 55.6% is Asian, of which 15.4% is Chinese and 33.3% is Filipino (City of Daly City 2013). What makes Daly City, often called "the adobo capital of the U.S.A.",[2] distinctive in terms of the Filipino immigrants is that, while other cities and counties have a higher Filipino population in total such as Los Angeles County in California (300,000), San Diego County (130,000), and Honolulu County in Hawaii (130,000), in terms of the ratio of Filipino immigrants to the total population of the County, Daly City is notably higher than any other County in the United States (Vergara 2009: 22–23).[3] Further, Daly City is characterised by a high ratio of the first and the 1.5-generation immigrants to the American-born second-generation immigrants (Vergara 2009: 23–24).

Daly City is located approximately 13 km south of downtown San Francisco, and approximately 50% of all workers are employed within San Francisco (City of Daly City 2013). On the other hand, major employers in the Daly City area include Seton Medical Center, a general hospital located in the centre of the city, Jefferson School District, City Hall, and Serramont Shopping Center

(City of Daly City 2013). Thus, Daly City can be described as a residential suburb of a large city with middle-class residents engaged in service industries such as healthcare, education, and retail (Pictures 9.1 and 9.2). Many Filipino immigrants work as nurses, care givers, and medical professionals, as described below. On the other hand, not a few immigrants are embedded in the lower strata of the service sector. For example, in the ethnography of Filipino immigrants in Daly City, Vergara argues that many white-collar workers who completed their college education in the Philippines are not given opportunities to use their qualifications and abilities after immigrating to the United States, and are forced to work as janitors in schools and businesses, security guards at airports, cashiers at shopping malls, and warehouse handlers (Vergara 2009: 55–60).

The immigration of the Filipinos into Daly City began in the 1970s, particularly because Seton Medical Center located at the centre of the city became a major employer of foreign-trained nurses. Eventually, the Filipino population in the city nearly doubled between 1980 and 1990 (Vergara 2009: 25). Today, more than 70% of the Filipinos in Daly City are Philippine-born immigrants. Thus, it is expected that everyday close interaction between each generation can be observed in Daly City, and this is the reason why Daly City was chosen as the site of this research.

Picture 9.1 Houses in Daly City

Picture 9.2 Daly City in the distance. The matchbox-like houses lined up side by side can be described as a typical American middle-class residential area

In this chapter, interviews were conducted for the 1.5 generations immigrants who were enrolling in the colleges and universities in and around Daly City at the time of research. These schools included four-year universities such as San Francisco State University, but many of the children attended two-year community colleges, where they took general education courses with the intention of later transferring to specialised courses at the same community college or to four-year universities. For immigrants who have just arrived in the United States, admission to a four-year university is difficult due to language skills and other academic hurdles, so they often attend community colleges first and then seek a higher education later. This may be the reason why many of the informants in this chapter are community college students (Picture 9.3).

A total of 44 people who belong to the 1.5 generation were interviewed during the fieldwork in March 2010, and March and September 2011.[4] Some interesting features can be gleaned from the demographic and immigration-related information on the interviewees. Firstly, a clear chain migration trend can be found, in which the mother or father of the 1.5-generation children was themselves immigrated to the United States through the petition by his/her parents who had come to the United States after around 1970s mostly as nurses. Secondly, and most significantly related to the discussion of this study, not a

Picture 9.3 A meeting of the Filipino students organisation. A venue for interaction between 1.5 and second generations (City College of San Francisco)

few of the mothers and female siblings of the 1.5 generation interviewed are working as nurses or caregivers, and more than half of the informants themselves are also willing to major in the nursing course after finishing the general education. Thirdly, most parents of the 1.5 generation experienced downward mobility of social class, in which they had to shift their jobs from middle-class white-collar jobs in the Philippines to miscellaneous blue-collar service labour, such as cleaning, janitors, shopping mall clerks, warehousing, airport services, and so on. These features indicate that the 44 interviewees of this study can be properly contextualised into the post-1965 Immigrant Act influx of the Filipino and Asian immigrants, who were mostly middle-class professionals, as explained in the Prologue to this part.

Migration Experiences of 1.5 Generation and Transition of Emotions: Sadness, Anger, and Acceptance

As mentioned earlier, the 1.5-generation migrants of this study experience the transition from enjoying middle-class amenities and comfort with many helping hands from extended family, such as helpers, nannies, and close relatives, in the Philippines into living a working-student lifestyle with their parents engaged in blue-collar labour. Such drastic downward social mobility of the parents often causes deep sadness for the 1.5-generation children. A 21-year-old female student, for example, suddenly shed tears when asked about her parents' jobs in the United States, saying "I cannot help but cry when I see the situation of my mother and father now". Her father used to work as an accountant in a big electric company in Metro Manila, but currently works as a cleaner in a bus company and is having a hard time getting along with his Latino co-workers. Her mother, on the other hand, who used to work in a major pharmaceutical company in Metro Manila, started to work in an outlet mall in the United States, where she was fired after having faced discriminatory treatment. Currently, she is working as a caregiver and also studying for the nursing license board exams. Aside from sadness, the decision made by the parents, as shown in Cases 9.1 and 9.2, sometimes causes "anger" among the 1.5-generation children.

Case 9.1: "I didn't have a choice in what to do with my life" (migration of Melissa)

Melissa, a 21-year-old sophomore student at Stanford University, came to the United States in 2001. Her father used to work in American Express in Cebu City, and her mother ran a restaurant and food catering business also in Cebu. It was during the political turmoil caused by the impeachment and arrest thereafter of former president Estrada when her parents decided to leave the country. At that time, Melissa, then 11 years old, was told by her parents that they were just going to have a vacation in the United States:

> My parents didn't tell us that we would settle here for good. What we were told was we were just going for a vacation and would be back for school in June. We were not told that we would settle here for good until we arrived here. So it was a really big surprise. (...) First I was so excited because I thought it was a vacation. When I got here, it was a different story. That was the day of our arrival. I was told in the car, on the way to the apartment, "We're staying here. We're not going back".
>
> When in Cebu, I had already made what I thought were pretty solid friendships. I thought the people I went to school with and my family friends were gonna be the people that I interacted with my whole life. I was already excited about the prospect of continuing my parent's business or my *lola*'s [grandmother] business, whichever one. I love Cebu, I love living there. I didn't see a need or a reason to move away. My cousins were there, my *titos* [uncles] and *titas* [aunts] who had watched me grow up were there so I wanted to stay and I didn't feel like we needed to move somewhere else.
>
> I thought they were joking at first, but when they told me they were serious, I was really very angry....and I fought with them. I thought that I'd been lied to and betrayed. I thought that I didn't have a choice in what to do with my life. And at the same time I was very sad, because I thought it was a vacation, and I thought I was coming back so I did not get to say a proper goodbye, like to my *lola*, or my friends and cousins.

Case 9.2: "They never included me in that decision" (migration of Jessica)

Jessica, also a student of Stanford University, came to the United States in 2006 at the age of 14. Her father managed a construction company owned by her grandfather, and her mother owned a salon business and sold cosmetics in

Laoag City, Ilocos Norte. Their business experienced a downturn during the economic crisis in the Philippines caused by the political chaos that accompanied the anomalies of the Estrada and Arroyo administrations. Jessica recollects her feeling when she realised that she had to leave the country:

> I felt like they never included me in that decision. So my Mom told me that I was moving there permanently on the day of my birthday, a month before she was gonna come and get me. I was sad of course because I was leaving everything. I really thought they decided for me, [but] they never really asked me.

Jessica narrated, in tears, that her parents had been separated and she felt like she had to leave so much in the Philippines including her father, brother, and friends. She continued, "I was against her decision but I couldn't do anything. So, I thought, 'OK, I'll go, I'll get to spend time with my Mom'".

Years after their migration, however, it appears that the anger and sadness among the 1.5-generation children have turned into understanding and acceptance of their parents' decision. For the toils made and pain experienced by their parents, the children now feel a sense of gratitude. Melissa, for example, explains such transition that has taken place inside of her:

> [Looking back at her parents' decision, she says] Now, I don't think I could be mad at them anymore because I think it was a good decision. I'm here in Stanford, I'm doing pretty well. I've gotten to see, learn and realise things that I don't think I would have [learned] if I had stayed in the Philippines.
>
> Also, a big part of my not being able to be angry at them anymore [happened that time] when we went back [to the Philippines] in 2006. My mom was really worried about me. For all those years, I was harbouring resentment, still having, sometimes, like, fits [and demanding] 'Why did you bring us here? Why are we here? We could have just been in the Philippines!'. So, that 2006 was kind of a "closure" for me. My sister, she didn't have a problem with [leaving], she didn't have a strong connection to living in Cebu as I did. She was younger; she was 7 when we moved.
>
> [She narrates the defining moment for her] When we went back in 2006, I really enjoyed it. I got to do what I used to do [when] I was [still] living there [in Cebu], I also saw some of my friends from school. But at the same time, I didn't feel like I could go back to living there anymore. In 2006, I had just finished my 1ˢᵗ year of high school, and at that point, we were pretty settled in New Jersey already. I had many cousins there, I made friends, and I was going to a really good school. I was starting to see why my parents moved us [to the United States]. I started to understand why they didn't just stay in the Philippines.

Jessica, whose mother left her behind in the Philippines and migrated first in the US, also narrates the change of her feeling towards her mother:

> Now, no more conflicts. Because I see everything that she's done for us, and I respect that. So I follow everything that she feels I need to do. [She interjects, "Why am I so teary-eyed?"] I see how hard the immigration process was for her, and leaving us behind. It was not just how we [would feel once we were] left behind, but [also] how she felt [with the thought of her] leaving us behind.

In this section, we examined the emotions experienced by children who were suddenly separated from the familiar and intimate environment of their childhood, left everything behind in the Philippines, and were forced to adjust to their new home in the United States. Of course, the 1.5 generation children do not uniformly experience a smooth, linear internal transition from anger to acceptance. The fact that Melissa and Jessica are able to view their current situation in a very positive light must be considered with the background that they are in an excellent educational environment at Stanford University. On the other hand, many students presented in the next section, who study at local community colleges and have various problems with their studies and future employment, cannot necessarily affirm the current situation and may continue to have deep sorrow caused by migration. Even for Melissa and Jessica, who view the current situation positively, their feelings towards their parents may change negatively again as their living environment changes in the future.

In any case, the cases in this section reveal that the relationship between the 1.5-generation children and their parents is not harmonious, but rather fluid in nature, based on acceptance and understanding that is always subject to manifest and latent ruptures, fissures, and conflicts, and is nevertheless achieved depending on a certain situation. Having pointed out this fluid nature of family fraught with implicit and explicit conflicts, I will examine in the following section the situation in which the "family" is represented as something being at the core of "us" in the narratives of 1.5-generation identity.

Identity of the 1.5-Generation Migrants: Aspects of Autonomy, Interdependence and Relational Self

In this section, I will examine the situation in which the identities of Filipino 1.5-generation immigrants are constructed in relation to the second generation, which can be regarded as their closest significant others in the host society of the United States. In particular, I will examine how the representation of the "family" becomes manifest in the narratives of various aspects of identity, such as the aspect of *autonomy, interdependence,* and *relational self.* First, it should be noted that the difference between the 1.5- and the second-generation Filipino migrants is often clearly recognised and told by both of these groups. For example, there are specific local terms of address that differentiate the 1.5 generation and second generation in the United States. According to a 17-year-old high school student, for example, "In my school, there are two groups, the 'Fil-Am' and 'Fil-born'. They don't like each other". Further, a 19-year-old male student said:

> From my experience in high school, there is a great divide between the Filipino immigrants and Filipino Americans. They always constantly clash and fight. I've got involved in it. I fought against Filipino Americans. In Union City where I live, there's always a clash and it's been going on for a long time. (...) Those Fil-Ams, they always stereotype us. Make fun of us about our accent. Bully us around. They always nitpick us. For little things,

they make fun of us. Then in response, Filipino immigrants retaliate against them. Definitely, it goes to a physical fight.

Interestingly, such comments by "Fil-born" children coincide with those of the "Fil-Ams". During a focus group discussion with second-generation students, a 22-year-old male stated:

> I have a group of friends who are from the Philippines but they have like their own crew. Immigrants have their own group of Filipino-borns. They won't join our community, because they would feel like they are left out, they are not up to par with us. That's how they think. They have a hard time coming hold of us (…). There is that 'mysterious force' between us that we cannot connect with each other. It's like a never ending battle.

A 20-year-old second-generation female, on the other hand, narrated the gap between them and Fil-born in this way:

> I remember some of Filipino immigrants make fun of Filipino-American and it would be vice-versa, like Filipino-Americans make fun of Filipinos and Filipinos make fun of Filipino-Americans. There is really a barrier between us. I definitely am looked down upon by Filipinos because I don't speak Tagalog. But I understand (Tagalog), which kind of doesn't make me fully underneath of them.

Thus, it can be said that the differences between the 1.5 generation and the second generation, whether implicitly or explicitly, are recognised in their daily interactions. In the following, I would like to focus on how the differences between the two generations, or the differences between the Philippines and the United States, which is perceived through the filter of "Fil-Am", are reflected in the identities of the 1.5 generation.

Aspect of Autonomy and Self-Reliance

In order to discuss an aspect of autonomy and self-reliance in the narrative of the 1.5 generation's identity, it is important to examine how the past life in the Philippines is remembered on one hand, and how the current life in the United States, surrounded by the second generation, on the other hand, is recognised contradistinctively to it. It had been found that the past life in the Philippines is recollected with a feeling of nostalgia, as a loose and freewheeling life where people used to live without any restriction of rule and regulation, or any time constraint. A 21-year-old female who was born and spent her life in Mindanao, the southernmost island of the country, until the age of 15, for example, narrates partially in Cebuano:

> *Dili ko ma-enjoy diri* [I cannot enjoy life here]. *Kana bitaw nga molakaw-lakaw…laag-laag…*[That roaming about for no special purpose]. I cannot

do that here. Here, everything is *"de-schedule"* [as scheduled]. Here everyone is too independent. Even if you are a teenager and want to visit your friends, you cannot visit them without prior appointment. *Kailangan de-schedule ka muna* [you have to make a prior appointment]. Some are at school, or at work... we cannot go around freely like in the Philippines.

In their recollection, it is suggested that their lives and activities were carried out mostly in the space of the "barangay", which is the most basic administrative unit of the Philippines. "Barangay" in the narratives of the 1.5 generation seems to indicate, rather than mere official administrative body, a symbolic space of community where their nostalgic recollections condense. A 20-year-old male student who used to spend his life until the age of 10 in a small town of southern Tagalog region, for example, narrates:

"In the Philippines, everybody knows everybody. Barangay is like family. Whichever house you go to, there is always food given to you. There is no limit to visit each other. You could relax. But here in the US, everyone is so hectic and there's always something going on, you need to do something. You cannot just sit down and relax".

Noticeably, the life in the United States, which is defined contradistinctively with such a nostalgic Philippine life, is not necessarily negative. Rather, the narrative shows that the life in the United States enabled the 1.5 generation to acquire independence and self-reliance, which they may not have attained had they remained in the Philippines. A 23-year-old female student who spent her life in Cainta of Rizal Province until the age of 13 narrates as follows:

During the sophomore years in high school [in the United States], I learned how to work. I learned how to be independent in the US. If in the Philippines, we are helped by *yaya* [nanny], but here you have to do everything by yourself. While I was in San Mateo High School, I started to work in KFC. *Mabilis ako makihalubilo sa* surroundings [I could mingle well in any surroundings]. If I had stayed in the Philippines, I would not have learned to be independent at this early age. I cannot imagine myself to be independent in the Philippines because there are my *titas* [aunts] and *yayas*. It's hard to imagine.

Another male student who is 21 years old and spent his life in Quezon City, says:

(Here in the United States) I don't want to rely on my parents as much. I know that in the Philippine culture, parents always want to give you something. But I don't really want to rely on them as much. Because I know that life here is tough too. Everything is going up... prices... and you are not really getting paid as much. I want to live on my own.

Further, the following long narrative indicates a characteristic feature of inner transformation, particularly a shift from indulgence to self-reliance, which is more or less commonly experienced by the 1.5-generation youth of this study.

Case 9.3: *"My life now is really straight" (migration of Arnold)*

Arnold, a 21-year-old male student, used to spend a wealthy upper-middle class life in the subdivision of Antipolo City but had to move to the United States in 2004 at the age of 16 after his father's business, having been heavily affected by the political turmoil of the Philippines during the early 2000s, went bankrupt. His father lost hope and trust in the government of the Philippines and hence sought for a new opportunity for the family's survival in the United States. Recollecting his indulgent and delinquent days in the Philippines, Arnold narrates how his life in the United States enabled him to nourish a sense of self-reliance and, as a result, "straightened" him out:

> In 2002, my Dad came to the US. Last straw *daw* [he said it was the last straw]. Dad's company incurred a debt of 5 million pesos. He declared bankruptcy. My Mom was crying in front of him asking "What are we gonna do, what are we gonna do", then my Dad, fed up, said "We are gonna get out of this country". He got fed up with doing business in the Philippines and losing money. Nothing is gonna happen in the Philippines, *lagi niyang sinasabi "walang mangyayari sa atin dito* [he always said that nothing is gonna happen here]". I remember my Dad said "there is no future in the Philippines. *Wala nang pagasa sa Pilipinas* [there is no hope in the Philippines]". Then he came to the US. He found a job in a bakery shop. Then we sold our property in Manila, then we came here to San Francisco.
>
> It was really hard because we had to start from scratch. (...) I was still 16 with two young sisters. You know, everything was just so chaotic. We didn't have *katulong* [domestic helper] anymore. I think that was the hardest part... we didn't have *katulong* anymore. We had everything in the Philippines, one time we had 6 maids, 2 drivers, gardener, and also a CNA [Certified Nursing Assistant] because my grandpa was sick.
>
> The time in the Philippines was bitter and sweet. I sometimes got hit by nostalgia. I miss it so much. It was so much fun there, all your friends were there. But on the other hand... its kind of... we were poor and I couldn't buy stuff I needed. It got to the point where your business consumed your family. When I was young we were wealthy but when I turned 13, 14, 15, it was like 'where did everything go?'. During my teenage years, it was like everything was so bad...my parents were fighting all the time, my grandpa had a stroke. You know all these things happening made me cut school. I didn't go to school a lot. My grades went into *palakol* [failing grade]. That was the time I started to smoke cigarette, smoking pot, smoking marijuana. You know, we had parties, drinking, having premarital sex. I didn't see any point in school, because I was getting my money through hustling. I wasn't in the house anymore. It was really a bad time.
>
> [When I had to leave the Philippines in 2004,] I was so pissed. I got really angry. Because I had a band there, I had two girlfriends there. I had all my friends. I was selling marijuana. I was getting money. I didn't care about my family anymore. And I truly regret whatever I was thinking back then, but [at that time] I really didn't want to leave

because it was so much fun. I had a fancy car... I had girls...having the time of my life. Then your Dad suddenly springs on you that you are going to America.

When I look back, coming to the US was really good for me. Because it straightened me out. My life now is really straight. You know...going here...having a shock and depending more on my family. It was kind of an eye opener for me. It kind of fixed me. I wasn't used to depend on my family, because I was delinquent in the Philippines. It was kind of a transformation. [When I was in the Philippines] I was so aggressive back then and fight all the time. But now, its kind of I chilled out. Probably, because I have to do everything by myself in the US. In the Philippines, somebody made my bed, somebody got my laundry, cooked my food, they drove me, but now I pay for my cell phone, I clean my clothes, I wash my dishes. [In the Philippines] I was a *katulong* baby (i.e. cared and indulged by the domestic helper). My family was always out for work. We just shared greetings. Family to me before was just a place to come back to. It was just that and nothing else. If you are done, you go there. That was family back then. But now I am supporting my sister and I saw that my Mom and Dad are trying to look out for us. Now, family is the only place you can come home to. In the Philippines they teach you "family first", but here they teach "you first". But [in the United States] my view switched to "family first". Because my Dad said to us when we came here "we are all in this together, whether you like it or not you have to help". Back in the Philippines I didn't need to shoulder any responsibility. Everything was shouldered by my father. But here everyone should bear responsibility for the lives of the family. It probably straightened up my life.

As suggested in the narratives above, while cherishing the free-wheeling past life spent in the "barangay" surrounded by the family which includes the nanny, helper, and many relatives, the children accept positively the new life in the United States which enabled them to be independent and self-reliant. As shown in the narrative by Arnold presented above, however, the independence and self-reliance acquired after migration do not simply result in American individualism of "you first" attitude. Rather what was found, or reaffirmed, by the 1.5-generation youth, simultaneously with independence and self-reliance, was the value of the "family". Narratives by the 1.5 generation that contrast the cohesion of "family" as a core value of the Filipino with "individualistic" American society and particularly with the "egotistic" lifestyle of the second generation would become clearer in the narrative examined below.

Aspect of Interdependence

For the 1.5 generation, the language ability, which is whether or not one can correctly speak Filipino, or Tagalog, is a significant marker which differentiates them from the second generation: "They cannot speak Tagalog. (...) They should know where they come from. I hope I don't forget Tagalog"; "Most of the Fil-Ams don't understand Tagalog. It is such a shame. You are Filipino, you should at least speak the language. They are Filipino in blood but it is difficult to associate with them".

Such reproach against the second generation is the flipside of an inferiority that the 1.5 generation actually entertains in terms of their English language ability. A female student who had already spent three years in the United States had this to say, "I have a fear that I will be laughed at by Fil-Ams if I talk to them in English". Such feeling easily turns to disgust with the term "FOB (Fresh Off the Boat)" which has a derogatory connotation towards the new immigrants who speak English with a strong Filipino accent:

> I hate how the Fil-Ams use the word 'FOB'. I heard that a million times and just don't like it. Even if it is a joke, I just don't like it. You know you are just born here but your parents are from the Philippines. So if you call someone a 'FOB', it is as good as saying your parents a 'FOB'. Just because you are born here, it doesn't give you a right to discriminate against people from your country. Because your blood came from the Philippines. Your feet just touch the US first. This is one thing that I don't like the Fil-Ams.

There are also other markers recognised by the 1.5 generation, which signify the behavioural differences between them and the second generation. Many from the 1.5 generation express such behavioural differences, stating that the second generation is "arrogant", "boastful", "outspoken", "extroverted", "individualistic", "self-indulgent", and more inclined towards "consumerism", behaviours with which the 1.5 generation identify themselves contradistinctively. Among these behavioural differences, most from the 1.5 generation consider a respect for the elders, particularly for the parents, close relatives, or teachers as a "core value" which most clearly differentiates them from the second generation:

> I do think there's a big difference [between Fil-born and Fil-Am], especially with the aspect of respect. I'm not saying they're not respectful but, compared to what I had to go through, I can't go without saying '*po*' (a Filipino particle connoting respect to the person whom one is speaking with) to an elder. I would '*mano*' (the gesture of taking an elder's hand on one's forehead as a show of respect). People born here do not have the sense to say '*po*'. (...) That's the biggest difference I see.

According to another 1.5-generation student, "Fil-Ams are lacking the core values. They are more focused on the consumerism in America. While Filipino immigrants have a core value of family, you stay together during breakfast, lunch, dinner, and you help each other".

Again, these comments by the 1.5 generation are somehow cross-validated by second-generation students, as follows. "Immigrants say they have to stay together. But we don't feel that way". "We do have dinner everyday, we talk with cousins, but we agree that immigrants are closer with the extended families than us". "They are more respectful. I became quite rebellious against my parents once. I demand for myself than my family. I became more selfish to a certain extent".

Such lack of a show of respect for elders and parents among the second generation is especially problematic in the context of the parent's migration to the United States:

> They don't appreciate their parents' hardship to move here. They just take it for granted that they have many opportunities here in the States. They are having too much fun. Some of their parents are nurses or caregivers [and having hard time in the severe working conditions], but they take it for granted in their current lives.

As Arnold narrates in the previous section, for the 1.5 generation, "family" is people on "one ship" in the uncertain ocean of the United States, and "whether we like it or not, we have to help each other". Such aspect of interdependence with the "family" would be another aspect of the 1.5 generation's identity that is recognised in relation to the second generation, which is spoken of as the "core value" of Filipinos.

An Aspect of Relational Self

As a third aspect which indicates the identity of the 1.5-generation youths, this part examines how the family is narrated in the context of their motivation of career choice which is one of the most urgent matters for the college students.

While, as mentioned above, it is true that more than half of the 1.5-generation students interviewed were willing to major in the nursing programme and become nurses thereafter, it should be noted that such choice was not always made by themselves but rather at times recommended, or quite often insisted on, by the parents. Firstly, for example, the narrative of a 21-year-old female student, who came to the United States at the age of 11 and currently majors in biology as a pre-med course at Stanford University, suggests what it means to be a nurse for the Filipino family in the United States:

> There is a Filipino stereotype that parents also have ... [that is] everyone should become doctors, engineers, or nurses. (...) Filipinos have a stereotype regarding health-related professions because these are something needed. Very noble job, you help people, care for people, it's useful (...) The other reason why health related jobs are so popular is that there is always a demand. People always pay to have a nurse, and a doctor. So it's a stable job. It provides security. Filipinos like the idea of security and stability. If you look at the historical and political challenges that the Philippines has faced, it hasn't been stable nor secured.

Thus, it is suggested that the Filipino immigrants view that to be a nurse is a normal thing, something that does not require any further justification. For the 1.5-generation students who internalise such "stereotype", it is sometimes unclear if the decision of becoming a nurse was actually arrived at solely by themselves or in accordance with their parent's will:

> I didn't like to take the nursing program. But there were people around me saying that if you become a nurse, that's what everyone needs. That career will not be replaced by machines or whatever. It is true that my Mom influenced me. Our family does not question about taking nursing. It is a normal thing for us. It's not like I was convinced by her. I am not pressured by my family. It was my own decision too.

Another female student expresses her sense of hesitation:

> Dad influenced me to take the nursing program. Actually, I am really undecided. I really don't know what I am good at. So I just took my Dad's suggestion. I am interested in web designing but it is just a hobby; I don't really find it as a job... I feel little pressure with my Dad but at the same time I am undecided so it's better to take what he wants me to do... than just do nothing... while if you are born in the US and raised in American way, the child will really push for what he wants [rather] than what his parents say.

There are also many 1.5-generation students who had no choice but to accept the decision made by their parents as reflected in the following narratives:

> I am going to take the nursing program. All my relatives were saying that nursing is the course that I should take. I didn't have any other course to choose from. That's why I decided to take nursing. I didn't have a passion for any other course anyway. It was like whatever course they recommend, that will be my course. (...) My parents are not actually convincing me to take the nursing program, but my cousins in the Philippines are convincing me. They said to me, "it is useless for your parents to come to the US if you don't take the nursing program and help your parents".

Such pressure from the parents often results in deep psychological confusion as told by another female student:

> *Mabigat ang sinabi nila, "Ikaw lang ang tangi naming pagasa para umangat", they always emphasize "Ikaw lang....", "Ikaw lang...". parang puro "Ikaw"... Paano naman ang gusto ko. Parang mapu-pressure ka masyado sa sinasabi nila... hindi mo magagawa ang gusto mo. Dahil sa pressure na iyan, parang naga-alala ka sa decisions mo...* [My parents say "You are our only hope for us to prosper". I am burdened by what they say. They always say "only you...", "only you..."...always "you". How about my own desire? It seems I am so pressured by what my parents say that I cannot proceed to do what I really want anymore. I became hesitant with my own decisions because of pressure coming from my parents].

A college counsellor, a Filipino immigrant herself, expressed her feeling of anxiety for those young Filipino immigrants who are just following their parents wish, or being pressured, being unaware of what they really want:

> It is true that the 1.5-generation has more inclination to think that they have to respect their parents. There are many students who come to counselling because they are forced to be a nurse by their parents but don't know how to communicate with their parents. (…) The 1.5-generation students are pressured by the parents but have no one to consult with. Especially when they want to major in the course that is not their parents' choice, they are worried that their parents will stop financial support. The students don't know how to talk to their parents. The reason why 1.5-generation students are offered nursing as the only choice of occupation is that to be a nurse, for their parents, is the only reliable and successful profession they know. That is the only reliable profession that their parents are familiar with and feel comfortable with. That's why the parents do not accept their children to major in courses that are not practical such as art and history. During my counselling, I try to teach them the importance of communication with their parents in order to tell their parents what they are really interested in, what are their real talents and abilities. I always tell the students that "it is important to make parents understand you, turn around and cooperate with you".

The meaning of nurses as "the only reliable profession" that the Filipino first-generation immigrants are familiar and comfortable with can only be understood properly when it is located in the context of colonial and post-colonial relationship between the United States and the Philippines since the end of the 19th century (Ong & Azores 1994). The American colonial period, which lasted from 1898 to 1946, instituted not only public education but also the general medical system and notion of public hygiene. The nursing education system initiated by the United States colonial government had been based on the medical practices in the United States and the textbook used in the United States (Choy 2003). Thus, the Filipino had been trained to be nurses with the ability to speak English fluently and possess knowledge of medical system and practice in the United States. Hence, it is no wonder that the Filipino comprised the majority of foreign-trained nurses who immigrated to the United States after the 1965 Immigration Act. Such background tells us that the nursing profession in the Philippines has been historically destined for overseas employment, and perceived as "the only reliable and successful profession" in the overseas labour market.

As shown in the narratives presented above, the pressure from their parents is sometimes negatively felt as a burden by the 1.5-generation children. It is also true, however, that most of them feel obliged to respect and prioritise their parents will, and, as shown in the case below (Case 9.4), do consider following what their parents say as a positive value, one that is at the centre of what it means to be Filipino.

Case 9.4: "It's not our lives, it's the family's lives" (the career choice of Philip)

Philip, a 20-year-old male student, who was still undecided if he should major in psychology or nursing, the latter having been recommended by his parents, suggests the idea that following his parents' will lies at the core of Filipino family and selfhood as narrated below.

> Under American values, you are not really attached to your parents, you are an individual, rather than a family. I'm not the closest thing to my parents but I still value them, I still do care for them. People who are born here, they take that for granted; they would leave at the age of 18... then they call the house their "parents' house", rather than "our house". Parents of the Fil-born think that "You were created so that you could help us". They expect us to help out. [However,] American-born are rebellious to say "no", they would say that "You could have chosen not to have me". I have that pressure on me that I have to help them out somehow, unlike the American-born who can say "I'm leaving" and live on [their] own. For me, I feel I do need to help out and I need to set time for them.
>
> [Asked if he has difficulty to go against his parents' will, he answered] Definitely, we were raised like that. We are raised to help them. There is always a sense of guilt that they would put upon you. You know, they say "We raised you; paid for everything. We don't ask for anything in return. We just want you to get a good education". They might not say "Once you grow up, help us out, pay the bills". but you would know, from the way they taught you, you're expected to help out. However wrongly it sounds, that's just how it is in the Philippine culture. That's why the Philippines is very populated, so that they can get more resources.
>
> [Asked further about the difference between the Fil-born and Fil-Am, he continues] they're really Americanised. You could really see how they're pretty much egotistic. They're very "me, me, me" kind of person. They would think, "I already pay for my own rent. I'm not supposed to get any nagging from you (their parents)". I see friends (who) were born in the Philippines and they have responsibility at the house. People who were born here would say to that person, "Oh why can't you go out? Is that your responsibility all the time?" I would tell the people born here, "That's just how it is". They can't accept the fact that we're expected somewhere at this time. We're expected to help at all times. It's not our lives; it's the family's lives. We're expected to be with the family when we are needed. That's why we were "created" to help out. That's our *utang na loob* [debt of gratitude] for them. We can't really do anything, and once we grow up and we have kids, that's what's gonna happen. I do see that conflict [where] Fil-Am people expect, "Oh you're not supposed to, they can't just chain you up at your house". Fil-born think, "That's just how it is. I'm expected to do this". (...) Filipino culture is based upon not yourself as an individual. Of course, you would expect in an Americanised kind of ideal, once you've done your share, you are okay to go out. But in Filipino culture, it doesn't go like that. You can never help enough. There's always something else you can do.

The narrative above suggests a notion of self which can only exist in relation with the family; a notion which is shared by most of the 1.5 generation in this study. A notion of self and sense of relatedness expressed in the narratives of the 1.5 generation in this section can be more clearly understood through a reference to the concept of "connective autonomy" discussed by George (2005) in the study of the selfhood of female immigrant nurses from Kerala, India settled in the United States. As an indication of such "connective autonomy" among the Keralite nurses in the United States, George discusses that "whereas entry into paid labor and emigration increase their mobility and independence—both financially and socially—they experience this autonomy only within a set of relationships and obligations" (George 2005: 40). Further, "the financial and social autonomy they gained (in the United States) did not lead to an individualised notion of the self, because the very definition of the self is embedded in a set of obligations and duties to others" (George 2005: 44). The choice of becoming a nurse among the Filipino 1.5 generation in the United States also indicates a notion of connective selfhood and identity which can be defined only by their relationships with their family and the obligation they owe them.

Further focusing on the aspect of "connective autonomy" among the Keralite female immigrant nurses in the United States, George argues that "in order to understand how women (and men) from non-Western cultures assess their own loss or gain of autonomy, we must first recognise that their notion of personhood may be very different from the notions of personhood found in Western cultures" (George 2005: 40). While such "connective autonomy" is indeed ingrained in the identity of the 1.5 generation in this study, it should not be reified as a notion indicating generalised "non-Western" selfhood. Rather, it is a notion that emerges under the specific context of countries of origin and host and particular interactions that 1.5-generation children maintain, especially those with their parents and also with the second generation.

Discussion

In this chapter, I focused on the marginalisation and identity construction experienced by the children of the Filipino middle-class migrants, who are dealt with in the previous chapter. By marginalisation, I mean the conflicts, contradictions, and confrontations that each migrant faces in the US, as well as the experience of being "uprooted" and "dislodged" from their familiar environment in the Philippines. In contrast, their identity construction is considered as an act of regaining an integrated "whole self" while recovering from such marginalisation. What this chapter has shown is that a symbolic resource mobilised for such identity construction is the "family".

What has been revealed in this chapter about the identity of the 1.5 generation children and the representation of the "family" that emerged with it? As discussed in the previous chapter, the migration of the first generation to United States was not motivated by the pure self-interest, but rather it was "for the sake of the children" and "for the sake of the family". However, contrary to the parents' wish, the children themselves felt being compelled, asking "why did we have to leave the Philippines?" and "my feelings were not taken into account at all", and they felt sadness and anger at being uprooted from the intimate and often indulgent environment surrounded by friends and the "family". As discussed in Cases 9.1–9.3, feelings towards parents may change to acceptance and gratitude during the process of adjustment and personal growth in the host country. However, many children of the 1.5 generation seem to oscillate between such feelings of sadness, anger, and acceptance. In other words, although many of the 1.5 generation said that "family ties are the core value of us Filipinos", we should avoid the static view on such ties that represents the essence of the relationship between the 1.5 generation children and parents. Rather, the cases presented in this chapter reveal the representation of the "family" and identity that emerge in spite of, or because of, the fissures, contradictions, and conflicts between the children and parents. Further, such representations and identities become prominent in the close interactions and negotiations between the first and second generations, the most familiar and important others in the everyday lives of the 1.5 generation.

As the first aspect that defines the identity of the 1.5-generation children, the emphasis on independence and autonomy from the "family" was pointed out. While they regretted being separated from the intimate sphere of the "family" including close relatives and nannies in the Philippines before migration, they positively valued their independence and autonomy after migration as a new aspect of self that "could only be obtained in America". However, this could not be equated with the "individualism" and "self-centeredness" that symbolised the second generation born in the United States. Rather, the identity of "we the 1.5 generation" was discussed as something that coexisted with the bonds and interdependence with the "family". Embedded in this is a criticism of the second generation, which in the eyes of the 1.5 generation is seen as forgetting (or trying to forget) its Filipino roots and trying to adapt excessively to mainstream American culture.

On the other hand, while the interdependence with parents and "family" was emphasised in the aspects of major and career choice in college, an ambivalent situation was revealed in which the 1.5 generation often felt constrained and oppressed by such ties. For them, becoming professionals in the health and care industry, especially nurses, was not considered simply as the fulfilment of their hopes and dreams. Rather, such a career choice was seen as the "only reliable career" to maintain a relational self based on interdependence with the "family". It can be said that the identity of the 1.5 generation was expressed in such occupational choices as something that should be differentiated from the "self-centred" second generation. At the same time, however, many of the 1.5 generation feel the conflict between the demands of their parents, or the "family", and their own will, or feel oppressed, and are trapped in the conflict of not being able to find the career or employment they truly want.

Thus, it can be said that the representation of the "family" of the 1.5 generation immigrants examined in this chapter is idealised as the core of their identity, but also contains various frictions, contradictions, and conflicts. It is true that their identities and representations of "family" clearly expressed the aspect of the relational self, in the sense of a self found only in relation to others. However, this is different from the static and essentialist notions of "connective autonomy" that George discussed with regard to the identity of the nurse who emigrated from India to the United States, which underpins the "non-Western self". Rather, it can be seen as a complex interplay of aspects such as "independence/autonomy", "interdependence", and "relational self" in relation to the "family", with one of these aspects taking precedence depending on a specific situation that the 1.5 generation lives.

Furthermore, it can be said that the identity and "family" representation of the 1.5 generation immigrants is not only determined by the other generations, but also by the institutional and structural factors in both the home and the host country, as discussed in the Prologue. In this chapter, I have focused on the nursing profession as an occupational choice closely related to the identity of the 1.5 generation. For them, the nursing profession has historically been a profession to support the American colonial system in terms of medical and sanitary care, and since the 1960s, it has been a profession to meet the increasing demand of the care industry in the post-industrial society of the West. Since the 1960s, it has been regarded as "the only secure and reliable occupation" to meet the growing demand of the care industry in the post-industrial society in the West. For many of the 1.5 generation, schooling, especially at community colleges today, is seen as a place of more practical training for such "only secure and reliable occupations" rather than a place to satisfy their academic and intellectual curiosity. In other words, it is a niche in the competitive immigrant labour market in the United States, a place to acquire the knowledge and skills needed for a workforce that is compatible with the nursing and care industry.

On the other hand, in the sending country, the Philippines, there existed a "brokering state" regime, as also explained in the Prologue. As discussed in the previous chapter, from the late 1990s to the mid-2000s, the parents of the 1.5 generation in this chapter were working at middle-class jobs in the Philippines, but were also seeking to obtain nursing certification in order to immigrate to the United States. At that time, private nursing schools, which proliferated to meet the demands of the US immigrant labour market, were indeed actors in the "brokering state" regime in the Philippines. As suggested in the various examples of motivations for migration presented in the previous chapter, under such a regime, the parents of the 1.5-generation children internalised and subjected themselves to the values and norms of entrepreneurship in pursuit of the skills and qualifications demanded by the global migrant labour market.

Due to these institutional and structural factors in both receiving and sending countries, the transnational social field that straddles the Philippines and the United States becomes a field of "struggle for social status" (Levitt & Glick Schiller 2004: 1008), rather than a space for mutuality and solidarity. The 1.5 generation's representation of the "family", and the construction of their identities based on it, are attempts to give meaning to the experiences of being uprooted and separated from their childhood environment, to regain an integrated self, and to reconstruct the relatedness and mutuality with others in order to tide over the tight struggle for social status in the host country.

Notes

1. A part of this chapter is reprinted in revision from *Mobile Childhoods in Filipino Transnational Families: Migrant Children with Similar Roots in Different Routes*, Nagasaka, Itaru and A. Fresnoza-Flot (eds.), (2015) London: Palgrave Macmillan, pp. 151–178, by permission of Palgrave MacMillan.
2. Adobo is popular Filipino cuisine with meat, usually chicken and pork, cooked in soy sauce, vinegar, and garlic.
3. More than the actual population figures, the image of Daly City as a "Filipino town" is pervasive among Filipino immigrants not only on the West Coast but throughout the United States. For example, a widely circulated joke among them is, "You know why Daly City is always covered in a thick morning haze? That's because Filipinos cook rice for breakfast all at once".
4. The schools visited for the interviews are as follows: City College of San Francisco, Skyline College, San Francisco State University. Some supplementary interviews were also conducted with the students in San Jose State University (San Jose, California), De Anza Community College (San Jose, California), and Stanford University (Palo Alto, California). Unfortunately, in these schools, the exact number of Filipino students who are of the 1.5 generation is not known. In order to find interviewees, the author visited Filipino student organizations and classes on history and culture of the Philippines, where most of the enrolees are Filipino students. On these occasions, questionnaires were distributed to all the Filipino students to gather basic information on their life histories. Based on this survey, those considered as 1.5 generation were contacted for an interview. The one-on-one semi-structured interviews were conducted usually for one hour to two, and English and Filipino languages were used for conversation. In order to cross check the narratives of the 1.5 generation, a focus group discussion with the second-generation students was also conducted. The names of all informants in this text are pseudonyms.

10 Transient Solidarity

A Case of the Movement to Revise the "Migrant Workers and Overseas Filipino Act of 1995"

Despair over Politics, Attachment to Country

In this chapter, I would like to deal again with the case of Filipino middle-class professionals discussed in Chapter 8, and discuss the possibility that the ambivalence that I pointed out as a characteristic of their identity can become an opportunity for mutuality and solidarity in the transnational social field.[1] First, I would like to present a case below (Case 10.1) in order to clarify the meaning of ambivalence in this chapter.

> **Case 10.1: Migration with leave of absence**
> **(Interview on September 4, 2005)[2]**
>
> Joshua Espinosa, born in 1967, is a medical doctor specializing in internal medicine. His wife, Gena, born in 1966, is an ophthalmologist. They had been working in Metro Manila as doctors in a military base and hospital for several years when Gena went to nursing school beginning in 2002. After securing her nursing license, she, together with Joshua and their two children, migrated to the Unites States in 2005. The reason behind their migration is their discontent with their salary, which is meagre compared to that of their doctor colleagues, and their dislike of their working conditions that often required them to transfer to different military hospitals, some located near the battle zones of Mindanao.
>
> At the time of the interview, they had been staying in the Unites States under a tourist visa with a two-year validity, putting pressure on Gena to swiftly find hospital employment before the visa's expiration. Joshua, for his part, has not resigned from the hospital he used to work for in the Philippines. He has been officially on a leave of absence for a year. That being the case, Joshua can go back to this hospital in the Philippines in case Gena's job hunt does not turn out to be fruitful.

Joshua and Gena exemplify the ambivalence of middle-class professionals. While these professionals seek to define themselves as being capable of attaining an alternative status and lifestyle abroad and are desirous of migrating, they are at the same time anxious and hesitant to carry out their enterprise. As has been clarified, the identity of the Filipino middle class can be said as being "pendulating" between two poles: to migrate on one end, and to stay in the country on the other. Gravitating towards the latter pole, to stay in the

DOI: 10.4324/9781003224273-13

Philippines, is caused not only by fear and anxiety observed in Mr. and Mrs. Espinosa's and other cases in Chapter 8, but also by a positive aspiration for social ties and networks with their countrymen. In other words, gravitation to stay can be motivated by a nationalistic sentiment harboured by middle-class professionals, that is, their wish to be connected to and allied with their countrymen. This chapter deals with this specific aspect of the middle class's ambivalence and its implication on the possibility for mutuality and solidary in the transnational social field. Presented below is an introductory case to such argument.

Case 10.2: *"We will simply repeat People Power again"* (Interview on August 29, 2005)

Born in 1972, Benjie Fajardo graduated from the University of the Philippines, majoring in Business Economy, and later pursued a law degree in the same university. Having passed the bar examination in 2001, he joined a law firm in Metro Manila where he continues to work at the time of the interview. His wife, Lea, after completing her college education from the University of Santo Tomas, was employed in a multinational pharmaceutical company in Metro Manila. They have thought about migrating to Canada since around 2002. They have passed some steps in the evaluation process required by the Canadian Embassy and attended several seminars in preparation for migration.

However, at the same time, they are hesitant to push through with their migration plan. Benjie has just started his career as a lawyer in the Philippines and they are unsure of the kind of job he can find in Canada. Further, it seems that Benjie entertains a more positive motivation to stay in the country. He says, "I realized that we should not give up on trying to change the government no matter how corrupt it is. If a revolution is necessary, I will join the revolution. Should People Power fail to bring a good government, we will simply repeat People Power again". Benjie and Lea recall that they were present almost every-day in Ortigas during People Power 2, which ousted Estrada from the presidency in 2001. Benjie's narrative suggests that, even after the Arroyo administration that replaced Estrada has been tainted by various scandals and corruption, he is willing to stay in the Philippines to help improve the government.

This case suggests that the identity, a definition of who they are, of the Filipino middle-class professionals, is not only constructed by their practice of distinction and differentiation through migration but also by their aspiration for social reform and the improvement of the government. Considering such aspiration, it is possible that the identity of the middle class leads them further to forge social alliances in an expansive space of civil society. However, such alliance is possible only as an ambivalent one. This is because, as shown in the case above, the middle-class professionals' aspiration for an alliance with their countrymen quite often coexists with their desire for migrating abroad, and this "pendulum" can easily gravitate to the other pole depending on contingencies in the country.

Yet, what should be pointed out here is that this seemingly unstable pendulum does not necessarily mean that the alliance is always weak and destined to fail in bringing about tangible achievements. Rather, as the following cases indicate, such an ambivalent alliance and network are capable of bringing about a degree of concrete social reform amid the apparent divisiveness and fragmentation of society.

National Anti-Poverty Commission and Movement to Revise "Migrant Workers and Overseas Filipino Act of 1995"

Here, I would like to focus on the National Anti-Poverty Commission (NAPC hereafter), a coalition of NGOs established under the Social Reform Agenda of the Ramos administration (1992–1998), and the middle-class people who gather under that coalition. While the NAPC is under the Office of the President, and therefore a government entity, every basic sector that comprises NAPC is composed of NGOs.[3] The NAPC is a recommendatory body to the government in regard to the policy for alleviating poverty of every sector. The migrant worker sector discussed here, composed of fourteen NGOs based in Metro Manila, is engaged in activities aimed at improving the welfare of vulnerable Overseas Contract Workers (OCWs). In the following, I will focus on the effort of the migrant worker sector to revise Republic Act No. 8042, commonly known as the Migrant Workers and Overseas Filipinos Act of 1995 (RA 8042 hereafter).

RA 8042 was hastily drafted and enforced amid severe criticisms of the perceived failure and inability of the government to protect the human rights of OCWs, as evinced by the execution of Flor Contemplacion in Singapore in 1995. The most significant feature of RA 8042 was that, for the first time, it made clear the government policy not to rely on the overseas employment as a means of economic growth but instead to create jobs at home and promotes the equitable wealth distribution within the nation (Ogaya 2016: 188–189). On the other hand, the law includes a provision requiring the deregulation of recruitment activities and the phase-out of all regulatory functions then undertaken by the Philippine Overseas Employment Administration (POEA) and their transfer to the private sector within five years from the time the law came into force (Art. VII, Sec. 29 and 30). The NGOs composing the Migrant Workers Sector of the NAPC had been vehemently demanding the repeal of this article on deregulation and phase out. According to those NGOs, when all administrative procedures and regulatory functions of the government concerning OCWs are phased out, the migrant workers would be exploited directly by private recruitment companies and foreign employers, and so the workers' rights and welfare would not be protected.

In 2006, at a time when the deregulation and phase-out requirement had not been implemented despite the law, several meetings were held in Metro

Manila by the NGOs of the Migrant Workers Sector in order to lobby some congressmen. In those meetings, the congressman, who was the Chairman of the Committee on Labor, or the Committee on Overseas Work, along with members of his staff were invited, and the negative effects on OCWs and the expected outcomes from the deregulation and phase out were fervently discussed. The NGOs were especially concerned about the Pre-Departure Orientation Seminar (PDOS), which is a mandatory training for the people set to be deployed for overseas employment.[4] Since the 1980s, the PDOS had been provided by six NGOs accredited by the government, particularly by the POEA (Picture 10.1). The NGOs contend that the deregulation of the PDOS and its administration by the private sector would diminish the seminar's standard of quality and contents, and it would emphasise more the rights of foreign employers rather than the security and welfare of the workers. After repeated discussions in the meetings, the NGOs finally won the repeal of the article on deregulation and phase out in March 2007.

Thus, the group of NGOs composed of the Migrant Workers Sector of the NAPC can be considered an actor of social reform that demands the revision of policy based on excessive liberalisation, and also the protection of the rights and welfare of OCWs. Here, it is important to note the difference in social class between migrant workers, such as those covered in Chapter 7, and middle-class professionals, such as those covered in Chapter 8. The former work under

Picture 10.1 Pre-Departure Orientation Seminar (PDOS) provided by NGO

temporary employment contracts ranging from one to several years as domestic workers or construction workers in various parts of Asia and the Middle East. Their migration abroad is appreciated by the domestic media as *sakripisyo* (sacrifice) for the sustenance of their families, and they are praised as "today's national heroes (*bagong bayani*)" for their contribution of remittance to the national economy. On the other hand, the latter group of people are the middle-class professionals, who are already living a comfortable life in the Philippines with hired drivers and housekeepers, and still migrate to the Western advanced countries in search of further security and comfort, or to escape political instability at home. Contrary to the praise for the "national heroes", they are often criticised as "national betrayal" (Aguilar 2004). As discussed in the following, the NGO members dealt with in this chapter have the same characteristic of social class as the middle-class professionals. Having realised such differences in social class, it can be considered that the movement to revise RA 8042 was made possible by the alliance of various actors who belong to the different social class backgrounds. To be specific, it was enabled through the negotiations and cooperation of NGOs with different social classes, such as the lower labour class comprising the main population of the OCWs, and with the upper class of congressmen and bureaucrats.

The Middle-Class Professionals Who Carried out the Movement

The case in this section indicates that a space for civic alliance, albeit transitory, was created for the purpose of the revision of the law. The questions that should be examined here are: Who are the members of those NGOs comprising the Migrant Workers Sectors of NAPC? What are their social status and class backgrounds? What are their motivations for their NGO activities? The following cases (Cases 10.3–10.5) introduce the members of NGOs which pursued the goal of revising the RA 8042, and they are examined to answer the queries just posed.

Case 10.3: Michael Rodrigo (Interview on September 25, 2006)

Michael was born in 1960 in Mindoro Island, southeast of Metro Manila. His parents are both public school teachers. He studied in a private university in Metro Manila during the late 1970s, when student activism against the Marcos dictatorship was at its peak. Michael also deeply involved himself in a nationalistic and leftist anti-government movement during those days. During the administration of Corazon Aquino, which started in 1986, Michael began to organise labour unions in various sectors. As part of such organising work, he formed an NGO in 1988 for the protection of the rights of OCWs. As of 2006, his NGO has gained 45,000 OCWs as members nationwide, and Michael has been working as Chairman of the Migrant Workers Sector of the NAPC.

Michael's wife graduated from the University of the Philippines and had worked as a teacher in an exclusive private high school in Metro Manila for eight years. She has immigrated to the Unites States and is currently working in Houston, Texas, as a public school teacher. Michael and the children are also planning to immigrate to the Unites States within a few years. Michael says,

> It is possible to continue an activity similar to what I am doing now even after I have settled in the United States. There are around 10,000 Filipinos in Houston. Some of them are professionals but there are also many who are suffering discrimination. Even if they are able to secure American citizenship, they are still looked down on as 'second class citizens.' The activities, such as the ones I am doing now in the Philippines, are also needed to protect the human rights of the Filipinos in the United States.

Case 10.4: Jorge Araneta (Interview on September 26, 2006)

Born in 1951, Jorge graduated from the University of the Philippines, College of Engineering, in 1975 and then received his MBA from the Ateneo de Manila University in 1979. He has long been working as a manager in the banking and financial sectors in Metro Manila before he organised an NGO, whose main activity is to provide the PDOS for the OCWs. Asked about his motivation for this NGO activity, Jorge answered, "Since I have accomplished a lot, I wanted to give back to the people".

Jorge's wife, on the other hand, has a BS degree in Business Administration, and more than one master's degree in related fields. She had been working as a government employee for quite a time, when she applied for a Canadian immigrant visa in 1995. Regarding the reason behind the application, Jorge explains, "At that time, since the economy was good under the Ramos administration (1992–1998), we were hesitant to apply for the immigrant visa. But there was quite a high possibility that Estrada was going to be elected as president in the succeeding election. That's why my wife thought we should apply 'for the security of the worst scenario'". He continues, "I am still supporting President Arroyo. But the political situation in this country has been chaotic since the People Power of 1986. I always feel insecure, haunted by the anxiety about the worst thing that might happen".

The immigrant visa was issued by the Canadian government in 1997. Jorge's wife, who migrated ahead of her family, has been residing in Canada for seven years now, doing various menial jobs such as that of a cashier, a bagger at a grocery or the supermarket, or a temporary clerk at the city hall. While staying in Canada, she has not resigned from her position in her government office in the Philippines, and keeps her status as a government employee under leave of absence. Jorge, who is also aiming for Canadian citizenship within three years, is shuttling between Canada and the Philippines because, in order to secure Canadian citizenship, he cannot be found to have been absent from his residency in Canada for more than six months for a period of three years. Jorge's son, who was born in 1982, graduated from the Ateneo de Manila University, and is wishing to immigrate to the Unites States. For that purpose, he has already secured his Philippine nursing license, and is currently preparing for the nursing board examination of the Unites States.

Case 10.5: Dante Paterno (Interview on September 27, 2006)

Dante was born in 1946 in San Pablo, Laguna, and was educated at San Beda College in Manila from elementary through college, graduating with a degree in Business Administration in the late 1960s. He obtained a Master's

Degree in Marketing Management from the University of Louisville in the Unites States, and later studied Traffic Engineering at the University of the Philippines. Since then, Dante has been working as an executive in several companies in the field of transportation and aviation. Aside from corporate work, he has involved himself in NGO activities since the 1970s, and he currently presides over an NGO that works for the environment, education, and human rights and welfare of OCWs. Dante's wife is a nurse working in the Philippines.

Many of Dante's uncles, aunts, and his own siblings have already left the Philippines and mainly live in the Unites States as American citizens. Dante himself possesses a multiple-entry visa to the Unites States and frequently travels there. For him, migrating to the Unites States is an option that he always entertains. He says, "America is attractive. The idea of migrating to America never escaped me. This is because the Unites States is where opportunity is available in all stages of your life". Regarding the motivation behind the migration of middle-class professionals including himself, he explains, "It is not because of financial reasons, but of the losing of trust for the system of the country, and the feeling of fear caused by it". He adds,

> My wish is to live in a place where I don't have any worry, anxiety, and fear when I wake up every morning. Particularly, what I need is a sense of security when I grow old. They say that New York has a higher crime rate than Manila, but I don't feel that is true. I can walk in the streets of Manhattan without any fear even during midnight. But in Parañaque, I can hear a gunshot sometimes emanating from the Muslim community near my residence. What we are looking for is not financial stability but quality of life.

However, denying his intention to migrate abroad right now, he confirms, "You should not ask only for personal comfort and convenience. What is needed is a concern for the needs of our community, society, and the people. I cannot simply depart for abroad and just leave all the NGO activities behind".

The Middle Class Caught up in a Pendulum

The cases of Michael, Jorge, and Dante who preside over NGOs comprising the Migrant Workers Sector of NAPC indicate that they and their families have high educational achievements and are engaged in professional and corporate executive jobs. In this sense, they share the same class background of the middle-class professionals presented in Chapter 8.[5] Similarly they are either planning to migrate abroad, mainly to the Unites States, or have families who have already settled abroad. What should be pointed out here is that, while they are entertaining their hope and have concrete plans of migrating to the Unites States, or Canada, they are also remaining in the country to pursue their NGO work in order to uplift the welfare of their countrymen, particularly the vulnerable OCWs.

Michael of Case 10.3 is keen on helping local labourers and OCWs and their families to improve their situation in the Philippines. Yet, his wife has already settled in the Unites States and Michael also plans to follow her soon. It seems that he is torn by contradictory desires—to help his countrymen, or migrate to the Unites States. His statement of "the activities, such as the ones I am doing now in the Philippines, are also needed to protect the human rights of the Filipinos in the United States" sounds like a compromise to solve such contradiction.

Jorge in Case 10.4, who is engaged in an NGO as a way of "giving back" to the people and society, would seem to now straddle between the Philippines and Canada. But it also appears that settling permanently in Canada is a fallback option for him, which has significance as "security of the worst scenario". Indeed, Jorge's wife, even after she secured the immigrant visa for Canada, is reluctant to resign entirely from her government post in the Philippines. Finally, migration to the Unites States is a quite realizable option for Dante in Case 10.5, who used to study in the Unites States and maintains rich networks and resources there. However, it is also difficult for him to leave behind the "interests of community, society, and the people".

As such, the middle-class professionals in this chapter are also identified by the same ambivalence that can be found in the cases discussed in Chapter 8. In a sense, they are both similarly swaying between two contrastive poles of a single "pendulum". For instance, while the group of middle-class professionals presented in Chapter 8 is gravitating towards migration as a way of distinction and differentiation, the middle class of this chapter on the other hand is gravitating towards staying in the country to help their countrymen through their NGO work.

This observation corresponds with the analysis made by a Filipino political scientist on the middle class in the contemporary Philippines. Rivera (2006: 195) discusses that the Filipino middle classes' quest for varying aspects of modernity is sought to be fulfilled "in the promises of foreign shores". It emphasises the threat and danger that former President Estrada's administration posed to middle-class lifestyle and aspirations, and the economic downturn that accompanied the series of scandals and corruption cases that "not only made it difficult to maintain middle-class amenities but also assailed its prevailing values of justice and fairness" (Rivera 2006: 195). As a number of trajectories middle-class participation in politics can assume in the context of "the continuing ineptness of state agency and the irresponsibility of many of the elites", Rivera (2006: 199–200) identifies the inclination that is similar to the "pendulum identity" discussed in this chapter: middle-class participation in politics, on one hand, "could lead to a cynical depoliticization in which the middle classes would try to prosper without consciously engaging the effete state agencies or by simply voting with their feet by further exploring opportunities outside the country", or, on the other hand, "within a reformist agenda, the middle classes could try to reinvigorate existing political institutions, particularly the electoral process and political parties through alliances with reformist politicians and bureaucrats".

What should be emphasised here is that the pendulum suggested here gravitates depending on the specific political-economic contingencies of the country, such as the unbearable political chaos and instability of the government, or the nationwide anger and demand for protection of rights of the vulnerable OCWs as shown in the case of revision of RA8042. As such, the pendulum metaphor suggests that it is not sufficient to focus only on the aspect of divisiveness and fragmentation of society, which is caused by the practice of distinction and differentiation of middle-class people; but attention should also be paid to the other pole of the pendulum, which is the aspiration of the middle class to remain in the country, further to be tied to its people, and even to forge a network and alliance in a civic social arena such as the NAPC.

Discussion

The identity and subjectivity forged under contemporary neoliberal governmentality are characterised by instability, fragmentation, individualisation, and social fluidity (Harvey 2005; Crompton 2008). Under such conditions, class identities, or consciousness, emerge not from a sense of collective belonging but from a process of differentiation from others (Crompton 2008: 92). The transnational migration of Filipino middle-class professionals examined in this chapter, and also in Chapter 8, is also considered a social practice of distinction and differentiation from others. The ambivalence reflected in the narratives of the informants suggests the middle class's "individualized identities, generated by a continuous process of comparison 'up' and 'down'" (Crompton 2008: 92).

While most anthropological studies of neoliberalism have focused on the counterhegemonic subalterns who participate in the "zones of resistance" against the neoliberal governmentality (Cahn 2008), there is also a growing number of articles that focus on "the loci and communities of social action and relation where the moves toward marketization and privatization seem to be embraced with open arms" (Richland 2009: 172) and middle-class people and corporate actors who actively participate in advancing neoliberal projects in order to realise their desired identities and lifestyles. The study of the Filipino middle-class professionals as enterprising selves who are engaged in the practices of distinction and differentiation through the utilisation of various networks and opportunities in transnational social fields can be properly contextualised in this burgeoning area of anthropological inquiry.

However, the middle-class selves that the data of this chapter suggest are not freewheeling entrepreneurs who, embracing the neoliberal project of marketisation and privatisation "with open arms", simply seek to improve their status and attain better lifestyles. The situation, as suggested by the data, is also not simply one of deepening divisiveness and disunity caused by the practices of such individualised middle class. Rather, the data suggest that the relations of social classes become more fluid and complicated owing to the ambivalence of members of the middle class who, while keenly involved in the practices of distinction and differentiation, cannot help but be hesitant to push through their enterprise, particularly transnational migration. As the informants of this chapter have frequently mentioned, emigration is a "fallback option" as it is not easy for them to leave the country for good despite their anxiety about and disappointment with its government.

Thus, while it is true that the practice of identity construction of the middle-class professionals in this study leads to a deepening polarisation and fragmentation of the society on one hand, the ambivalent character of their identity, on the other hand, results in networks and social ties with people of different social classes in the Philippines. Such social alliances might neither share a coherent identity nor have a unified moral or long-term endurance. Rather such alliances tend to be loose and transient networks of people. This study, however, maintains that under the neoliberal situation of deepening fragmentation and polarisation of social classes, and also the individualisation accompanied by the gaps and inequalities in various social fields, no association and civil society movement can be coherent entities with members having unified goals and a homogeneous identity. Rather, what should be emphasised here is that a "pendulum" of middle-class identity suggests that even individualistic pursuits for distinction and differentiation quite often include the possibility of forging networks and alliances with others such as the one we have seen in the case of the movement to revise RA8042 and other activities to protect and enhance the welfare of the migrant workers. The transient solidarity observed in this chapter contains seemingly contradicting dual aspects of sociality such as alliance and differentiation, solidarity and fragmentation, division and mutuality, and articulation and disarticulation. While it is transient and ambivalent in nature, it can still form a network to demand and achieve certain political reform as observed in this chapter. In this sense, such solidarity, while transient and ephemeral, suggests the possibility of the emergence of alternative public sphere.

Notes

1. A part of this chapter is reprinted in a revised form from *Philippine Studies* Vol.60.2 (2012): 187–222, by permission of the Ateneo de Manila University.
2. At the time of the interview, Joshua and Gena Espinosa had already moved to the United States. This interview was conducted with Gina's sister in Pasig City, Metro Manila. The interviews for this chapter had been conducted in August and September 2005, and September 2006 in various parts of Metro Manila.
3. The NAPC consists of fourteen basic sectors: farmers and landless rural workers, artisanal fisherfolk, urban poor, indigenous cultural communities/indigenous peoples, workers in the formal sector and migrant workers, workers in the informal sector, women, youth and students, persons with disabilities, victims of disasters and calamities, senior citizens, nongovernment organizations, children, and cooperatives.
4. The contents provided during the PDOS include general information on the region/country of destination; requirements and procedures for overseas employment; OCW's rights and duties; empowerment and coping mechanism of the OCWs in foreign countries; effects of migration on family life; programs and services for the OCWs; financial management of earnings gained from overseas employment; basic steps for OCW's reintegration preparedness, and so on.

5. The other members of the NGOs that comprise the Migrant Workers Sector of the NAPC are also middle-class professionals: medical doctors, corporate managers and executives, nuns from Catholic covenants, maritime engineers, and so on. Generally, NGOs in the Philippines are composed of middle-class professionals. By virtue of their proficiency with the English language, knowledge of technical terms, and skills of drafting technical papers and documents, they tend to monopolise the negotiation process with the government and international donors. As such, a certain power gap has been observed between NGOs composed of middle-class professionals and People's Organisations (POs) composed mainly of the lower-class residents of indigent neighbourhoods (Ferrer 1997; Hilhorst 2003).

11 Conclusion

As a conclusion, I would like to summarise the discussions of each chapter on how neoliberalism has been restructuring "the social" and what kind of alternative public sphere is emerging in such a process. As discussed in the Introduction, compared with the mutuality based on personal and face-to-face connections, such as family, kinship, and community, "the social" is considered mutuality based on impersonal, anonymous, and formal connections. Such a formal mutuality played an important role in the institutionalisation of modern welfare states, particularly in the history of the West, where redistribution as a formal system has been realised within the nation-state. Neoliberal restructuring, however, resulted in the "rolling back" of the welfare state and the fragmentation of the public sphere in both the Global North and Global South. If "the social" as a formal mutuality cannot be maintained at this time of new precarities and uncertainties, then what can the alternative form of the public sphere particularly needed for the protection and security of lives in the Global South be? Such an attempt at reimagining and reconceptualising "the social" has been the task of this book.

Neoliberal Restructuring of "the Social"

As has been observed in the chapters of this book, the implementation of social policies in the Philippines clearly indicates the process of the neoliberal restructuring of "the social". Under such restructuring, the state is increasingly becoming an "enabler", or a "facilitator", rather than a "provider" of resources and protection, whose role is "the conduct of conduct" of non-state actors by activating citizens, empowering the poor, and fostering productive communities. The ethnographies of the chapters of this book, however, have suggested the various dilemmas, contradictions, and unexpected consequences brought about by such social policies and development relying on active citizens, the empowered poor, and productive communities.

In the case of the Community Mortgage Program (CMP) in Chapter 2, homeowners associations consisting of neighbourhood residents are expected to be the main drivers. The use of homeowners associations is in line with the "empowerment approach" that has become the mainstream of social development in

DOI: 10.4324/9781003224273-14

the Philippines since the end of the 1980s, during which time, the processes of democratisation and decentralisation were accelerated. Indeed, as shown in the chapter, such programs have created a certain number of legal landowners from among former "squatters" in an urban slum community. In contrast, land ownership is still a distant dream for those who cannot engage in the "productive work" emphasised by these associations. The conditional cash transfer program (4Ps) discussed in Chapter 3 has "investment in human capital" as its basic principle, which is also effective in justifying criticism from the middle class that the program is just an another "dole-out" policy for the poor. As such, the neoliberal logic of activating citizens is the driving force behind the implementation of the program. It is true that a certain number of beneficiaries spoke positively about the program by suggesting how it nurtured diligence and discipline in them and their children. However, the program did not reduce the risks and vulnerabilities inherent in daily life within the slum, and some citizens questioned the effectiveness of the intended empowerment, while others simply remained indifferent. Despite the program's philosophy of social inclusion through "investment in human capital", people continued to face the challenges of disasters, informal employment, illness, and the difficulty of keeping their children in school.

Under the neoliberal restructuring of the coastal resource management discussed in the chapters of Part II, actors such as the local government, non-governmental organisations (NGOs), and communities were encouraged to become guardians of nature to enhance its value as a commodity. Eco-governmentality in coastal resource management shifted the rationale of resource use from the subsistence of community members to the maximisation of the market value of nature. Under this new regime of resource use and management, the livelihood activities that used to secure the subsistence of fishermen and their families, but can no longer produce high profitability, are increasingly marginalised and eliminated in the community.

The chapters of Part III examined the neoliberal restructuring of the transnational social field. Macro-level factors such as the restructuring of the international division of reproductive labour have created a huge new market for the Philippine labour force. Responding to such newly created opportunities, the "brokering state" regime of the Philippines sought to enhance its emotional capacity, such as "docility", "hospitality", and "tender loving care", which became vital "added-export value" in marketing its own people to meet the global demands for foreign reproductive labour as a backdrop. Furthermore, by "professionalizing" reproductive labour, migrants are expected to become self-reliant "super-maids" or caregivers who can deal with the various risks and uncertainties inherent in overseas employment through their own responsibility and self-help. Such a retreat of the state from the transnational social field, however, further proliferated the risks that could not be borne by individuals, such as war and conflict, abuse by employers, and the breakdown of the family, as discussed in Chapter 7.

In contrast to temporary migrant workers, it was the middle-class professionals who attempted to migrate abroad as a way of distinction and differentiation from both the lower-class masses (*masa*) and the upper-class elites. As discussed in Chapter 8, the nursing schools that had been mushrooming in Metro Manila and other major cities in the Philippines during the mid-2000s became part of the "brokering state" regime that embodied and further incited the desire of middle-class professionals to increase the "added-export value" highly demanded in the global market for reproductive labour. Contrary to the general expectation for the middle class to play a vital role in creating a robust civil public sphere in the new democracies, the cases in Chapter 8 suggested that their desire for and practice of migration accelerated the fragmentation and individualisation of the transnational social field. Chapter 9 shifted the focus to the children who migrate to the United States with their middle-class professional parents. These young migrants, who are called the 1.5 generation, engage in everyday "struggles for social status" (Levitt & Glick Schiller 2004: 1008) through interactions with various others in the transnational social field, characterised by the unequal exchange of resources and asymmetrical power relations. These immigrants were experiencing deep dilemmas and conflicts while being faced with the first generation, who want their children to have the "only reliable profession", particularly nursing, in exchange for the sacrifice of their migration to the United States, and also with the second generation, who seemed to have overly internalised American individualism.

In this study, "the social" is defined as ideas and institutions that enable us to live, protect our subsistence, and liberate our lives from dependence on various primordial relationships. At the same time, it is a power that normalises, disciplines, and standardises our lives under a uniform bureaucratic grid. Such fundamental ambivalence inherent in "the social" becomes further prominent under the neoliberal restructuring of today's world. Furthermore, the neoliberal restructuring of "the social" directs our lives to become "a permanent enterprise", whereby society is penetrated by the model of enterprise "down to the fine grain of its texture" (Foucault 2008: 241). The contradictions and dilemmas observed in the ethnographies presented in this book can be discussed as a consequence of such an "enterprise model" under which individuals are subjected to become "human capital", the value of which is measured by the criteria of "productivity/unproductivity" and "efficiency/inefficiency".

Emergence of the "Vernacular Public Sphere" in the Global South

Along with this restructuring of the "social", it became clear that the localised mutuality of the intimate sphere has been activated and mobilised to form an alternative public sphere, which in this work, is referred to as the "vernacular public sphere" (Figure 1.1 in the Introduction). Localised mutualities such as family and kin, patron–client relationships, and neighbourhood and community should not be considered remnants of tradition that would be phased out with the progress of modernisation, nor are they primordial ties that stubbornly resist neoliberal governance. As already mentioned in the Introduction, this book avoids the dichotomy of "(post)modernity/tradition" or "civil society/community". Rather, what became clear from the ethnographies in each chapter is that an emerging vernacular public sphere can be observed at the interface between the neoliberal restructuring of "the social" and localised mutualities. In the following, I would like to elaborate on this point by reviewing the arguments in each chapter.

The chapters of Part I discussed the implications of the clientelistic connections that emerge in the process of implementing social policies targeting the urban poor. The homeowners association discussed in Chapter 2 had become one of the prominent actors in realising the "participatory democracy" that appeared in the post-authoritarian era in the Philippines in the late 1980s. In the implementation process of the CMP, however, they were no longer associated with the abstract and formal value of "participatory democracy", but rather, were interpreted by residents as another route to access resources for subsistence. The poor residents of urban communities maintain a number of personal ties as channels through which various resources are accessed. Specifically, these include local politicians, such as barangay councillors and city councillors, congresspersons of local districts and other politicians, relatives and neighbours, friends living abroad, and even, when life is difficult, loan sharks such as the *Bombai* (immigrant Indian merchants). Also in this implementation process, associations were incorporated into existing networks of the people as another channel of access to new resources, namely land. Of course, when some association officials and local politicians develop personal relationships based on their vested interests, the association stops its operation because of the suspicion and distrust of other members. However, while maintaining strong patron–client relationships with the mayor and other local politicians, several associations have been successful in gaining the trust of residents by emphasising transparency and achieving land tenure security for informal residents. By interpreting associations not in terms of the abstract and formal concept of "participatory democracy", but rather, in terms of the more familiar and understandable logic of clientelism, residents were able to "tame" the institution as an informal channel for the distribution of goods and services, thereby making life security possible.

In Chapter 3, I examined the implications of the logic of "investment in human capital" as a rationale of the Conditional Cash Transfer Program (4Ps). I argued that the neoliberal logic of self-reliance incited, unexpectedly and ironically as well, a desire of the people for redistribution through clientelistic interdependence. Such a desire is not simply a reflection of a "culture of dependency" among the poor nor is it an indication that the people are still embedded in feudalistic patron–client relationships; rather, it is a reaffirmation of interdependence and reciprocity based on intimate connections by the people who, having faced the overwhelming precarity and vulnerabilities inherent in slum communities, reasserted the value contrary to an "investment in human capital". Such reaffirmation and reassertion are not "retrograde yearning for paternalism and inequality" (Ferguson 2013:223) but rather an active pursuit of full social personhood through subordination and dependency by the people who have been marginalised by liberal democracy and free civil society. As Ferguson asserts, these are "declarations of dependence" by the people to achieve a "new politics of redistribution" (Ferguson 2015) following all the contradictions that occurred under the neoliberal restructuring of social policies.

The chapters of Part II, particularly Chapter 5, suggested that the articulation of the community in regard to the coastal resource management regime, which I called the "contextualization" process of institutions, opened up the community to various external actors, thereby enabling alternative resource use. The community, while maintaining the personal bonds of family and kin, started to collaborate with the actors who implemented the co-management of coastal resources, namely the Municipal Fisheries and Aquatic Resources Management Council (MFARMC) under the local government, central governmental agencies such as the Bureau of Fisheries and Aquatic Resources (BFAR), and civil society organisations such as local and foreign NGOs. Here, too, personal and intimate ties were not the residue of a primordial attachment that stubbornly resists the public interest of resource management; rather, the intimate ties of family, kinship, and community are reactivated in a manner that realises an alternative mode of livelihood by interacting and negotiating with the public rationale of resource management and conservation, along with the discipline it demands (Case 5.4). Here again, as discussed by the "new politics of redistribution" by Ferguson, the people openly accepted inequality and hierarchy in order to achieve a certain balance in resource redistribution among community members (Chapter 5). Similarly, social relations in the maritime world, characterised by high mobility, are not defined by static identities based on rigid group membership or blood ties. As discussed by Carsten, their identity and membership to the community are flexibly constructed through the everyday exchanges of various substances such as food, clothing, and shelter (Carsten 1995a, 1995b). As discussed in Chapter 6, the lives of fisherman, who have been marginalised by the neoliberal restructuring of coastal resource management, were also made possible by such flexible interdependence within the community.

The chapters in Part III focused on the narratives and representations of intimate connections, such as the family, by the people living in the transnational social field, which is increasingly permeated by neoliberal governmentality. As observed in Chapter 7, risks created by the widespread deployment of overseas temporary contract workers are being dealt with by activating neighbourhood ties and creating new linkages with NGOs and the government. Although the presence of the state and NGOs is certainly essential in dealing with these risks, the intimate connections based on neighbourhood relations were what mobilised the actors to form a broad network, which was made possible by the people's ability to not only affect, but also to be affected by others by sharing emotions such as misery, sorrow, and anger. The alternative public sphere described in this chapter consisted of an affective agency that caught up with others through compassion, rather than by formal civil society organisations based on the civil rationality, logical deliberation, or professional knowledge.

In Chapter 9, the representation of the "family" served as a symbolic resource for identity among the children and youths who were living in the differentiated and fragmented transnational social field, which is characterised by the "struggle for social status". Amidst the highly competitive environment in the US, where economic independence, achievement, and individualism are prioritised, the representation of the "family" is said to be at the core of "we, the Filipinos" for the young 1.5-generation immigrants who are still in the process of unstable socialisation and identification in an unfamiliar host country. However, the harmonious representation of the "family" does not actually reflect the families that existed in their childhood in the Philippines or the current state of families in the United States; this is because the families of the 1.5-generation immigrants were already losing their economic foundations and psychological unity after facing the depressing situation in the Philippines, which was expressed in ways such as "this country has nowhere to go" and "there is no hope in this country". Meanwhile, in the United States, families are often oppressive and restrictive for 1.5-generation children, pressuring them, either directly or indirectly, to enter into the competitive reproductive labour market. Nevertheless, reaffirming the "family", and reasserting their ties to it, made it possible for 1.5-generation immigrants to reinterpret, and give new meaning to, their experiences of "being uprooted" and to recover an integrated whole self in the host country.

The final chapter argued the significance of loose and transient solidarity among middle-class professionals caught up in the fragmented transnational social field. Ambivalence characterised their NGO work and political movement, which is carried out by middle-class professionals who have one foot in the Philippines and the other in the United States or Canada. Their solidarity and movement were mobilised by a concern for their compatriots, or *"kapwa"* in Filipino. Even though they are anxiously seeking to secure backup options in case the political situation in the Philippines worsens, at the same time, they feel obliged to "give back to the people". Although the solidarity observed in Chapter 10 was not a robust and lasting one based on a cohesive identity and shared morals among middle-class citizens, the case study suggested that even such loose and transient solidarity never excludes the possibility of concrete social reforms and political action.

In this book, I have presented ethnographies that indicate the consequences of the contemporary neoliberal restructuring of "the social" and the kind of alternative public sphere for the people's security that can be observed in such a restructuring process. Particularly, this book argues that localised mutualities based on the social relationships embedded in the community have been reactivated in the process of the neoliberal restructuring of "the social" and mobilised to form an alternative public sphere, which I call the "vernacular public sphere" (Figure 1.1 in the Introduction). Although this vernacular public sphere is made possible by personal, informal, and localised sociality such as the family, kin, neighbours, and patron–client relationships, it would be inappropriate to view such connections as the residue of the traditional and primordial relationships that will be phased out with the further penetration of neoliberal governmentality into "the social". This is because the vernacular public sphere observed in this study emerged at the interface between neoliberal restructuring and localised mutualities, while being activated by neoliberal ideas such as self-help, autonomy, empowerment, an active citizenry, productive communities, and institutions based on those ideas. Activated and mobilised by both neoliberal restructuring and localised mutualities, the vernacular public sphere emerges to provide security for life in precarious and uncertain times. To further clarify the concept of the "vernacular public sphere", I briefly touch on the literature that deals with similar ideas.

Chatterjee's argument on "popular politics" (Chatterjee 2004), which was based on the case of a slum colony in Kolkata, India, suggests a version of the vernacular public sphere described in this book. Chatterjee argues that popular politics is made possible by counterposing a "political society" to a "civil society". Chatterjee defines "civil society" as "the closed association of modern elite groups, sequestered from the wider popular life of the communities, walled up within enclaves of civil freedom and rational law" (Chatterjee 2004: 4). "Political society", by contrast, emerges out of government policies that target subaltern groups.

> [These groups are] organized into associations, transgress[ing] the strict lines of legality in struggling to live and work. They may live in illegal squatter settlements, make illegal use of water or electricity, travel without tickets in public transport. Yet state agencies (…) cannot ignore them either, since they are among thousands of similar associations representing groups of [the] population whose very livelihood or habitation involve violation[s] of the law.
>
> (Chatterjee 2004: 40)

Popular politics in India cannot be realised by liberal democracy or the formal rationality of civil society. Rather, popular politics is mobilised by the informal, and sometimes illegal, practices of subaltern populations. Although informal and illegal, government agencies, as providers of the welfare and well-being of the people, must respond to the demands for legitimacy made by political society owing to the huge subaltern populations. Thus, it can be argued that popular politics would emerge at the interface between civil and political society to demand the survival and welfare of subaltern populations.

In another study from India, Tanabe (2007) introduced the concept of "vernacular democracy" in relation to contemporary India's subaltern politics, which resonates strongly with Chatterjee's political society. According to Tanabe, vernacular democracy is based on "people's creative mediation of embodied cultural resources and ideas and institutions of democracy" (Tanabe 2007: 589). Such embodied cultural resources signify the nonofficial cultural resources that are historically embedded in the life-worlds of the villagers. Tanabe refers specifically to the egalitarian sacrificial ethics that prevail among villagers, entailing indigenous notions of service, duty, and sharing. Thus, vernacular democracy is founded on a moral society in which morality is premised on the indigenous notion of concrete connections forged between the body, land, and duty of exchanging services, as opposed to abstract universal norms such as freedom, equality, and citizenship. Within a moral society, individuals are connected through various modes of informal sociality, including community, kinship, caste, and patron–client relationships. The efforts of subalterns in contemporary India to acquire proper representation, and their entitlements within local politics, are more successfully accomplished through vernacular democracy than through formal institutional democracy. Another important point to note is that a moral society and the vernacular democracy that it fosters function in a manner that is complementary, but not reducible to, civil society, which is based on the abstract membership of individuals and citizens and their equally formal ideals of liberty, rights, and equality. As an abstract and formal association, civil society provides limited opportunities for subalterns to access resources. The democratic participation of subalterns in contemporary India today is secured through vernacular democracy and a moral society. Vernacular democracy enables the coalescing of the "public life" of civil society with the "private life" of communities, wherein villagers' existing cultural–ethical resources, which relate to the "care of life" itself, determining what they eat, with whom they interact, and whom they marry, are critically important (Tanabe 2002, 2007).

The studies that have been reviewed thus far clearly reveal a focus on the interface of, and negotiation between, formal institutions such as civil society or democracy, and localised mutualities, such as political or moral society. Popular politics and vernacular democracy as discussed by Chatterjee and Tanabe can be considered to contain similar characteristics to the vernacular public sphere proposed in this book. The localised mutuality embedded in the community would not simply fade out with the penetration of neoliberalism, but rather, would be reactivated and reinvented to emerge as a vernacular public sphere. To what degree, and in what way, the vernacular public sphere is effective at providing protection and security for those face precarity and uncertainty in the Global South and beyond remains to be answered in the future study.[1]

Note

1. The author is fully aware that the precarity and uncertainty of the Anthropocene derive not only from humans but also from the interaction between humans and non-humans. As the "reassembling the social" (Latour 2005) should be conducted through focusing on the entanglement of culture and nature, anthropological discussions on "the social" should accordingly focus on the entanglement of humans and non-humans. A discussion of the vernacular public sphere from the standpoint of human and non-human interactions is thus a remaining task to be examined in the future.

Bibliography

Abinales, Patriciao N. and Donna J. Amoroso 2005 *State and Society in the Philippines*, Quezon City: Anvil.

Adams, William M. and Jon Hutton 2007 People, Parks and Poverty: Political Ecology and Biodiversity Conservation, *Conservation and Society* 5(2): 147–183.

Agoncillo, Jodee A. 2017 Gunmen Took Baby in Mom's Arms Before Killing Her in Front of Kids, *Philippine Daily Inquirer*, March 1, 2017.

Agrawal, Arun 2003 Sustainable Governance of Common-Pool Resources: Context, Methods, and Politics, *Annual Review of Anthropology* 32: 243–262.

———— 2005a Environmentality: Community, Intimate Government, and the Making of Environmental Subjects in Kumaon, India, *Current Anthropology* 46(2): 161–190.

———— 2005b *Environmentality: Technologies of Government and the Making of Subjects*. Durham: Duke University Press.

Agrawal, Arun and Clarke C. Gibson 2001 Introduction: The Role of Community in Natural Resource Conservation, In Agrawal, Arun and Clarke C. Gibson (eds.), *Communities and the Environment: Ethnicity, Gender, and the State in Community-Based Conservation*, New Brunswick, NJ: Rutgers University Press, pp.1–31.

Aguilar, Filomeno 2003 Global Migrations, Old Forms of Labor, and New Transborder Class Relations, *Japanese Journal of Southeast Asian Studies* 41(2): 137–161.

———— 2004 Is There a Transnation? Migrancy and the National Homeland among Overseas Filipinos, In Brenda, S. A. Yeoh and Katie Willis (eds.), *State/Nation/Transnation: Perspective on Transnationalism in the Asia-Pacific*, Abingdon and New York: Routledge, pp.93–119.

Allison, Anne and Charlie Piot 2011 New Editors' Greeting, *Cultural Anthropology* 26(1): 1–5.

Anderson, Benedict 1998 *The Specter of Comparison: Nationalism, Southeast Asia and the World*, Brooklyn, NY: Verso.

Ansell, Aaron 2014 *Zero Hunger: Political Culture and Antipoverty Policy in Northeast Brazil*, Chapel Hill, NC: The University of North Carolina Press.

Antolihao, Lou 2004 *Culture of Improvisation: Informal Settlements and Slum Upgrading in a Metro Manila Locality*. Quezon City: Institute of Philippine Culture, Ateneo de Manila University.

Appadurai, Arjun 2002 Deep Democracy: Urban Governmentality and the Horizon of Politics, *Public Culture* 14(1): 21–47.

Astuti, Rita 1995 *People of the Sea: Identity and Descent among the Vezo of Madagascar*, Cambridge: Cambridge University Press.

Austin, Rebecca et al. 2009 The Accidental Scholar as Activist: From Ecocolonialism to Effective Transnational Alliances in Palawan's Environmental Movement (Poster Presentation at Society for Applied Anthropology, 69th Annual Meeting, Santa Fe, New Mexico).

Auyero, Javier 2001 *Poor People's Politics: Peronist Survival Networks and the Legacy of Evita*, Durham, NC: Duke University Press.

Azuma, Kentaro, Junpei Ichinosawa, Shuhei Kimura and Taku Iida (eds.) 2014 *Risk no Jinruigaku: Fukakujitsu na Sekai wo Ikiru*, Kyoto: Sekaishisosha.

Ballesteros, Marife M. 2005 *Rethinking Institutional Reforms in the Philippine Housing Sector*, Quezon City: Philippine Institute for Development Studies.

Bakker, Karen 2005 Neoliberalizing Nature? Market Environmentalism in Water Supply in England and Wales, *Annals of the Association of American Geographers* 95(3): 542–565.

Bautista, Maria Cynthia Rose Banzon 2001 People Power 2: 'The Revenge of the Elite on the Masses'?, In Doronila, Amando (ed.), *Between Fires: Fifteen Perspectives on the Estrada Crisis*, Quezon City: An Inquirer Books Publication, pp.1–42.

Beck, Ulrich 1992 *Risk Society: Toward a New Modernity*, Thousand Oaks, CA: Sage Publications.

Berlanga, Mauro and Betty B. Faust 2007 We Thought We Wanted a Reserve: One Community's Disillusionment with Government Conservation Management, *Conservation and Society* 5(4): 450–477.

Berner, Erhard 1997 *Defending a Place in the City: Localities and the Struggle for Urban Land in Metro Manila*, Quezon City: Ateneo de Manila University Press.

——— 2000 Poverty Alleviation and the Eviction of the Poorest: Towards Urban Land Reform in the Philippines, *International Journal of Urban and Regional Research* 24(3): 554–566.

——— 2001 Learning from Informal Markets: Innovative Approaches to Land and Housing Provision, *Development in Practice* 11(2&3): 292–307.

Biersack, Aletta 2006 Reimagining Political Ecology: Culture/Power/History/Nature, In Biersack, Aletta and James B. Greenberg (eds.) *Reimagining Political Ecology*, Durham, NC: Duke University Press, pp.3–40.

Bird, Richard and Edgard R. Rodriguez 1999 Decentralization and Poverty Alleviation: International Experience and the Case of the Philippines, *Public Administration and Development* 19: 299–319.

Boris, Eileen and Rhacel Salazar Parreñas (eds.) 2010 *Intimate Labors: Cultures, Technologies, and the Politics of Care*, Stanford, CA: Stanford University Press.

Bourdieu, Pierre 1984 *Distinction: A Social Critique of the Judgement of Taste*, Cambridhe, MA: Harvard University Press.

Bridge, Gavin 2007 Acts of Enclosure: Claim Staking and Land Conversion in Guyana's Gold Fields, In Heynen, Nik, James McCarthy, Scott Prudham and Paul Robbins (eds.), *Neoliberal Environments: False Promises and Unnatural Consequences*, Abingdon and New York: Routledge, pp.74–86.

Bryant, Raymond L. and Sinéad Bailey 1997 *Third World Political Ecology*, London and New York: Routledge.

Brockington, Dan 2004 Community Conservation, Inequality and Injustice: Myths of Power in Protected Area Management, *Conservation & Society* 2(2): 411–432.

——— 2008 Powerful Environmentalisms: Conservation, Celebrity and Capitalism, *Media, Culture & Society* 30(4): 551–568.

_____ 2009 *Celebrity and the Environment: Fame, Wealth and Power in Conservation*, London: Zed Books.

Brockington, Dan and Rosaleen Duffy 2010 Capitalism and Conservation: The Production and Reproduction of Biodiversity Conservation, *Antipode* 42(3): 469–484.

Brockington, Dan and Katherine Scholfield 2010 The Conservation Mode of Production and Conservation NGOs in Sub-Saharan Africa, *Antipode* 42(3): 551–575.

Burchell, Graham 1996 Liberal Government and Techniques of the Self, In Barry, Andrew, Thomas Osborne and Nicholas Rose (eds.), *Foucault and Political Reason: Liberalism, Neo-liberalism, and Rationalities of Government*, Chicago: University of Chicago Press, pp.19–36.

Büscher, Bram and Wolfram Dressler 2007 Linking Neoprotectionism and Environmental Governance: On the Rapidly Increasing Tensions between Actors in the Environment-Development Nexus, *Conservation and Society* 5(4): 586–611.

Butcher, John G. 2004 *The Closing of the Frontier: A History of the Marine Fisheries of Southeast Asia c. 1850-2000*, Singapore: ISEAS Publications.

Cahn, Peter S. 2008 Consuming Class: Multilevel Marketers in Neoliberal Mexico, *Cultural Anthropology* 23(3): 429–452.

Cannell, Fanella 1999 *Power and Intimacy in the Christian Philippines*. Cambridge: Cambridge University Press.

Carrier, James G. 2010 Protecting the Environment the Natural Way: Ethical Consumption and Commodity Fetishism, *Antipode* 42(3): 672–689.

Carrier, James G. and Donald Macleod V.L. 2005 Bursting the Bubble: The Socio-Cultural Context of Ecotourism, *Journal of Royal Anthropological Institute* 11: 315–334.

Carsten, Janet 1995 The Politics of Forgetting: Migration, Kinship and Memory on the Periphery of the Southeast Asian State, *Journal of the Royal Anthropological Institute* 1(2): 317–335.

Castel, Robert 2003 *From Manual Workers to Wage Laborers: Transformation of the Social Question*, New Brunswick, NJ and London: Transaction Publishers.

_____ 2009 *La Montée des Incertitudes: Travail, Protections, Statut de L'individu*, Paris: Seul

Castree, Noel 2008 Neoliberalising Nature: Processes, Effects, and Evaluations, *Environment and Planning A* 40: 153–173.

Casino, Faith Christian Q. 2001 *Microfinance Approach to Housing: The Community Mortgage Program*. Discussion Paper Series No. 2001-28, Makati City: Philippine Institute for Development Studies.

CFO (Commission on Filipino Overseas) 2016 Stock Estimate of Overseas Filipinos as of Dec. 2013, http://www.cfo.gov.ph/index.php?option=com_content&view=article&id=1340:stock-estimate-of-overseas-filipinos&catid=134:statisticsstock-estimate&Itemid=814 (accessed May 23, 2016).

CFO (Commission on Filipino Overseas) 2013 Number of Registered Filipino Emigrants by Major Countries of Destination: 1981-2012, http://www.cfo.gov.ph/images/stories/pdf/bymajorcountry2012pdf (accessed July 18, 2012).

Chakrabarty, Dipesh 2000 *Provincializing Europe: Postcolonial Thought and Historical Difference*, Princeton, NJ: Princeton University Press.

Chatterjee, Partha 2004 *The Politics of the Governed: Reflections on Popular Politics in Most of the World*, New York: Columbia University Press.

Choy, Catherine Ceniza 2003 *Empire of Care: Nursing and Migration in Filipino American History*. Durham, NC: Duke University Press.

City of Daly City (City Profile) 2013 http://www.dalycity.org/About_Daly_City/City_Profile.htm (accessed October 10, 2013).

Clarke, John, Dave Bainton, Noémi Lendvai and Paul Stubbs 2015 *Making Policy Move: Towards a Politics of Translation and Assemblage*, Cambridge: Policy Press.

Claudio, Lisandro E. 2017 *Liberalism and the Postcolony: Thinking the State in 20th-Century Philippines*, Quezon City: Ateneo de Manila University Press.

Clough, Patricia Ticineto 2007 Introduction, In Clough, Patricia Ticineto and Jean Halley (eds.) *The Affective Turn: Theorizing the Social*, Durham, NC: Duke University Press, pp.1–33.

Clough, Patricia Ticineto and Jean Halley 2007 *The Affective Turn: Theorizing the Social*, Durham, NC: Duke University Press.

Comaroff, Jean and John Comaroff 1999 Introduction, In Comaroff, Jean and John L. Comaroff (eds.), *Civil Society and the Political Imagination in Africa: Critical Perspective*, Chicago, IL: The University of Chicago Press, pp.1–43.

Correia, David 2005 From Agropastoralism to Sustained Yield Forestry: Industrial Restructuring, Rural Change, and the Land-grant Commons in Northern Mexico, *Capitalism Nature Socialism* 16(1): 25–44.

Crompton, Rosemary 2008 *Class & Stratification*, 3rd edition. Cambridge: Polity Press.

Cruikshank, Barbara 1999 *The Will to Empower: Democratic Citizens and Other Subjects*, Ithaca and London: Cornell University Press.

Curato, Nicole 2019 *Democracy in a Time of Misery: From Spectacular Tragedy to Deliberative Action*, Oxford: Oxford University Press.

Danico, Mary Yu 2004 *The 1.5 Generation: Becoming Korean American in Hawai'i*, Honolulu, HI: University of Hawai'i Press.

David, Randy 2005 *Change, Philippine Daily Inquirer*, August 7, 2005.

Dean, Mitchell 2010 *Governmentality: Power and Rule in Modern Society*, 2nd edition. London: Sage.

Donzelot, Jacques 1979 *The Policing of Family*, New York: Pantheon Books.

———— 1984 *L'invention du Social: Essai sur le déclin des passions politiques*, Paris: Libraire Artheme Fayard.

———— 1988 The Promotion of the Social, *Economy and Society* 17(3): 395–427.

———— 1991 The Mobilization of Society, In Burchell, Graham, Colin Gordon and Peter Miller (eds.), *The Foucault Effect: Studies in Governmentality*, Chicago: The University of Chicago Press, pp.169–179.

Donzelot, Jacques and Philippe Estèbe 1994 *L'Etat Animateur: Essai sur la Politique de la Ville*, Paris: Edition Esprit.

Dressler, Wolfram H. 2009 *Old Thoughts in New Ideas: State Conservation Measures, Development and Livelihood on Palawan Island*, Quezon City: Ateneo de Manila University Press.

Dreyfus, Hubert I. and Rabinow Paul 1983 *Michael Foucault: Beyond Structuralism and Hermeneutics*, 2nd edition. Chicago: The University of Chicago Press.

Duffy, Rosaleen and Lorraine Moore 2010 Neoliberalising Nature? Elephant-Back Tourism in Thailand and Botswana, *Antipode* 42(3): 742–766.

Dunn, Elizabeth C. 2004 *Privatizing Poland: Baby Food, Big Business, and the Remaking of Labor*, Ithaca: Cornell University Press.

Eaton, Kent 2001 Political Obstacles to Decentralization: Evidence from Argentina and the Philippines, *Development and Change* 32: 101–127.

Eder, James F. and Janet O. Fernandez 1996 Palawan, A Last Frontier. In Eder, James F. and Janet O. Fernandez (eds.), *Palawan at the Crossroads: Development and the Environment on a Philippine Frontier*, Quezon City: Ateneo de Manila University Press, pp.1–22.

Ehrenreich, Barbara 1990 *Fear of Falling: The Inner Life of the Middle Class*, New York: Harper Perennial.

Espin-Andersen, Gosta 1999 *Social Foundations of Postindustrial Economies*, Oxford: Oxford University Press.

Espiritu, Yen Le 2003 *Home Bound: Filipino American Lives across Cultures, Communities, and Countries*, Oakland, CA: University of California Press.

Espiritu, Yen Le and Diane Wolf 2001 The Paradox of Assimilation: Children of Filipino Immigrants in San Diego, In Ruben, Rumbaut G. and Alejandro Portes (eds.), *Ethnicities: Children of Immigrants in America*, Oakland, CA: University of California Press, pp.157–186.

Fabinyi, Michael 2014 Fishing and Socio Economic Change in the Calamianes Islands, In Eder, James and Oscar L. Evangelista (eds.), *Palawan and Its Global Connections*, Quezon City: Ateneo de Manila University, pp.140–160.

Fallow, James. 1987 "A Damaged Culture: A New Philippines?", *The Atlantic Monthly*, November 1987 (http://www.theatlantic.com/technology/archive/1987/11/a-damaged-culture-a-new-philippines/7414/).

Ferguson, James 2009 The Use of Neoliberalism, *Antipode* 41(S1): 166–184.

———— 2013 Declarations of Dependence: Labour, Personhood, and Welfare in Southern Africa, *Journal of the Royal Anthropological Institute (N.S.)*19: 223–242.

———— 2015 *Give a Man a Fish: Reflections on the New Politics of Distribution*, Durham, NC: Duke University Press.

Ferguson, James, and Akhil Gupta 2002 Spatializing States: Toward an Ethnography of Neoliberal Governmentality, *American Ethnologist* 29(4): 981–1002.

Fernando, Marides C. and Eric C. Maliwat 2009 *Urbanidad: Responsible Living, Rewarding Life*, Quezon City: CROSSOVER Books.

Ferrer, Miriam Coronel (ed.) 1997 *Civil Society Making Civil Society*, Quezon City: The Third World Study Center.

Fiszbein, A. and N. Schady 2009 *Conditional Cash Transfer: Reducing Present and Future Poverty*, Washington, DC: The World Bank.

Fletcher, Robert 2010 Neoliberal Environmentality: Towards a Poststructuralist Political Ecology of the Conservation Debate, *Conservation and Society* 8(3): 171–181.

Fortwangler, Crystal 2007 Friends with Money: Private Support for a National Park in the US Virgin Islands, *Conservation and Society* 5(4): 504–533.

Foucault, Michael 1990 *The History of Sexuality, Vol. 1: An Introduction*, New York: Random House.

———— 2008 *The Birth of Biopolitics: Lectures at the Collège de France, 1978–1979*, London: Palgrave Macmillan.

———— 2009 *Security, Territory, Population: Lectures at the Collège de France 1977–1978*, London: Palgrave Macmillan.

Fraser, Nancy 1992 Rethinking the Public Sphere: A Contribution to the Critique of Actually Existing Democracy, In Calhoun, Craig (ed.), *Habermas and the Public Sphere*, Boston, MA: MIT Press: 109–142.

——— 1995 Politics, Culture, and the Public Sphere: Toward a Postmodern Conception, In Nicholson, Linda and Steven Seidman (eds.), *Social Postmodernism: Beyond Identity Politics*, Cambridge: Cambridge University Press: 287–312.

Fukuda, Shingo 2012 The Inflow of Foreign Cheap Products and Local Manufacturing in the Philippines: Case of the Footwear Manufacturing Industry, *Japanese Journal of Southeast Asian Studies* 50(1): 72–108.

Ganti, Tejaswini 2014 Neoliberalism, *Annual Review of Anthropology*, 43: 89–104.

Gardner, Katy 2012 Transnational Migration and the Study of Children: An Introduction, *Journal of Ethnic and Migration Studies* 38(6): 889–912.

Garrido, Marco 2008 Civil and Uncivil Society: Symbolic Boundaries and Civic Exclusion in Metro Manila, *Philippine Studies* 56(4): 443–465.

———— 2013a. The Ideology of the Dual City: The Modernist Ethic in the Corporate Development of Makati City, Metro Manila, *International Journal of Urban and Regional Research* 37(1): 165–85.

———— 2013b. The Sense of Place behind Segregating Practices: An Ethnographic Approach to the Symbolic Partitioning of Metro Manila, *Social Forces* 91(4): 1343–1363.

———— 2019 *The Patchwork City: Class, Space, and Politics in Metro Manila*, Chicago, IL: University of Chicago Press.

George, Sheba M. 2005 *When Women Come First: Gender and Class in Transnational Migration*, Oakland, CA: University of California Press.

Giddens, Anthony 1998 *The Third Way: The Renewal of Social Democracy*, Cambridge: Polity.

Glick Schiller, Nina 2011 Localized Neoliberalism, Multiculturalism and Global Religion: Exploring the Agency of Migrants and City Boosters, *Economy and Society* 40(2): 211–238.

Goldman, Michael 2001 The Birth of a Discipline: Producing Authoritative Green Knowledge, World Bank-Style, *Ethnography* 2(2): 191–217.

———— 2004 Eco-Governmentality and Other Transnational Practices of a 'Green' World Bank, In Peet, Richard and Michael Watts (eds.), *Liberation Ecologies: Environment, Development, Social Movements*, 2nd edition. New York: Routledge, pp.166–192.

———— 2005 *Imperial Nature: The World Bank and Struggles for Social Justice in the Age of Globalization*, New Haven, CT: Yale University Press.

Gonzalez, Dennis T. 2009 *The Will to Change: Marikina and Its Innovations*, Marikina City: City of Marikina & Ateneo School of Governance.

Goode, Judith and Jeff Maskovsky (eds.) 2001 *The New Poverty Studies: The Ethnography of Power, Politics, and Impoverished People in the United States*. New York and London: New York University Press.

Gordon, Colin 1991 Governmental Rationality: An Introduction, In Burchell, Graham, Collin Gordon and Peter Miller (eds.), *The Foucault Effect: Studies in Governmentality*, Chicago: The University of Chicago Press, pp.1–51.

Gough, Ian and Geof Wood 2004 *Insecurity and Welfare Regimes in Asia, Africa and Latin America: Social Policy in Development Context*, Cambridge: Cambridge University Press.

Grandia, Liza 2007 Between Bolivar and Bureaucracy: The Mesoamerican Biological Corridor, *Conservation and Society* 5(4): 478–503.

Guevarra, Anna Romina 2010 *Marketing Dreams, Manufacturing Heroes: The Transnational Labor Brokering of Filipino Workers*, New Brunswick, NJ: Rutgers University Press.

Gupta, Akhil 1995 Blurred Boundaries: The Discourse of Corruption, the Culture of Politics, and the Imagined State, *American Ethnologist* 22(3): 375–402.

Hacking, Ian 1990 *The Taming of Chance*, New York: Cambridge University Press.

Hann, Chris 1996 Introduction: Political Society and Civil Anthropology, In Hann, Chris and Elizabeth Dunn (eds.), *Civil Society: Challenging Western Models*, Abingdon and New York: Routledge, pp.1–26.

Hardt, Michael and Antonio Negri 2000 *Empire*, Cambridge, MA: Harvard University Press.

Harvey, David 1989 From Managerialism to Entrepreneurialism: The Transformation in Urban Governance in Late Capitalism, *Geografika Annaler* 71B(1): 3–17.

234   Bibliography

_____ 2005 *A Brief History of Neoliberalism*, Oxford and New York: Oxford University Press.

Hedman, Eva-Lotta E. 2006 *In the Name of Civil Society: From Free Election Movements to People Power in the Philippines*, Honolulu, HI: University of Hawaii Press.

Heynen, Nik and Harold A. Perkins 2005 Scalar Dialectics in Green: Urban Private Property and the Contradictions of the Neoliberalization of Nature, *Capitalism Nature Socialism* 16(1): 99–113.

Heynen, Nik and Paul Robbins 2005 The Neoliberalization of Nature: Governance, Privatization, Enclosure and Valuation, *Capitalism Nature Socialism* 16(1): 5–8.

Heynen, Nik, James McCarthy, Scott Prudham and Paul Robbins 2007 Introduction: False Promises, In Heynen, Nik, James McCarthy, Scott Prudham and Paul Robbins (eds.), *Neoliberal Environments: False Promises and Unnatural Consequences*, Abingdon and New York: Routledge, pp.1–21.

Higaki, Tatsuya (ed.) 2011 *Seikenryokuron no Genzai: Foucault kara Gendai wo Yomu*, Tokyo: Keiso Shobo.

Hilhorst, Dorothea 2003 *The Real World of NGOs: Discourses, Diversity and Development*, Quezon City: Ateneo de Manila University Press.

Hochschild, Arile Russel 1983 *The Managed Heart: Commercialization of Human Feeling*, Oakland, CA: University of California Press.

_____ 2000 Global Care Chains and Emotional Surplus Value, In Hutton, W. and A. Giddens (eds.), *On the Edge: Living with Global Capitalism*, London: Jonathan Cape, pp.130–146.

Holifield, Ryan 2004 Neoliberalism and Environmental Justice in the United States Environmental Protection Agency: Translating Policy into Managerial Practice in Hazardous Waste Remediation, *Geoforum* 35: 285–297.

Hollander, Gail 2007 Weak or Strong Multifunctionality? Agri-environmental Resistance to Neoliberal Trade Policies, In Heynen, Nik, James McCarthy, Scott Prudham and Paul Robbins (eds.), *Neoliberal Environments: False Promises and Unnatural Consequences*, Abingdon and New York: Routledge, pp.126–138.

Holmes, George 2010 The Rich, the Powerful and the Endangered: Conservation Elites, Networks and the Dominican Republic, *Antipode* 42(3): 624–646.

Hutchcroft, Paul D. 1998 *Booty Capitalism: The Politics of Banking in the Philippines*, Ithaca, NY: Cornell University Press.

Hutchison, Jane 2007 The 'Disallowed' Political Participation of Manila's Urban Poor, *Democratization* 14(5): 853–872.

Hyatt, Susan Brin, Boone W. Shear and Susan Wright (eds.), 2015 *Learning Under Neoliberalism: Ethnographies of Governance in Higher Education*, New York and Oxford: Berghahn.

Igoe, Jim 2004 *Conservation and Globalization: A Study of National Parks and Indigenous Communities from East Africa to South Dakota*, Belmont, CA: Wadsworth.

Igoe, Jim and Dan Brockington 2007 Neoliberal Conservation: A Brief Introduction, *Conservation and Society* 5(4): 432–449.

Igoe, Jim and Beth Croucher 2007 Conservation, Commerce, and Communities: The Story of Community-Based Wildlife Management Areas in Tanzania's Northern Tourist Circuit, *Conservation and Society* 5(4): 534–561.

Igoe, Jim, Katja Neves and Dan Brockington 2010 A Spectacular Eco-Tour around the Historic Bloc: Theorising the Convergence of Biodiversity Conservation and Capitalist Expansion, *Antipode* 42(3): 486–512.

Ileto, Reynaldo C. 1999. *Knowing America's Colony: A Hundred Years from the Philippine War*, Philippine Studies Occasional Papers Series No.13, Honolulu, HI: Center for Philippine Studies, University of Hawai'i.

Ishi, Tomoji 1987 Class Conflict, the State, and Linkage: The International Migration of Nurses from the Philippines, *Berkeley Journal of Sociology* 32: 281–312.

Jocano, Landa F. 1975 *Slum as a Way of Life: A Study of Coping Behavior in an Urban Environment*, Quezon City: New Day Publishers.

Karaos, Anna Marie A. and Gerald M. Nicolas 2009 More than Building Homes: Institutionalizing Innovation through the Community Mortgage Program, In Hermoso, Reuel R., Fernando Aldaba and Mary Racelis (eds.), *Agenda for Hope: Ideas on Building a Nation*, Quezon City: Ateneo de Manila University Loyola Schools, pp.79–98.

Kerkvliet, Benedict, 1991 *Everyday Politics in the Philippines: Class and Status Relations in a Central Luzon Village*, Berkeley: University of California Press.

Kingfisher, Catherine 2002 Introduction: The Global Feminization of Poverty, In Kingfisher, Catherine (ed.), *Western Welfare in Decline: Globalization and Women's Poverty*, Philadelphia, PA: University of Pennsylvania Press, pp.3–12.

_____ 2013 *A Policy Travelogue: Tracing Welfare Reform in Aoteroa/New Zealand and Canada*, New York and Oxford: Berghahn.

Kipnis, Andrew 2008 Audit Cultures: Neoliberal Governmentality, Socialist Legacy, or Technologies of Governing? *American Anthropologist* 35(2): 275–289.

_____ 2011 *Governing Educational Desire: Culture, politics, and Schooling in China*, Chicago, IL: The University of Chicago Press.

Kusaka, Wataru 2017 *Moral Politics in the Philippines: Inequality, Democracy and the Urban Poor*, Singapore: NUS Press.

Latour, Bruno 2005 *Reassembling the Social: An Introduction to Actor-Network-Theory*, Oxford and New York: Oxford University Press.

Lazar, Sian 2004 Education for Credit: Development as Citizenship Project in Bolovia, *Critique of Anthropology* 24(3): 301–319.

Lee, Michael 1995 The Community Mortgage Program: An Almost-Successful Alternative for some Urban Poor, *Habitat International* 19(4): 529–546.

Lemos, Maria Carmen and Arun Agrawal 2006 Environmental Governance, *Annual Review of Environment and Resources* 31: 297–325.

Levine, Arielle 2007 Staying Afloat: State Agencies, Local Communities, and International Involvement in Marine Protected Area Management in Zanzibar, Tanzania, *Conservation and Society* 5(4): 562–585.

Levitt, Peggy and Nina Glick Schiller 2004 Conceptualizing Simultaneity: A Transnational Social Field Perspective on Society. *International Migration Review* 38(3): 1002–1039.

Levitt, Peggy and Mary C. Waters (eds.) 2002 *The Changing Face of Home: The Transnational Lives of the Second Generation*, New York: Russell Sage Foundation.

Li, Tania Murray 2005 Beyond "the State" and Failed Schemes, *American Anthropologist* 107(3): 383–394.

_____ 2007a. *The Will to Improve: Governmentality, Development, and the Practice of Politics*, Durham: Duke University Press.

_____ 2007b. Practices of Assemblage and Community Forest Management, *Economy and Society* 36(2): 263–293.

_____ 2009 To Make Live or Let Die? Rural Dispossession and the Protection of Surplus Populations, *Antipode* 41(s1): 63–93.

Llanto, Gilberto M. and Aniceto C. Orbeta 2001 *The State of Philippine Housing Programs: A Critical Look at How Philippine Housing Subsidies Work*, Makati City: Philippine Institute for Development Studies.

Luke, Timothy W. 1999 Environmentality as Green Governmentality, In Darier, Eric (ed.), *Discourses of the Environment*, Hoboken, NJ: Blackwell Publishers, pp.121–151.

――――― 2005 On Environmentality: Geo-Power and Eco-Knowledge in the Discourses of Contemporary Environmentalism, In Haenn, Nora and Richard R. Wilk (eds.), *The Environment in Anthropology: A Reader in Ecology, Culture, and Sustainable Development*, New York: New York University Press, pp.257–269.

Lynch, Frank 2004 Big and Little People: Social Class in the Rural Philippines, In Yengoyan, Aram A. and Perla Q. Makil (eds.) *Philippine Society and the Individual: Selected Essay of Frank Lynch*, Quezon City: Ateneo de Manila University Press, pp.104–111.

MacDonald, Kenneth Iain 2010 The Devil is in the (Bio)diversity: Private Sector 'Engagement' and the Restructuring of Biodiversity Conservation, *Antipode* 42(3): 513–550.

Majima, Ichiro 2006 Chukanshudanron: Shakaitekinarumono no Kiten kara Kaikie, *Japanese Journal of Cultural Anthropology*, 71(1): 24–49.

Manasan, Rosario G. (ed.) 2002 *Managing Urbanization: Under a Decentralized Governance Framework*, Makati City: Philippine Institute of Development Studies.

Mansfield, Becky 2004a. Neoliberalism in the Oceans: 'Rationalization,' Property Rights, and the Commons Question, *Geoforum* 35: 313–326.

――――― 2004b. Rules of Privatization: Contradictions ion Neoliberal Regulation of North Pacific Fisheries, *Annals of the Association of American Geographers* 94(3): 565–584.

McAfee, Kathleen 1999 Selling Nature to Save It? Biodiversity and Green Developmentalism, *Environment and Planning D* 17: 133–154.

――――― 2003 Neoliberalism on the Molecular Scale: Economics and Genetic Reductionism in Biotechnology Battles, *Geoforum* 34: 203–219.

McCarthy, James 2004 Privatizing Condition of Production: Trade Agreements as Neoliberal Environmental Governance, *Geoforum* 35: 327–341.

――――― 2005 Commons as Counterhegemonic Projects, *Capitalism Nature Socialism* 16(1): 9–24.

McCarthy, James and Scott Prudham 2004 Neoliberal Nature and the Nature of Neoliberalism, *Geoforum* 35: 275–283.

McCoy, Alfred W. (ed.) 1994a *An Anarchy of Families: State and Family in the Philippines*, Quezon City: Ateneo de Manila University Press.

McCoy, Alfred W. 1994b 'An Anarchy of Families': The Historiography of State and Family in the Philippines, In McCoy, Alfred W. (ed.), *An Anarchy of Families: State and Family in the Philippines*, Quezon City: Ateneo de Manila University Press, pp.1–32.

Miller, Peter and Nikolas Rose 2008 *Governing the Present: Administering Economic, Social and Personal Life*, Cambridge: Polity.

Morgan, Sandra and Jeff Maskovsky 2003 The Anthropology of Welfare "Reform": New Perspective on U.S. Urban Poverty in the Post-Welfare Era, *Annual Review of Anthropology* 32: 315–338.

Mori, Akiko (ed.) 2014 *Europe Jinruigaku no Shiza: Social na Mono wo Toinaosu*, Kyoto: Sekaishisosya.

Muehlebach, A. 2012 *The Moral Neoliberal: Welfare and Citizenship in Italy*, Chicago, IL: The University of Chicago Press.

Murphy, Denis (ed). 2008 *Philippine NGO Report on the Implementation of the International Covenant on Economic, Social and Cultural Rights Concerning the Right to Adequate Housing*, Quezon City: John Carrol Institute on Church and Social Issues.

Neves, Katja 2010 Cashing in on Cetourism: A Critical Ecological Engagement with Dominant E-NGO Discourses on Whaling, Cetacean Conservation, and Whale Watching, *Antipode* 43(3): 719–741.

Neyazi, Taberez Ahmed, Tanabe, Akio and Ishizaka, Shinya (eds.) 2014 *Democratic Transformation and the Vernacular Public Arena in India*, Abingdon and New York: Routledge.

NSCB (National Statistical Coordination Board) 2009 Statistics – Labor and Employment, http://www.nscb.gov.ph/secstat/d_labor.asp (accessed October 14, 2009).

Ogaya, Chiho 2016 *Ido wo Ikiru: Philippine Iju Josei to Fukusu no Mobility*, Tokyo: Yushindo.

Okongwu, Anne Francis and Joan P. Mencher 2000 The Anthropology of Public Policy: Shifting Terrains, *Annual Review of Anthropology* 29: 107–24.

Olofson, Harold and Araceli Tiukinhoy 1992 'Plain Soldiers': *Muro-ami* Fishing in Cebu, *Philippine Studies* 40(1): 35–52.

Olofson, Harold, Bernie Cañizares and Farah de Jose 2000 A People in Travail I: Labor Relations History of Veteran *Muro-ami* Fisherfolk in the Central Philippines, *Philippine Quarterly of Culture and Society* 28(2): 224–262.

Omoda, Sonoe 2010 *Rentai no Tetsugaku I: France Shakai Rentai Shugi*, Tokyo: Keiso Shobo.

Ong, Aihwa 1999 *Flexible Citizenship: The Cultural Logic of Transnationality*, Durham, NC: Duke University Press.

——— 2006 *Neoliberalism as Exception: Mutations in Citizenship and Sovereignty*, Durham, NC: Duke University Press.

Ong, Paul and Tania Azores 1994 The Migration and Incorporation of Filipino Nurses, In Ong, Paul, Edna Banocich and Lucie Cheng (eds.), *The New Asian Immigration in Los Angeles and Global Restructuring*, Philadelphia, PA: Temple University Press, pp.164–195.

Ong, Paul, Edna Bonacich and Lucie Cheng 1994 The Political Economy of Capitalist Restructuring and the New Asian Immigration, In Ong, Paul, Edna Banocich and Lucie Cheng (eds.), *The New Asian Immigration in Los Angeles and Global Restructuring*, Philadelphia, PA: Temple University Press, pp.3–35.

Ong, Paul and John M. Liu 1994 U.S. Immigration Policies and Asian Migration, In Ong, Paul, Edna Banocich and Lucie Cheng (eds.), *The New Asian Immigration in Los Angeles and Global Restructuring*, Philadelphia, PA :Temple University Press, pp.45–73.

Ortega, Arnisson Andre 2016 *Neoliberalizing Spaces in the Philippines: Suburbanization, Transnational Migration, and Dispossession*, Lanham, MD: Lexington Books.

Ortiga, Yasmin Y. 2018 *Emigration, Employability and Higher Education in the Philippines*, Abingdon and New York: Routledge.

Osborne, Thomas and Nikolas Rose 1999 Governing Cities: Notes on the Spatialisation of Virtue, *Environment and Planning D: Society and Space* 17: 737–760.

Parreñas, Rhacel Salazar 2001 *Servants of Globalization: Women, Migration, and Domestic Work*, Redwood City, CA: Stanford University Press.

——— 2005 *Children of Global Migration: Transnational Families and Gendered Woes*, Redwod City, CA: Stanford University Press.

_____ 2008 *The Force of Domesticity: Filipina Migrants and Globalization*, New York and London: New York University Press.

Parnell, Phillip C. 2002 The Composite State: The Poor and the Nation in Manila, In Carol Greenhouse, J. et al. (eds.), *Ethnography in Unstable Places: Everyday Lives in Contexts of Dramatic Political Change*, Durham, NC: Duke University Press, pp.146–177.

Peck, Jamie 2001 *Workfare States*, New York and London: Guilford Press.

Peet, Richard and Michael Watts (eds.). 2004 *Liberation Ecologies: Environment, Development, Social Movements*, 2nd edition. Abingdon and New York: Routledge.

Philippine National Statistics Office 2012 National Quick Stat, http://www.census.gov.ph/sites/default/files/attachments/ird/quickstat/October2012.pdf (accessed November 28, 2012).

Pinches, Michael 1992a 'All that we have is our muscle and sweat': The Rise of Wage Labor in a Manila Squatter Community, In Pinches, Michael and S. Lakha (eds.), *Wage Labor and Social Change: The Proletariat in Asia and the Pacific*, Quezon City: New Day Publishing, pp.105–138.

_____ 1992b. Proletarian Ritual: Class Degradation and the Dialectics of Resistance in Manila, *Pilipinas* 19: 69–92.

_____ 1994 Modernisation and the Quest for Modernity: Architectural Form, Squatter Settlements and the New Society in Manila, In Askew, Mark and William Logan (eds.), *Cultural Identity and Urban Change in Southeast Asia: Interpretative Essays*, Geelong: Deakin University Press, pp.13–42.

_____ 1996 The Philippines' New Rich: Capitalist Transformation Amidst Economic Gloom, In Robison, Richard and David S. G. Goodman (eds.), *The New Rich in Asia: Mobile Phones, McDonalds and Middle-Class Revolution*, Abingdon and New York: Routledge, pp.105–133.

_____ 1999 Cultural Relations, Class and the New Rich of Asia, In Pinches, Michael (ed.), *Culture and Privilege in Capitalist Asia*, Abingdon and New York: Routledge, pp.1–55.

_____ 2001 Class and National Identity: The Case of Filipino Migrant Workers, In Hutchison, Jane and Andrew Brown (eds.), *Organising Labour in Globalising Asia*, Abingdon and New York: Routledge, pp.187–243.

Philippine Overseas Employment Administration 2008 Overseas Employment Statistics, http://www.poea.gov.ph/html/statistics.html (accessed August 5, 2009).

Polanyi, Karl 1944 *The Great Transformation: The Political and Economic Origins of Our Time*, New York City: Farrar & Rinehart.

Pomeroy, Robert and Melvin Carlos 1997 Community-Based Coastal Resource Management in the Philippines: A Review and Evaluation of Programs and Projects, 1984–1994, *Marine Policy* 21 (5): 445–464.

Porio, Emma 2004 The Community Mortgage Programme: An Innovative Social Housing Programme in the Philippines and Its Outcomes, In Mitlin, Diana and David Satterthwaite (eds.), *Empowering Squatter Citizen: Local Government, Civil Society and Urban Poverty Reduction*, London and Sterling, VA: Earthscan, pp.54–81.

Portes, Alejandro and Ruben G. Rumbaut 2001 *Legacies: The Story of the Immigrant Second Generation*, Oakland, CA: University of California Press.

Prudham, Scott 2004 Poisoning the Well: Neoliberalism and the Contamination of Municipal Water in Walkerton, Ontario, *Geoforum* 2004: 343–359.

Rebullia, M. Lourdes et.al. 1999 *Housing the Urban Poor: Policies, Approaches, Issues*, Quezon City: UP Center for Integrative and Development Studies.

Reid, Ben 2005 Poverty Alleviation and Participatory Development in the Philippines. *Journal of Contemporary Asia* 35(1): 29–52.

Richland, Justin B. 2009 On Neoliberalism and Other Social Diseases: The 2008 Sociocultural Anthropology Year in Review, *American Anthropologist* 111(2): 170–176.

Rivera, Temario C. 2006 The Middle Classes in Philippine Politics. In Tadem, Teresa S. and Noel M. Morada (eds.), *Philippine Politics and Governance: Challenges to Democratization and Development*, Quezon City: Department of Political Science, College of Social Sciences and Philosophy, University of the Philippines, pp.179–203.

Robbins, Paul and April Luginbuhl 2005 The Last Enclosure: Resisting Privatization of Wildlife in the Western United States, *Capitalism Nature Socialism* 16(1): 45–61.

Robertson, Morgan M. 2004 The Neoliberalization of Ecosystem Services: Wetland Mitigation Banking and Problems in Environmental Governance, *Geoforum* 35 (2004): 361–373.

Robison, Richard and David S.G. Goodman (eds.) 1996 *The New Rich in Asia: Mobile Phones, McDonalds and Middle-Class Revolution*, Abingdon and New York: Routledge.

Rodriguez, Robyn Magalit 2010 *Migrants for Export: How the Philippine State Brokers Labor to the World*, Minneapolis, MN: University of Minnesota Press.

Rose, Nikolas 1996a The Death of the Social?: Refiguring the Territory of Government, *Economy and Society* 25(3): 327–56.

———— 1996b Governing 'advanced' liberal democracies. In Barry, A., T. Osborne and N. Rose (eds.), *Foucault and Political Reason: Liberalism, Neo-liberalism, and Rationalities of Government*, Chicago: University of Chicago Press, pp.37–64.

———— 1999 *Powers of Freedom: Reframing Political Thought*, Cambridge: Cambridge University Press.

Rose, Nikolas, Pat O'Malley and Mariana Valverde 2006 Governmentality, *Annual Review of Law and Social Science* 2006(2): 83–104.

Rumbaut, Ruben G. and Alejandro Portes (eds.) 2001 *Ethnicities: Children of Immigrants in America*, Oalkland, CA: University of California Press.

Russel, Andrew and Iain R. Edgar (eds.) 1998 *The Anthropology of Welfare*, Abingdon and New York: Routledge.

Salaverria, Leila 2010 More Lawmakers Oppose Cash Transfer Scheme, *Philippine Daily Inquirer*, August 1, 2010

Sachedina, Hassanali T. 2010 Disconnected Nature: The Scaling Up of African Wildlife Foundation and its Impacts on Biodiversity Conservation and Local Livelihoods, *Antipode* 42(3): 603–623.

Schaffer, Frederic C. 2005 Clean Elections and the Great Unwashed: Vote Buying and Voter Education in the Philippines, Occasional Paper No. 21 (Institute for Advanced Study), http://www.sss.ias.edu/publications/papers/paper21.pdf (accessed February 19, 2009).

———— 2008 *The Hidden Costs of Clean Election Reform*, Ithaca, NY: Cornell University Press.

Scott, James C. 1998 *Seeing Like a State: How Certain Schemes to Improve the Human Condition Have Failed*, New Haven and London: Yale University Press.

Seki, Koki 2000 Wherever the Waves Carry Us: Historical Development of a Visayan Fisherfolk's Livelihood Strategies, *Philippine Quarterly of Culture and Society* 28(2): 133–157.

———— 2012 Difference and Alliance in Transnational Social Fields: The Pendular Identity of the Filipino Middle Class, *Philippine Studies* 60(2): 187–222.

———— 2020 Introduction: Emergent Sociality, or What Comes After 'the Social'? In Seki, K. (ed.), *Ethnographies of Development and Globalization in the Philippines: Emergent Socialities and the Governing of Precarity*, Abingdon and New York: Routledge, pp.1–16.

Sharma, Aradhana 2006 Crossbreeding Institutions, Breeding Struggle: Women's Empowerment, Neoliberal Governmentality, and State (Re)formation in India, *Cultural Anthropology* 21(1): 60–95.

Shatkin, Gavin 2000 Obstacles to Empowerment: Local Politics and Civil Society in Metropolitan Manila, the Philippines, *Urban Studies* 37(12): 2357–2375.

——— 2004 Planning to Forget: Informal Settlements as 'Forgotten Places' in Globalizing Metro Manila, *Urban Studies* 41(12): 2469–2484.

——— 2007 *Collective Action and Urban Poverty Alleviation: Community Organization and the Struggle for Shelter in Manila*, London: Ashgate.

——— 2008 The City and the Bottom Line: Urban megaprojects and the Privatization of Planning in Southeast Asia, *Environment and Planning A* 40: 383–401.

Shore, Cris and Susan Wright (eds.) 1997 *The Anthropology of Policy*, London and New York: Routledge.

Shore, Cris and Susan Wright 2000 Coercive Accountability: The Rise of Audit Culture in Higher Education, In Strathern, M. (ed.), *Audit Cultures: Anthropological Studies in Accountability, Ethics and the Academy*, Abingdon and New York: Routledge, pp.57–89.

——— 2011 Conceptualising Policy: Technologies of Governance and the Politics of Visibility, In Shore, Cris, Susan Wright and Davide Però (eds.), *Policy Worlds: Anthropology and the Analysis of Contemporary Power*, New York and Oxford: Berghahn Books, pp.1–25.

Shore, Cris, Susan Wright and Davide Però 2011 *Policy Worlds: Anthropology and the Analysis of Contemporary Power*, New York and Oxford: Berghahn Books.

Sidel, John T. 1999 *Capital, Coercion, and Crime: Bossism in the Philippines*, Redwood City, CA: Stanford University Press.

Silliman, Sidney G., and Garner Lela Noble (eds.) 1998 *Organizing for Democracy: NGOs, Civil Society, and the Philippine State*, Honolulu, HI: University of Hawai'i Press.

Snelder, Denyse J. and G. Persoon 2005 Comanagement of Natural Resources: Introduction. In Snelder, Denyse and Eileen C. Bernardo (eds.), *Comanagement in Practice: The Challenges and Complexities of Implementation in the Northen Sierra Madre Mountain Region*, Quezon City: Ateneo de Manila University Press, pp.3–34.

Social Weather Station 2014 Social Weather Indicators, http://www.sws.org.ph/ (accessed March 12, 2016).

Sodikoff, Genese 2007 An Exceptional Strike: A Micro-history of 'People versus Park' in Madagascar, *Journal of Political Ecology* 14: 10–33.

Soon, Chuan Yean 2015 *Tulong: An Articulation of Politics in the Christian Philippines*, Manila: University of Santo Tomas Publishing House.

Spierenburg, Marja and Wels, Harry 2010 Conservation Philanthropists, Royalty and Business Elites in Nature Conservation in Southern Africa, *Antipode* 42(3): 647–670.

St. Martin, Kevin 2005 Disrupting Enclosure in New England Fisheries, *Capitalism Nature Socialism* 16(1): 63–80.

Strathern, M. (ed.) 2000 *Audit Cultures: Anthropological Studies in Accountability, Ethics and the Academy*, Abingdon and New York: Routledge

Swyngedouw, Erik 2005 Dispossessing H_2O: The Contested Terrain of Water Privatization, *Capitalism Nature Socialism* 16(1): 81–98.

Swyngedouw, Eric, Frank Moulaert and Arantxa Rodriguez 2002 Neoliberal Urbanization in Europe: Large-Scale Urban Development Projects and the New Urban Policy, *Antipode* 34(3): 542–577.

Szanton, David L. 1970 *Entrepreneurship in a Rural Philippine Community*, Ph.D. dissertation, University of Chicago.

_____ 1981[1971] *Estancia in Transition: Economic Growth in a Rural Philippine Community*, Quezon City: Ateneo de Manila University Press.

Szanton, Maria Cristina Blanc 1972 *A Right to Survive: Subsistence Marketing in a Lowland Philippine Town*, Quezon City: Ateneo de Manila University Press.

Tanabe, Akio 2002 Moral Society, Political Society and Civil Society in Post-Colonial India: A View from Orissa Locality, *Journal of Japanese Association for South Asian Studies*, 14: 40–67.

_____ 2007 Toward Vernacular Democracy: Moral Society and Post-Colonial Transformation in Rural Orissa, India, *American Ethnologist*, 34(3): 558–574.

Tanaka, Takuji 2006 *Hinkon to Kyowakoku: Jukyuseiki France ni okerru shakaitekirentai no Tanjo*, Jinbunshoin

Umali, Agustin F. 1950 *Guide to the Classification of Fishing Gear in the Philippines*, Washington DC.: Fish and Wildlife Service, United States Department of Interior.

United Nations Human Settlements Programme 2003 *The Challenge of Slums: Global Report on Human Settlements*, London: Earthscan Publications Ltd.

Veneracion, Cynthia C. 2004 *Partnerships for Slum Improvement: The ADB-JFPR and DSWD Projections in Muntinlupa City and Payatas*, Quezon City: Institute of Philippine Culture, Ateneo de Manila University.

Vergara, Benito M. 2009 *Pinoy Capital: The Filipino Nation in Daly City*, Philadelphia, PA: Temple University Press.

Vigilia, Wendell 2010 Cash Transfers: Dole-out or Lifebuoy?, *Malaya News*, September 21, 2010.

Weber, Rachel 2002 Extracting Value from the City: Neoliberalism and Urban Redevelopment, *Antipode* 34(3): 519–540.

West, Paige 2005 Translation, Value, and Space: Theorizing an Ethnographic and Engaged Environmental Anthropology, *American Anthropologist* 107(4): 632–642.

_____ 2006 *Conservation is Our Government Now: The Politics of Ecology in Papua New Guinea*, Durham, NC: Duke University Press.

_____ 2010 Making the Market: Specialty Coffee, Generational Pitches, and Papua New Guinea, *Antipode* 42(3): 690–718.

West, Paige and Dan Brockington 2006 An Anthropological Perspective on Some Unexpected Consequences of Protected Areas, *Conservation Biology* 20(3): 609–616.

West, Paige and James G. Carrier 2004 Ecotourism and Authenticity: Getting Away From It All?, *Current Anthropology* 45(4): 483–498.

West, Paige, James Igoe and Dan Brockington 2006 Parks and Peoples: The Social Impact of Protected Areas, *Annual Review of Anthropology* 35: 251–277.

Wilshusen, Peter R. 2010 The Receiving End of Reform: Everyday Reponses to Neoliberalisation in Southern Mexico, *Antipode* 42(3): 767–799.

Wolf, Diane L. 2002 There's No Place Like 'Home': Emotional Transnationalism and the Struggles of Second-Generation Filipinos, In Levitt, Peggy and Mary C. Waters (eds.), *The Changing Face of Home: The Transnational Lives of the Second Generation*, New York City: Russell Sage Foundation, pp.255–294.

Yoneya, Sonoe 1996 Michal Foucault no Tochisei Kenkyu, *Shiso* 870: 77–105.

Young, Douglas and Roger Keil 2007 Re-regulating the Urban Water Regime in Neoliberal Toronto, In Heynen, Nik, James McCarthy, Scott Prudham and Paul Robbins (eds.), *Neoliberal Environments: False Promises and Unnatural Consequences*, Abingdon and New York: Routledge, pp.139–150.

Index